EVERYTHING IS NEGOTIABLE

EVERYTHING
IS NEGOTIABLE

Gavin Kennedy

ARROW BOOKS

Arrow Books Limited
20 Vauxhall Bridge Road, London SW1V 2SA

An imprint of the Random Century Group

London Melbourne Sydney Auckland Johannesburg
and agencies throughout the world

First published in Great Britain
by Century Hutchinson 1982
Reprinted 1983, 1984, 1985, 1986
Second edition 1989
Arrow edition 1991

Printed and bound in Great Britain by
Cox & Wyman Ltd, Reading

ISBN 0 09 998070 3

FOR PATRICIA

'How much do I want, sir?'

'Yes. Give it a name. We won't haggle.'

He pursed his lips.

'I'm afraid,' he said, having unpursed them, 'I couldn't do it as cheap as I'd like, sir . . . I'd have to make it twenty pounds.'

I was relieved. I had been expecting something higher. He, too, seemed to feel he had erred on the side of moderation, for he immediately added:

'Or, rather thirty.'

'Thirty?'

'Thirty, sir.'

'Let's haggle,' I said.

But when I suggested twenty-five, a nicer looking sort of number than thirty, he shook his grey head regretfully, so we went on haggling, and he haggled better than me, so that eventually we settled on thirty-five.

It wasn't one of my best haggling days.

[*Aunts Aren't Gentlemen*, by P. G. Wodehouse]

Contents

Preface to the second edition

The first edition of Everything is Negotiable was a success for the many thousands of readers who were inspired by the message asserted in its title. Many wrote, telexed and faxed me stories of how they had applied its techniques to secure better deals than the ones they were first offered. One or two complained that my publisher appeared unwilling to negotiate on the price! Perhaps they should have tried harder by offering Mr Hutchinson a better deal too?

By reflecting on the messages of the book and applying them in your daily negotiations (be they business, pleasure, domestic or neighbourly) you too can improve your performance as a negotiator and compare yourself with the professionals.

I continue to make the learning task as enjoyable and entertaining as possible. It is not flippancy on my part but a sturdy belief that people learn most when they are exploring new ideas while relying on their sense of fun. The alternative approaches to learning (of which bookshops are crammed full) soon lose their impact. However, Everything is Negotiable has a serious message. For this reason I have extended the second edition by including some new chapters on negotiating abroad and by updating some of the examples.

My old friends remain active as ever, though they have moved on over the years. Angus still regrets his decision to buy the former Commodore's boat (though because he still sails it I suspect that he and his wife have overcome their initial reservations – it seemed perfectly OK to me when I last took a trip with them through the Crinan Canal in Argyll, where at the delightful Cairbaan Inn, we got gloriously inebriated one evening celebrating his election as Commodore); Helmut Weber has since taken over the family business of manufacturing and selling industrial pumps around the world (Fritz is his Vice-President), and what a success Helmut is making of it too (his wife runs their chocolate business on the side); Bob in Sydney has gone from strength to strength, even buying into a tv channel, while his wife has become a Member of Parliament; Jack in California has changed professions from Professor of Economics to Attorney at Law and is specialising, somewhat surprisingly, in reconciling the aggrieved parties rather than supporting them suing each other into bankruptcy (he still buys and sells Jaguar cars); the Summers and Hang families now have two grandchildren between them, plus several Hang children working in the store (Gilbert is resisting letting them loose on the check-outs!); Nelson is now a leading barrister in London (I recently met the computer salesman who fell victim to Nelson's Mother Hubbard – he still dines out on the story).

Likewise, to a large extent, my negotiating experiences have moved on a long way since 1982. My one-man consultancy, Negotiate Ltd, now has six consultant negotiators on the pay-roll, plus an admirable administration staff of four. We also have made many new friends and associates around the world, including a list of regular correspondents whose letters have brought much joy and interest to myself and my colleagues. The negotiating challenges we cope with are increasing in scope, seriousness, and, hopefully, reward. My colleagues, John Benson, Peter Curran, Douglas Henderson, Roy Webb, Trevor Webster and Peter Glasgow, and the dedicated team who run the office (Karen, Alison, Teresa and Vivien) have continued to make major contributions to my thinking and practice as a negotiator. As have Colin and Judy Rose in Australia and Ira Ascherman in New York. Our clients, however, deserve the warmest of thanks we can muster (without it affecting the prices we charge!).

My family continues to cope with my absences and wandering attentions and they support me in ways which are impossible to quantify. While my negotiations with our children, Florence, Beatrice and Gavin, have moved on from the ratio of cabbage to ice cream at dinner to the ever-increasing ratio of their monthly allowances to the UK's Gross Domestic Product, they remain major inspirations for all of what I do while I am away on business and a major source of my contentment when I am home. Of Patricia, I can say no more than ask you to note that this book (as I am) is dedicated to her.

To you the reader, I invite you to write to me about your negotiating experiences, and your views on the book (critical or otherwise). The first edition provoked a massive mail; I challenge you all to beat that response with this one. You can write to me at 22 Braid Avenue, Edinburgh EH10 6EE, Scotland, or Fax me on 031 452 8388.

Lastly, if you are passing through an airport, a hotel, a corridor, a company office, or whatever, and see me sitting about with not too much to do (if I am up to my ears in a deal I will soon let you know!), why not amble across, introduce yourself, and swap experiences with me? We can have a chat and a coffee, or, if we are both in funds and on expenses, we might stretch ourselves, and our clients' budgets, to a glass or two of the local nectar!

GAVIN KENNEDY
June 1989

Self-assessment tests

Opposite the beginning of most chapters is a short (and painless!) self-assessment test. Read the questions carefully and then mark the answer you consider to be most appropriate, given the information available.

My opinions of the answers are set out at the end of the chapter. The opinions I express are my own and you might have cause to differ with them. You are invited to question my opinions, and anybody else's, on negotiating!

I believe the views I have expressed of the answers represent the most regular notions of 'best practice' for the majority of occasions but, as every negotiator knows, some people see things differently from the way we do – that is why we need to negotiate – so I am not going to be upset if you decide to differ!

Introduction
or how to beat the competition!

If you go about your daily business assuming that nothing is negotiable unless the other party indicates otherwise, you are missing opportunities galore to get better deals both for yourself *and* the people you deal with.

Ironical isn't it? Not only are *you* poorer as a result of not trying to negotiate, but so are those you deal with.

Why?

Because in many cases there is a better deal than the one on offer waiting to be discovered. A deal that is better for *you* can also be better for *them*. So, if working for your own interests strikes you as being selfish (perish the thought!), then consider it as a favour to them.

However, you don't have to be a dedicated altruist to be a negotiator. Far from it. It is my belief that persons who strive to look after their own interests are more likely to contribute to the common good than those who assume the world owes them a living.

By striving to negotiate a better deal than the one that is on offer, you can make our world a more pleasant place to be in. Everything is negotiable – but only if *you* make it so.

On some issues you may choose not to negotiate – that is your right and it is perfectly sensible too, if you haven't the time to look for a different deal or if the outcome isn't worth the effort on some occasions – but if you do decide to negotiate, and you want to do the best you can, you should know that your negotiating behaviour can make or break the deal.

This book will show you how to avoid basic negotiating errors that are committed everywhere and every day by someone or other (and even the world's best negotiators screw up a deal occasionally).

1

Trade or stay poor – that is the bottom line for every country that aspires to compete in the world economic system. It doesn't matter whether you are exporting or importing, piling up raw materials, processing bits and pieces, assembling parts, packaging entire plants or selling on what others have sold to you, nor does it matter whether you are a capitalist or a communist (or anything in-between), a saint or a sinner, a Christian, a Muslim, a Hindu, a Confucian, a Jew, an atheist or even a devotee of voodoo, and it certainly doesn't matter whether you are rich or poor, deserving a break or due a come-uppance: if you don't trade profitably you won't trade for long and if you don't trade at all you will have sealed your fate as surely as if you had gone in for free-fall parachuting – without a parachute.

There is just no way in which the goods and services that the rich countries take for granted can be got by those who can pay for them without the act of trading. And there is no way in which the goods and services that the poor countries quite rightly aspire to possess can be got on a long-term basis unless they trade for them.

Those societies that attempt to distribute their goods and services without trade must almost always compromise their no-trade principles or face a steady ruin of their people. What is not permitted by law breaks through illicitly: the people will trade whatever the risks, whatever the bureaucrats threaten to do to them, and whatever names they are called by the dictators. Those whom the dictators condemn as 'bandits', 'social parasites', and 'traitors' are actually regarded by the people they serve and supply as heroes: they provide the people with the one thing the dictators usually keep for themselves, namely, *choice* of things to consume. So-called 'black-market' traders are the very creation of any society that suppresses the freedom of trade. Destroy them and you immediately reduce living standards.

In the 1770s, about the time when George Washington and his friends were stirring themselves to fight for the right to trade without English interference, a Scotsman, Adam Smith, had recognized the importance to civilized society of the act of trading and was working on it as the major theme of his magnum opus, *An Inquiry into The Nature and Causes of the Wealth of Nations* (1776).

Smith took twelve years to write his great work (much of it dictated to his sister while warming his rearquarters over his coal fire and drinking claret); it became what publishers today would hype as a 'number one best seller'. On this occasion it thoroughly deserved to be so regarded, for it is still in print in many languages throughout the world and almost every MBA student hears of it (though few, too few, actually get round to reading it).

Smith distinguished himself in his book by identifying a 'certain propensity' in human society to 'truck, barter, and exchange one thing for another'. Bargaining is unique to the human species and it has a long pedigree back into the mists of time. His ideas on the significance of this propensity are worth considering.

First, he noted that the propensity to truck, barter and exchange was common to all people but was not to be found in any other species on the planet:

'Nobody,' Smith wrote, 'ever saw a dog make a fair and deliberate exchange of one bone for another with another dog. Nobody ever saw one animal by its gestures and natural cries signify to another, this is mine, that yours: I am willing to give this for that.'

Second, he noted that people in any civilized society require the co-operation of others for their very survival and yet a person's 'whole life is scarce sufficient to gain the friendship of a few persons'. Think about that. How would you have fared if the services of the millions of people who have co-operated to produce just the goods and services that you have consumed this very day were withdrawn from your end of the market?

You would have had to feed yourself, provide for your own safety, perhaps cope with a medical problem, attend to your needs in every respect, and also think about what you have to do to ensure your survival tomorrow (and through tonight!). There is no doubt that, whatever else this would mean to you personally, it would certainly mean a drastic reduction in your standard of living, and, perhaps, a shortening of your life.

Friends always come in handy – a friend in need is a friend indeed – but the majority of people whom you depend upon for the many things you take for granted will never have time to get to know you, let alone get to know you in a way which makes them feel positive about helping you. Indeed, getting to know you might have the effect of encouraging entirely negative feelings towards you.

Third, Smith posed the question as to why people co-operate to produce things for people they will never meet, never know and probably would never like even if they knew them? Smith's answer

3

was controversial. It still offends some people. He said that people co-operate not for love of their fellows, nor indeed because of their humanity, but because it is in their *self-interest* to do so:

> 'It is not', he wrote in his famous assertion, 'from the benevolence of the butcher, the brewer, or the baker, that we expect our dinner, but from their regard to their self-interest.'

What is the nature of this self-interest? Quite simply it is people's desire for what you are going to give them in exchange for their meat, beer and bread. They certainly ain't going to give you their goods for nothing.

Relying on their benevolence will not loosen their hold on their meat, beer and bread sufficient to ensure you a long and contented life as much as will relying on offering them something in trade. In a contest between benevolence and trade as a motivator of human beings, it is more likely that trade will induce people voluntarily to part with what they have that you desire.

In effect, said Smith, you are showing them that parting with their wares in exchange for yours is to their own advantage – you are appealing, in other words, to that most powerful of human motives: self-interest.

'Give me that which I want, and you shall have this which you want' is, for Smith and the majority of us, the one sure way to obtain the greater part of the things we are in most need of. This is the essential meaning of trading. And we trade by making offers and counter-offers, or bargaining.

All who produce anything that somebody else might want can participate in trade. Someone, somewhere, who wants what you have to trade can trade what they have for what they want, perhaps through long chains of intermediaries who know nothing about anybody one or two links along the chain in either direction, and thereby they can satisfy their desires without even knowing about you. It does not matter what kind of person you are, what race, nationality or religion you are blessed with, what your politics are, what your age, your sex, or likes and dislikes are.

If you engage in trade you become connected with those others who trade with you, and with the people who trade with them, in a world economic system that has raised living standards to levels undreamt of by Adam Smith and his contemporaries.

Smith's powerful insight into the propensity to truck, barter and exchange remains one of the most challenging concepts in business. Experience since 1776 suggests that those countries that live closer to the principles of free trade do better than those that have abandoned them.

If you want to trade you have to negotiate, or accept what the other person offers. By negotiating you can improve on what you are first offered for what you have that the other person wants. Smith certainly saw it that way: people truck, barter and exchange, they do not just accept what's on offer.

Negotiating is the name of the game. How to negotiate, how to get better deals, how to improve your share of the cake – how to get a bigger cake for both of you! – that's what this book is about. And more!

In business, you can be intimidated into believing that certain things are not negotiable, and, if you give in without a struggle, you will pay whatever they demand, or do without whatever they have to offer.

As a result, you can only get what they want you to have in the form they decide is good for you and for a price that they decide will make them – not you – better off. This book will show you how to recognize intimidation and how to overcome it.

You are challenged to consider testing the prices you come across, no matter how prestigious the vendor, no matter what the 'normal rules' of business. Indeed, the more prestigious (read: intimidating) the vendor's reputation, the more vulnerable they are to the methods outlined in this book.

And what is true of the big guys, is also true of all the smaller guys who also want to secure your business. Hence the challenge: *do not be intimidated by fixed prices. Never mind what the price tag says, or what the vendor tells you* – just keep haggling. Somewhere, sooner or later, a better deal will emerge, and that's got to be good for you (and for them).

This book is about finding those better deals; about getting them irrespective of the obstacles put in your way by whomsoever is trying (or expecting) to intimidate you. You will be shown how to find those better deals and how to make a negotiator happy by haggling.

* * *

This is a practical book, packed with advice on how to handle negotiations. It is not a theoretical treatise. The methods outlined in the text are the methods tried and tested where it matters – in face-to-face negotiations in the real world of international business.

Negotiating as a technique can be applied no matter what the issues or their gravity, no matter who the parties are, or their cultures, or the amounts at stake. But the particular principles applicable to each negotiation can differ for each culture depending on local business and social norms.

In scores of examples throughout the text you will see different ways to play the same shots, depending on the circumstances. When you change the issues, parties, cultures or amounts, only the *way* you play the shots needs to be different.

The book discusses negotiations for *big* stakes (ships, real estate, long-term contracts, rent reviews, mainframe computers, companies, high-volume outputs, airlines, territory, hostages, your life, etc.) and *smaller* stakes (accommodation, travel, food and drink, low volumes, small offices, and such like).

Sometimes I demonstrate the appropriate moves to get results by illustrations from everyday domestic negotiations, many of which are essential to domestic happiness and security. And yet hardly any attention is given to domestic negotiations, even by those experienced in handling big deals for their companies.

Top company negotiators, handling accounts in the $20 million-plus range, often 'confess' at the Negotiating Clinics that they are hopeless when it comes to negotiating for a set of tyres, or a discount off a case of wine.

Somehow the skills they use professionally are forgotten when it is their own personal interests at stake and not their company's. For these people, this book has an important message: what works when buying tankers or selling refineries works when getting your car fixed, the roof repaired and the garden dug over.

Why?

Because Everything is Negotiable!

And for those more familiar with the smaller deals, remember the moves that work for those tyres also work for the buying of tankers, options on land or a million gross of widgets.

Hence, we look at how to get better deals when buying or selling a new or used car, or getting it fixed at the garage; buying or selling your house; getting plumbers, plasterers, double-glazers, electricians and painters to improve it, plus getting them to do what they promised to do for the money.

You will also read how to negotiate with such people to get them to do even more for the same money. We also look at negotiations to buy refrigerators, TVs, video recorders, furniture, washing machines, and cookers, etc.

En passant I show you how to negotiate a night out without provoking a divorce; how to get discounts for poor service in hotels and restaurants; how to negotiate disputes with spouses, lovers, in-laws, friends, neighbours, strangers, workforces, bosses and bureaucrats. There is even some advice on negotiating with kidnappers, hijackers, burglars and pests!

Negotiating is a big activity

Over 50,000 international agreements have been negotiated in the 20th Century – so far. These are increasing at the rate of over 1,100 a year (up from 550 a year in the late 1940s).

But nobody knows exactly how many international agreements there are and even the United Nations has great difficulty keeping track of them all.

The League of Nations published 205 volumes of Treaties before its demise and the United Nations series was running at 1,000 volumes in 1987.

With 250 international organizations operating around the world, we can expect the number of negotiated agreements to keep rising throughout the rest of this century – and the next!

---

* * *

In life everybody negotiates about almost everything.

We don't always realize we are negotiating – that is one reason why we get worse deals than we need to, and why sometimes we don't realize we are being ripped-off into the bargain!

In business we negotiate with customers and suppliers. We also negotiate within our organizations with colleagues *and* rivals. Behind our every move as a business negotiator there is a whole hierarchy of interested parties watching, not all of them benevolently inclined to enhance our own interests, or even grateful for our efforts.

Because negotiating is such a common activity you probably hardly think about it. You may think that you only negotiate on big deals. But if you look more closely at the hundreds of little deals you make every year – with your boss, your customers, your suppliers, your spouse, your children, your in-laws, your neighbours, your conscience – you would realize that poor negotiating performance costs you money, time, and, perhaps, lost chances for happiness.

Most good negotiating practice is 'common sense', but, unfortunately, common sense is a lot less common than is commonly thought! Also, the majority of people do not review their everyday negotiations – they are not, in the main, motivated to do so. Therefore, they do not learn to identify their mistakes and correct them for next time.

* * *

Negotiations in practice are a messy, almost chaotic, experience. People do not negotiate as if they are playing chess: 'first you move, then I move'. Human beings are given to wandering attention, digressions, circular arguments, repetition, interruptions, crosstalk, irrelevancies, and a whole range of emotional responses from the passive sulk to the violent outburst.

But in all the chaos there are underlying patterns. This book identifies the underlying patterns of the negotiating process and presents them in a manageable form.

You will be shown how to improve your judgment in preparing for your negotiations, how to think clearly about the choices you must make as the negotiation unfolds, how to improve your performance while under the stress of negotiating, and how to get better deals *almost* every time (you can't win 'em all, but you won't win any unless you try).

* * *

The message is serious – in some negotiations, the stakes are literally life or death – but 17 years' experience in negotiating training has convinced me that most people learn more about negotiating when they are relaxed than when they are tense or wearied by the sobriety of the style or presentation. Hence, my presentation style is sometimes a trifle lighthearted.

The book is composed of a central text in chapter form, supported by boxed inserts illustrating the experiences of negotiators in a wide variety of real-world settings. Each chapter begins with a *self-assessment test* consisting of three or four multiple-choice questions. The negotiating scenarios in the tests are highly simplified and you are asked to mark the answer you think is the most appropriate, given the information to hand. You should test yourself before reading the chapter that follows the test.

My answers are given at the end of the chapters, but don't worry if you disagree strongly with *some* of my answers – negotiating is a question of style and some styles suit one person but not another – but in the main the answers given are the ones that will produce, in my opinion, the best results in the long run.

The questions have been tested with hundreds of negotiators and their comments and suggestions have been taken into account for the versions used in this book. You can work through the central text independently of the self-assessment tests and the boxed insert examples. Or you can choose any combination of the three elements that suits your particular needs.

How you use the book is entirely up to you, but I believe that you will gain most from it by working diligently through the self-assessment tests, followed by the relevant chapters. You can look up the answers before or after reading the chapter.

* * *

There is one additional activity that you might find helpful while reading the book, and that is to try to think up negotiating scenarios, either from your own experience or from other sources (colleagues, friends, the media, etc) that are relevant to the material in the chapter you are reading.

We learn best by counterposing concepts (new or familiar) with our experience and this seems to be a productive way to bring out the important, though often subtle, principles of negotiating.

No matter how bad or good you are *now* as a negotiator you can improve your performance, to your own and your company's benefit, if you apply yourself with an open mind to the methods outlined in this book.

Then as you secure more confidence as a negotiator – mainly from securing better deals – you will actively seek opportunities to practise negotiating. And, like learning to ride a bike, the more practice, the more confidence. Each reinforces the other.

The end-result could be a new beginning. For a start, it could get you past the competition in better shape than you think possible at the moment. And if you can learn to do well when you are learning, think what you might achieve when you get ahead!

9

Self-assessment test 1

1   You want to sell your yacht and you know that you would
    be very fortunate to get as much as £50,000 for it. While you
    are considering placing the advertisement, a keen yachts-
    man approaches you and offers £65,000 in cash immedi-
    ately for your boat. Do you:
    (a) Accept his offer without further ado?
    (b) Tell him to wait until the boat is advertised?
    (c) Haggle?

2   You are in the market for a yacht and have taken a fancy to
    the 'Isabella' which is advertised at £50,000. The most that
    you can raise is £43,000 from selling your own boat and
    borrowing from the bank. You meet the owner in the
    clubhouse and casually tell him of your (strong) interest.
    You mention that you could raise £43,000. He agrees to sell
    you the 'Isabella' for that sum. Is this:
    (a) An offer you can't refuse?
    (b) A lousy situation?
    (c) An occasion to celebrate your bargain?

3   A young talented actress wants to get into the 'big time' and
    she meets a television producer who is desirous of securing
    her services for an important part in a detective film. He tells
    her that she cannot get top rates until she is 'known' but if
    she does this one 'cheap' and gets famous, she will see 'train
    loads of money' coming her way for her future work.
    Should she:
    (a) Tell the producer to 'offski'?
    (b) Agree, as she needs to start somewhere?
    (c) Demand top rates if she is to do a top job?

Chapter One

The worst thing you can do to a negotiator
or how to avoid a 'bargain'

What is the *worst* thing you can do to a negotiator? At the Negotiating Clinics we invariably get answers like:

'Insult him.'
'Get her annoyed.'
'Go over her head to the boss.'
'Make him look stupid.'

All or any of these behaviours are to be avoided, perhaps. However, none of these responses is the *worst* thing you can do to a negotiator. The worst thing you can do is:

ACCEPT HIS FIRST OFFER!

Why is it so bad to accept a negotiator's first offer, especially if it is one of those offers which is 'too good to refuse'?

Junior sales staff are most given to thoughtlessly dancing to the 'offer-I-could-not-refuse' tune. Partly, it is the fault of their sales training that turns them into 'order-takers'. 'The order, any order, and nothing but the order' is drummed into them by trainers who have forgotten to beat the drum as loudly about the equally important business message of profitability. Graduates of these training programmes end up like computer-programmed football players who only know about scoring goals – including own goals! – because the programmer forgot to distinguish between them.

Partly also, junior sales staff make the cardinal mistake of first-offer-acceptance as a result of their lack of experience.

Euphoria is always generated when a difficult task is accomplished, and those readers who have been 'baptised' in cold-canvas selling will know how difficult it can be to get that first order from a prospective customer. It is the euphoria (or relief) that somebody wants to buy that leads junior sales staff to say 'Yes' to the first offer.

They sign, grab it and run. This is why women often make the best negotiators – they learn at their mother's knee never to accept a man's first offer!

If this proclivity to first-offer-acceptance was confined to the inexperienced it would be a minor problem, and self-correcting as time goes by. Sales staff gain experience – if they can't, or don't, they find another career – and experience will teach them never to accept a negotiator's first offer.

However, first-offer-acceptance is widespread among negotiators, some of whom have considerable experience. This presents you with the first challenge, and opportunity, to improve your negotiating performance, because you are bound to find yourself, sometime in the near future, in a situation where first-offer-acceptance is a likely temptation, either for you, or for the other person.

Let me illustrate the traumas that first-offer-acceptance can cause to even the most experienced of negotiators. In the West of Scotland we have several famous yacht clubs. These clubs are patronized by a fair cross-section of the community, but, as with everything in life, there are various layers of affluence between the owners of the most expensive boats and those of the more modest.

The size and capacity of a boat helps in these circles to distinguish its owner's social position – such foibles are our ruin but few escape from them, which explains why somebody once described boating as a hole in the sea into which the owner pours money.

Some people buy boats for the pleasure of sailing, which in the West of Scotland tends to produce experts in handling boats in Force 8 gales, whereas in Bermuda or the Mediterranean it is about getting a sun tan. Indeed, at St Tropez, in France, people pay thousands of dollars to hire a boat for a few days and have absolutely no intention of leaving the harbour – the hirers of the most expensive boats sit on deck and sip champagne, and watch the crowds on the quayside watching them sitting on deck sipping champagne.

The owners of the boats are obviously meeting some deeply felt tribal need among their customers so are not ashamed to charge outrageously for meeting it.

Back in Scotland a modestly affluent small businessman (Angus McTavish) was looking for a bigger boat recently and took a fancy to the boat on sale in his club belonging to the Commodore (roughly equivalent to a Golf Club's 'Captain'). The Commodore wanted

Watch those first offers!

An impatient wholesale watch-seller, having experience of negotiating with his country clients, decided to short-circuit the higgling and haggling and get straight to a price near where he and the buyers settled last time.

He tried out this plan on his first call at a store right off the highway up in the Catskills: 'Let's save ourselves a lot of time and sweat,' he told the owner, 'and cut out the ritual haggle between my high price and your low one.'

The buyer looked suspicious but said nothing. The seller took this for agreement with his proposal. 'OK,' he said, 'I'll give you my absolute best price – no kidding, no padding, and you tell me how many watches you want at that price. Then we can settle up and both go fishing this sunny afternoon.'

He opened with a good price, much lower than he normally started at and below that at which they had settled last time. The price was good enough to warn the buyer slightly.

'How many watches do you want at my absolute best price?', asked the watch-seller.

'None', replied the buyer. 'None?', queried the astonished seller. 'That price is better than last year's and it is my absolute best price. So how many do you want?'

'You must think we country folk are stupid or something,' replied the buyer. 'I learned long ago that any city slicker who tells you he is opening with his "absolute *best* price" still has some way to go before he reaches his absolute *bottom* price, and even when we get to that price, I might just tell you I don't want any watches at all!'

They haggled all that afternoon and long after the sun went down. In the end they settled below the seller's 'absolute best price' giving him a profit that wouldn't cover his gasoline for the sales trip.

This taught him how to make a negotiator happy: give him haggling room; and also that country folk never accept a city slicker's (or anybody else's) first offer.

£53,000 for his boat. He too was looking for a bigger boat, being even more affluent than Angus.

The most that Angus could get together to purchase the Commodore's boat was circa £45,000. This was composed of the price he could get for his own smaller boat, plus a small loan from his bank.

It happened that Angus was in the club one afternoon and got into conversation with the Commodore. The subject of bigger boats came up and Angus expressed an interest in the Commodore's. The Commodore said he would be delighted to sell his boat to Angus, him being 'such a good club member', etc.

Angus decided to go in near his top price and said: 'The absolute most I can offer you for your boat is £43,000, but I don't suppose you'll take that for it?'. He was stunned by the Commodore's reply: 'OK. I'll sell you the boat, Angus, for £43,000.'

The shook hands there and then and each went away to arrange the transaction (both are solicitors and in Scotland a verbal agreement is a legally binding contract).

Literally, within minutes Angus had doubts. In fact he felt somewhat sick about the whole business. Instead of rushing off to tell Mrs McTavish the good news that they had acquired the Commodore's boat (she being a keen sailor too and not just an indulgent wife) he wondered whether he had done the right thing.

What would Mrs McTavish say when she found that he had bought a £53,000 boat for only £43,000? She would ask how long the obviously prolonged negotiations took and what concessions had her husband made to get the boat at that price? If he told her it only took 15 seconds to clinch the deal, she would be sceptical, either about her husband's truthfulness ('was he paying much more than £43,000 and hiding the true price from her?'), or about the boat's seaworthiness.

Indeed, Angus himself could think of all sorts of blemishes in the Commodore's boat (he had sailed in it several times) and he began to worry about any blemishes he did not know about. Before the deal he was prepared to ignore these blemishes, even excuse them; after the deal they loomed before him. In fact the Commodore's acceptance of his first offer depressed him no end. Instead of a bargain, he wondered if he had a lemon.

We don't know how the Commodore felt as I got the sorry tale from Angus himself, but I guess that he was in no less of a torment than Angus once he thought about what he had done.

14

Send us your invoice!

Recently, I was approached by a multinational company with a view to my conducting a two-hour negotiating seminar for their senior managers.

The company president interviewed me before approving the arrangements for the seminar. He asked about the proposed contents and I showed a slide presentation on 'the worst thing you can do to a negotiator – accept his first offer!'. He expressed strong approval for the topic and desired it to be included as 'my people could do with that message'.

After various other details were agreed he said I could go ahead. He was about to close the meeting when I suggested we agree my fee for conducting the seminar.

'How much do you charge?', asked the company president.

'Normally, £1,800 a day', I replied, expecting to have this challenged.

'Fine', said the company president, 'Just send us your invoice!'

Exit one much demoralized negotiator, who to this day wonders what fee he should have shot for.

How would Mrs Commodore feel about her husband selling their £53,000 boat for £43,000 in a 15-second 'negotiation'? She would hardly be impressed with his business acumen.

Angus would forever ponder: what price might the Commodore have gone down to as he had accepted £43,000 without blinking? Should Angus have opened at £41,000 or £40,000 or – why not? – £30,000? He would never know.

And not knowing worried him. In fact it worried him so much he derived little pleasure out of the entire transaction.

What had the Commodore done to Angus by accepting his first offer?

He had made Angus miserable.

Instead of a good bargain he had made it into a doubtful deal.

He had undermined Angus's self-confidence as a negotiator. He had also done the same to himself, if he thought about it. Instead of two guys happy with their deal, he had made it likely that neither would be happy with it.

15

By treating Angus's first offer with due respect as one negotiator to another, the Commodore could have made them both happier with the deal, even if Angus had to pay *more* than £43,000 for the boat.

How could the Commodore achieve the remarkable situation of an agreement on apparently worse money terms than the 15-second deal he arranged in the club?

Think what would have happened if the Commodore had haggled with Angus over his first offer of £43,000. How he haggles is not the point here (we look at haggling techniques later), only that he does so in some way.

Suppose after due time has elapsed, he gets Angus to raise his offer from £43,000 to his limit of £45,000 (or perhaps even higher by forcing Angus to see his bank manager). If they settle at a higher price than the first offer, will Angus be happier?

Yes!

He would rush home to Mrs McTavish to tell her what a brilliant negotiator he was. He had got them a £53,000 boat for '*only* £45,000'; 'an absolute snip at the price'.

He would minimize the 'very minor' blemishes in the boat ('normal wear and tear; overall the boat is as sound as a battleship'), and he would promote the family image in owning such a 'magnificent' boat, – 'that's one in the eye for them next door and their holidays in St Tropez!'.

Altogether he would be feeling very very pleased with himself.

So, too, would the Commodore. He would have negotiated a better price than he was first offered. He would be £2,000 or more better off. His wife would be duly impressed, or at least less unimpressed as a result. He would have proven his ability as a negotiator.

All this would remain true even if *the final deal was at exactly the same price as the original one*.

How so?

If the Commodore had haggled and found he could not get the price up, but made an effort to bargain ('cash deposit now and the rest in two days, bare boat minus all moveables and less the radar', say) he would have made Angus *work* for the deal. And a deal somebody works for is a deal that they are happier with. I know. I've heard Angus on the subject.

It wasn't the money terms of the deal that were wrong. It was the way they were arrived at.

Even smart guys get 'bargains'

University professors generally believe themselves to be among the brightest people in the world and they often congratulate themselves on the 'bargains' they negotiate out of others.

A marketing professor at a European business school was asked to team up with an American professor and run a four-week top-level marketing course at a US mid-west university during the summer vacation.

He was asked to quote his fee for conducting the course. He sat and thought about it for a week and asked for £24,000 (being the equivalent of his annual university salary). He justified this to himself on all kinds of grounds, including the joy he felt in 'showing the Americans that when they want the best, they have to pay for it'.

He was a trifle surprised, but nevertheless delighted, when the US university accepted his fee without a quibble, and he duly conducted the course in a euphoric mood at the bargain he had struck with them.

During the first week he got into conversation on the subject of fees with the other marketing professor (who came from Texas and whose constant refrain was: 'you get what you pay for').

He declared his own joy with his fee of £24,000 and how it had enabled him to bring his wife over for the course and for a holiday in New York afterwards.

However, he was mortified to discover that the Texan had obtained his 'normal' rate for top-level executive courses: £52,000 plus the family's expenses for accompanying him!

From this moment on the European professor's enthusiasm for the course sank to zero.

People like to get bargains.

Much of the retail trade plays on the desire for bargains in its promotion campaign and so-called 'sales'. 'Save 15 per cent by buying now', shouts the advertising. And it works. People who had no intention of buying the item, reduced by a notional 15 per cent, flock in to buy it. In effect they are not saving 15 per cent at all – they are *dis*saving 85 per cent!

But they are happy with the deal because they believe they have paid less than they would have done if they had bought the item yesterday.

Negotiators expect to negotiate. They feel cheated if somebody does not recognize this. A first offer accepted without a haggle undermines their confidence in both the deal and themselves.

If the first offer is acceptable, what other offer might have been accepted if it had been tried first?

Answers to self-assessment test 1

1 *(a)* You are thinking only of the profit you might make and not about the problems you might create. *Never* accept a first offer.

   (b) How crazy can you get? His offer is already more than you were hoping for and to delay a decision by sending him out of your sight is foolhardy – he might see another boat on the way back to his car.

   (c) Absolutely right! No matter how good the first offer, haggle: he might offer even more and anyway he will be happier with the boat if he thinks he squeezed you.

2 *(a)* Oh dear, you are impetuous aren't you?

   (b) Because he has accepted your first offer it must cast doubts in your mind about the 'Isabella' and/or what you might have got it for if you had opened lower.

   (c) How do you know it is a bargain?

3 *(a)* Obviously a very determined young woman! But consider the risks that she blows it by trying to intimidate the producer. He might 'offski' and she might 'neverski'. However, if she thinks she can batter him into a higher price through *(c)*, then it is a good move.

   (b) Terrible! He has pulled the 'sell cheap/get famous' gambit beloved by casting producers the world over.

   (c) Has the implications of *(a)* without its risks. Shows she knows what she is worth. She can come down a *little* without losing out or relying on vague hopes and fantasies as in *(b)*. If you sell yourself/your products cheap, then you will get exactly what you demonstrate they are worth!

Self-assessment test 2

1 You are in dispute with a supplier over items he has charged you for in his monthly account which, in your firm opinion, were delivered in a faulty condition. Do you:
   (a) Stall on payment of the total amount?
   (b) Stall only on the amount in dispute?
   (c) Offer to compromise on the disputed amount?

2 Your office is due for a rent review and you expect the landlord to demand an increase of 20 per cent. Do you:
   (a) Make a 'reasonable' offer of 10 per cent?
   (b) Demand a rent reduction?
   (c) Offer to go to arbitration?
   (d) Itemize all the defects that you want rectified?

3 You are managing a civil project for the Saudis, who have imposed a time-delay penalty clause on you. A sub-contractor has missed a delivery of important machinery. Planned start-up times may not be met. Do you:
   (a) Check through the supply contract to discover their liability?
   (b) Ask the site agent to list all the failures associated with the defaulting contractor since the job began and telex their head office with your complaints?
   (c) Telephone their managing director and threaten to sue for any penalty costs imposed on you by the Saudis?
   (d) Arrange an immediate meeting with the contractor to put into operation an alternative delivery programme that your own engineers have drawn up?

Chapter Two

Why you can't negotiate a grievance
or how not to get your room changed

Have you ever been on the wrong end of somebody else's incompetence?

Of course you have.

People let you down. In fact, the only thing that is certain about some people is that they let you down, incessantly. The divorce courts are full of claims of broken promises, unrealized expectations and unfulfilled dreams.

And not just the divorce courts. Sit in any court for a few hours, and watch the litigious in pursuit of retribution for real or imaginary failings on the part of those they were happy to do business with, until the roof fell in.

The distribution of short straws is random enough for all of us to get one sooner or later, and not just in business. You can draw them at home, in a restaurant, hotel, or bar, at an airline check-in, theatre ticket office, passport control, shop counter, taxi rank, or even your local PTA.

Anywhere that Joe Citizen meets Fred Citizen there is a possibilty that one or other, or both, will find cause (real or imaginary) to complain about something the other does, or does not, do that they expected them to do, or not do. (Throw in their in-laws and you can have a real bust up, especially after a breach in the Christmas 'ceasefire'.)

Don't just take my word for it!

How many hours is it since you last thought you had cause to complain about something or somebody, either in your professional business or elsewhere? If you answer more than eight you are either

20

of divine origin or you've been asleep (and if you were asleep I bet you *dreamt* you had a complaint). Complaining is part of the social intercourse of human beings.

This chapter is not a plea for moderation in the habit of complaining – far from it, but unless King Canute's humiliation against the waves was in vain we have no call to struggle against the irresistible tide of human nature!

My purpose here is quite different. It is to improve the effectiveness of your complaining about the failings of others by giving *them* an alternative to merely telling *you* to get stuffed.

Not all negotiating relationships are sweetness and light. Some can get very acrimonious, and I am not just thinking of industrial or international relations. Commercial deals can fall apart when one of the parties believes the other is failing to meet its commitments in some way.

Not only are promises not kept, but deliveries are not always made on schedule, quality controls sometimes fail, performance can fall short of specification, and earnings may be less than expected, etc.

Agreeing on a deal is only part of the commercial relationship – keeping the deal implemented is the other part. In complex production systems, there are many opportunities for failings to occur and some way has to be found for resolving the conflicting interests that arise after contracts have been signed.

The problem with most people faced with a business (or domestic) grievance is that they have a remarkable facility for doing the one thing that is *least* important to them and their grievance, while at the same time, they display an astonishing incapacity to do the only thing that *is* important.

People, almost without exception, play their strongest suit in the pure mechanics of *complaining*. People, undoubtedly, are good at complaining, especially when their grievance is tinged with a perceived slight of some kind or when an element of unfairness is felt to be present.

But they are usually absolutely bereft of ideas about their most important interest, namely, getting their grievance *remedied* in some way. That's why I urge:

DON'T JUST COMPLAIN, NEGOTIATE A REMEDY!

Remember, it is not the other person's failings that need sorting out – it's your *interests* that need attention.

Don't ring them, call us instead!

A large property development company, operating in a rapidly changing market, relied heavily on information of its financial status. This was particularly critical during the first hour of business each day.

If their funds ran down overnight, they needed to know *before* they placed deals that day in case they were forced into borrowing short-term 'hot' money at high interest rates to bridge gaps of a few days. A firm of their nature going into the market for temporary funds more than a few times a year could start damaging speculation.

However, a problem developed when the accountants found it increasingly difficult to get through to the local bank on the telephones early in the morning. This caused friction between the bank tellers and the firm's accountants.

Relations got so bad that pressure appeared for the account to be moved to another bank on the grounds of the bank's 'incompetence', 'delay' and 'bad faith'.

A 'crisis' meeting was arranged with the bank, and the accountants spent a weekend documenting the 'failings' of the bank over the past month, itemizing the alleged costs of telephone delays to the property company's finances.

Before the meeting, the managing director of the property company rejected the entire approach of his accountants and threw their thick report into the wastepaper basket.

Instead, he asked them what arrangement would suit their needs either with the current bank or a new one. In lieu of an answer, he suggested that they get the bank to ring them each morning at 9.05 on a special line instead of them fruitlessly ringing the bank. He also noted that this would save them the cost of the phone calls!

The bank willingly agreed to this proposal.

There is no doubt that had the accountants' report been discussed there would have been a bitter row and a breakdown in the relationship.

I can illustrate how easy it is to fall into the lack-of-a-remedy trap, by recounting an incident from my own experience. (The best lessons are our own mistakes.) In October 1977 I arrived in Rome late one wet Sunday evening, having driven there by car from sunny Edinburgh (via a North Sea ferry, of course). I was very tired, to put it mildly.

I had been seconded to a United Nations agency for three months and they had reserved me a room in a small hotel on the Aventino. The room I was given had one major failing: it was damp. In fact it was very damp. It was like a sauna – only a cold one!

It was also late, I was tired and had nowhere else to stay that night, so I remained dressed, put on my overcoat and spent a very restless night on the damp bed.

By now you have the picture: *I had a grievance*.

In the frequent moments when the dampness woke me I rehearsed the speech I intended to make to the hotel management next morning. My imaginary agenda began with a description of the lousy room I was in, the management's total lack of consideration of my health, let alone my comfort, and the extortionate price they were charging the United Nations for a cold sauna. My *piéce de résistance* was a sarcastic 'joke' about the ancient Roman proclivity for bathing being taken too far when it was brought into the bedrooms! My imaginary speech ended with an account of the exhausting extent of *my* car journey and finally what *I* thought of their Roman welcome to strangers.

Believe me, through the night the agenda was altered several times and the levels of authority I considered invoking escalated – a telex to the United Nations in New York, perhaps even a meeting of the Security Council (you can see how delirious I was as a result of the dampness).

I had no doubt that the force of my complaint, if not natural justice alone, would immediately provoke the management to apologize profusely and move me to a magnificent room, complete with marbled bathroom and private balcony.

Next morning, I marched to the reception desk ready with my complaints, and spoke to a young man – he had that Roman air of authority and also that charming Italian indifference to anybody other than good-looking women.

So I told him about the dampness in the room, but copped out of the more outrageous of my prepared agenda – including my 'joke' about Roman baths.

What was his reaction? *He suggested I tried shutting the window!* What he did *not* do was offer me another room. I was flabbergasted, and withdrew a defeated and demoralized complainer.

But reflecting on this episode – as I did later that day from my dry room in *another* hotel – the excellent S. Anselmo, Aventino, Roma – I had nobody to blame but myself:

AS I HAD NOT ASKED FOR ANOTHER ROOM WHY ON EARTH SHOULD HE OFFER ME ONE?

If my remedy was to be given another room – a perfectly reasonable proposal unless the hotel specialized in damp rooms – it was up to me to say so.

By not stating *my* remedy, I left the initiative of suggesting a remedy to the other guy – and one thing you can be certain about, if you leave the initiative to somebody else, it is likely that they will only consider their own interests in framing their remedy rather than yours. Hence, his suggestion that I shut the window.

This is all the more certain if, as is usual in situations where you feel aggrieved about something, you colourfully blame the other person for their failings.

Attack someone and they defend themselves.

Attack them ferociously and their defence is returned with interest.

Impugn their competence and stand back while they dissect yours.

Challenge their parentage and they will challenge that of your children.

Tempers are never calmed by being tested and the longer the row goes on the less the likelihood that you will get anything other than a sore throat – and perhaps even a thump on the nose for your trouble. Try the hopeless tack of making them responsible for the problem and they will deny responsibility.

In Italy, for instance, hotel receptionists, car hire people and airline check-ins have a devastating way of shrugging their shoulders and blowing hard through tight mouths when they want to deny either responsibility or concern for your plight. (Though, I must say in defence of Italian *waiters*, they are the best in the world.)

The lesson is clear. Time spent preparing for a blazing row about your grievance is totally wasted – so is the nervous energy.

What of the alternative? To negotiate a remedy you have to have

The case of mother's 'mile high' applie pie

A harassed mother was trying to cope with the tears and tantrums of her youngest son who was loudly complaining that he always got the smallest piece of apple pie because his elder brother always took the biggest piece.

She decided not to bore her children with another lesson on the morality of sharing in families but instead asked:

'Who cut the pie?'

'I did', said the eldest boy, adding sarcastically, '*he's* too little to be trusted with a knife.'

'I agree,' the mother replied, 'but he is not too little to know which is the biggest slice of my apple pie on the plate. So he chooses which slice to eat first.'

The youngest son triumphantly chose the biggest slice of applie pie and the eldest boy was livid.

'In future,' the mother added, 'the rule will be clear; one of you will cut the pie and the other will choose which slice they want.'

At this the elder boy whispered to his brother that as he always cut the pie he would get even next time by making sure that the two slices were the same size!

The mother returned to her TV show happy to have solved a problem so constructively.

one. And thinking through what your remedy ought to be requires preparation – another reason for not wasting time thinking up articulate insults about the other person's incompetence. The case for you negotiating a remedy is fourfold:

1   You take the initiative in choosing the remedy and your remedy is more likely to start with your interests in mind than theirs.
2   The negotiation will be on your remedy and not stuck in an argument about the legitimacy of your grievance.
3   By proposing a remedy you provide helpful information to the other person – he does not have to guess what will assure him of your future business.
4   The other person may very well be relieved that you want so little and are not demanding, like an American attorney, grossly exaggerated recompense for your 'losses'.

Putting the discussion into a business context, suppose, say, you just complain to a supplier about a missed delivery of components. You can be fairly sure that their shipping department will justify, excuse, explain, blame or even apologize for the delay. They might just tell you to 'offski' – they have bad days too.

But, remember, if you have no remedy prepared you leave it to them to choose whether to do anything or nothing about deliveries in future. If you attack them they are unlikely to be motivated to do anything other than defend themselves.

It is not always within your power to withhold business from them – at least in the short run – and if you haven't clout like that you had better be careful that you don't provoke them into turning their system's 'gremlins' loose on your deliveries in the future.

The capacity for people in large organizations to quietly screw up their own systems in pursuit of private revenge on 'difficult' customers is known among the *cognoscenti* as the 'buggeration factor'.

Anybody who has ever suffered the 'run around' in business will recognize the seriousness of my caution.

But even if you have clout, you have no guarantee that pushing them will produce a remedy suitable to your interests. If pushed they might do something for you, but only the minimum possible. If, however, you state your (reasonable) remedy you could be half way to getting them to agree to it.

The greatest source of grievances is vague promises.

Plumbers and electricians who offer to fix something in your house are notorious for many things (including not doing it, or not finishing it when they promised – though garage mechanics are by far the worst story-tellers in this respect), but their notoriety is unbounded in the way they calculate their bills, especially if they are not working to an agreed estimate.

Never accept a promise to fix anything in your house that is not supported by an estimate of the likely cost, complete with a breakdown of the individual items, before they start work. Get it in writing or write it down in front of them. That way you will not get a nasty surprise when they send in their account, and if you do not agree with their estimate you can tell them before they start. They might suggest a cheaper way of doing it – ask them – or they might suggest you use out-of-fashion materials instead of the superduper gadgets that have just arrived in their shop.

On not being served

On entering an Italian restaurant in Edinburgh last year, we were confronted with an Italian scale row between the leader of a party of six and the owner. The issue appeared to be the inability of the restaurant to sit the party at their booked table because the people already there had not finished their meal. The spokesman was adamant that his party be seated immediately (clearly an impossible demand unless the owner phsyically ejected the party at the table), and went on to lambast the restaurant for accepting his booking and then not having a table ready for when he and his guests arrived.

We were swept aside as he led his party out to the street to cries of "I'll never return to this so-called restaurant again" and "What an outrageous way to be treated". I stepped forward and the visibly angry owner turned to me, no doubt expecting a repeat run of "what a way to run a restaurant". He explained that my table was still occupied by the earlier diners and that it would be 15 minutes or so (which means 25 minutes at least) before we could be seated.

"I see," I said. "In that case, myself and my guests will avail ourselves of complimentary drinks at your bar until the table is free." To which he replied: "Fine, no problem. Luigi, serve Mr Kennedy's party with whatever they want, no charge." Which is precisely what we did. More than halfway through a bottle of Chianti Classico we took our seats, much the merrier for the free drink. Also, the owner and Luigi danced around our table with Italian style attention all night, grateful no doubt that somebody loved them.

A reasonable solution is often acceptable to those embarrassed by a failure in their usually reasonable service; embarrassing them by unreasonable abuse usually means no service at all and no compensation for their embarrassment at failing to serve you reasonably.

Remember, before they get the job they are in the business of selling, not supplying, and they are more keen to persuade you to give them the order than they are to pad the account later.

Also, if in the course of the work you want to change something from the original plan, don't ask them how much they will charge you for the change (what an invitation that is!) – tell them the changes you want and leave it to them to raise the issue of extra payment, and if they do, negotiate!

When something goes wrong you should think what (realistic) options you have, and you must concentrate entirely on the issue in dispute and not irrelevant side-issues. If the meal was rotten, make that the issue and not the way they took your coat (that's a separate issue). In the same way, if your spouse is late, that is the issue and not your mother-in-law or last year's missed anniversary.

Lastly, look for trade-offs that will meet your interests. Will a reduction of the bill make up for the lousy lasagne? How about a free video for the machine that needed repair within two days of purchase? Why not a free meal in the hotel where the room TV is not working, or a free taxi when reception forgot to call you for your train?

Recently, British Airways mislaid my luggage in Amsterdam and through overbooking shunted me into the Economy cabin from Business Class. I told the cabin crew that I was not best-pleased with British Airways at that moment but that a free brandy would go a long way to making me smile again. I was instantly given two brandies! (And they found my luggage too.)

Answers to self-assessment test 2

1 (a) The first thing you must do. This is also the most commonly chosen response by managers.

   (b) A move that reduces your bargaining power.

   (c) Never! Let *them* offer to compromise.

2 (a) You are in danger of implying a 15 per cent compromise before you know how strongly he feels about his demands.

   (b) A strong opening – better left as a support for (d).

   (c) Arbitration removes your veto on the decision.

   (d) Open with the defects in order to get something back for what you pay – support it with (b) if possible. Could reduce the pressure of his demands.

3 *(a)* It's a bit late to check liability and anyway it does not resolve your own liability to the Saudis.

(b) A waste of time and telex money as it does not move the machinery to your site.

(c) Threats won't get the machinery to the site.

(d) Don't just state a grievance, negotiate a remedy!

Self-assessment test 3

1 You run a courier business and one of your vehicles breaks its big-end just before a busy weekend. A friend has a spare van and agrees to loan it to you until your own vehicle is back on the road. He asks you to sign a receipt that reads: 'One vehicle, £500, one week's rental'. Do you:
   (a) Sign as asked?
   (b) Insist on a properly drawn up legal contract?
   (c) Tell him a receipt is not necessary between friends?
   (d) Ask for more details?

2 You have been approached by a Saudi Arabian company to handle the management contract of a large civil project. Do you:
   (a) See this as an opportunity to get into a lucrative Middle East business and therefore go in easy on your initial fee?
   (b) Assume that as the market is strong enough to take a high fee you can go in 'high'?
   (c) Prefer to 'wait and see' what fee is likely to be acceptable to the Saudi company?
   (d) Base your fee on what is profitable to you?

3 You are a manufacturer of engine parts and have been granted an interview, after many last-minute cancellations, with the boss of Europe's largest car firm who insists that you meet him at Terminal 3, Heathrow, a few minutes before he flies off to Australia. This is your big chance! While walking towards Passport Control, he opens with a demand for your 'best price' for a six months' contract to supply fuel-injection pumps. Do you:
   (a) Show him what you can do by quoting the lowest price you can in order to get your foot in the door?
   (b) Go in slightly above your lowest price?
   (c) Go in high to leave yourself room to negotiate?
   (d) Wish him a pleasant flight.

Chapter Three

The negotiator's most useful question

or how to avoid a one-truck contract

Experience is a great help in dealing with the routine – you know what to expect if you know your line of business and there are few, if any, surprises left. Experience in one field of negotiation can also help in another where you are totally ignorant of what is considered 'normal' and what is 'out of the question'.

But how can you make up for lack of experience other than by taking the time, which you may not have, to get it?

If you have to make a decision, perhaps with a lot of money (or something more important) riding on the outcome, and you have almost no experience to draw upon, you will need more than just luck to help you out.

Fortunately you can apply the principles of negotiating to give you the elbow room to make your decisions. Some years ago, for example, three authors were involved in negotiating the sale of the video rights of a book they had written. In the field of negotiating author's rights they had some experience, but video rights were a new game altogether.

The question posed by the video company's offer was whether it was a 'good' or 'lousy' deal? The three of them spent a not inconsiderable time pondering that question but none of them had a clue to the right answer.

Their problem was that they had no idea what the rights were worth *to* the video company or what to look for – and what to avoid – by way of contractual obligation. The amount of cash they were offered could have been a small fortune in the video business or a mere bagatelle. The proposed contract could have been normal or outrageous.

In other words, they could have been offered a deal that

experienced authors would have been delighted with, or they could have been giving away the video rights for next to nothing.

Now it is important here that you do not concern yourself with the actual amount of cash involved. That is of no relevance to anybody in a *new* market, though it is often the first rationalization made by newcomers for why they accepted the first offer.

If your money flow tends to be stuck in the tens and units range, try not to show that you are overly impressed when someone opens their offer with a number followed by several zeros – it weakens your negotiating position.

Likewise, don't fall into the opposite trap of being unable to negotiate seriously for what are bagatelles compared to your daily business quotas – more than one top negotiator, handling millions of dollars a deal, has confessed at a workshop how they tend to get done in the little deals worth a few hundred dollars or less.

If anybody offers you what appear to be '*big*' sums of money for what you value relatively lightly (or its converse, pennies for what you value greatly), remember:

they may not be nuts – *you* may just be naive!

Therefore, don't sign, grab it and run. The bargain price for a product in one market can be sheer robbery in another. And there is nothing worse for your ego than finding out later that you cheated yourself.

An offer you 'can't refuse' is one you ought to think carefully about. Consider: what is the price for a gallon of water for a thirsty tourist in the middle of Glasgow?

Not much, considering the amount of water that falls on Glasgow at most times of the year. Certainly you are unlikely to get mugged for water in Glasgow – though, I cannot discount the possibility of you being taken for a half-bottle of the local 'water of life'!

But what of the price for a gallon of water in the middle of the Arabian desert? In 1980 I was driving a Range Rover round up-country Oman selling diamonds to ex-patriate Brits working in oil exploration, and such was the dehydration that I drank a gallon of water every 20 miles – just to stop my mouth cracking like sandpaper.

And that was only part of the discomfort. I was under strict instructions from the Old Arabia Hands in Muscat not to drink alcohol even if I found an unlocked brewery; not to complain about having sand in every orifice of the body; and under no circumstance was I even to *think* of women – 'If you must look at a camel, make sure it's a male one' I was advised! I can tell you straight, if for any reason I had been cut short of water for any length of time in that climate I would have traded all my diamond samples for a glass of water, and probably thrown in the company's Range Rover as well.

So, a bargain can look different depending on from where you are looking at it. Faced with an offer from the video people the authors needed to know the market price for video rights: should they take the deal or count their fingers? That is, they needed a lot more information about the *appropriate* money worth, and implications, of the deal if they were to prepare a negotiating position quickly.

Their efforts were aided by the use of a single question, asked over and over again and, in the event, they got the up-front money considerably increased and eventually reached agreement on the wider issues. So they're glad they asked their questions. It is with these questions, and the wider implications of going into deals where the market is new to you, that this chapter is concerned.

So many deals come undone that it is a wonder any get put together, but the time to concern yourself with the small print of a deal is *before* pen is put to paper, not afterwards in your lawyer's office. And bringing in the lawyers doesn't help too much – they tend to throw spanners in the works of any deal they are associated with and always deny any responsibility for the deals that get past them.

In new business fields – particularly in countries new in your itinerary – you will have to handle the negotiations yourself and hope that you survive long enough to acquire the experience that will protect you from the pitfalls that are obvious to the old hands.

You can start improving your performance in 'one-off' negotiations by first of all not trusting to luck to take care of your interests. Look after them yourself, instead. And to look after your interests you have to identify them.

The simple two-word question that was used in the video negotiation can get you started and to this I now turn.

Because hindsight is a cheap forecaster of the deals we should avoid, the bars and dinner parties of the world are full of smart guys willing to give you advice on what you should have done after you have already done something else. Foresight, a much scarcer commodity, is all the more valuable for that.

One type of deal we must avoid, though circumstances often

conspire against us, is known as the 'one-truck' contract. These are lethal because everything that can go wrong probably will (Murphy's famous law) and anything you insure against only happens after you miss a premium (floor joke at Lloyds).

The time to avoid the disasters of ill-thought deals is when the deals are being negotiated and this can be illustrated by considering the following contract to hire a truck offered by a 'pal' in Muscat:

'One truck, $1000, one month's rental'

What is wrong with a clean and simple 'one-truck, etc.' contract like that? No complications, no red tape, and no hassle, just pay your cash and drive off. The basic problem with 'one-truck' contracts is that they leave almost everything to the mercies of Murphy's law.

And this is true for *both* parties to the deal.

Neither of you is protected in the slightest by the 'one-truck' contract you have negotiated: if you sue them you will either lose the case or waste your cash in a deadlock. Either way the only people laughing in the court are the lawyers, and their bank managers (and if you think your own country's lawyers are expensive, they are positively penurious compared to any foreign lot).

If you are the hirer, you have no assurance that you will get the truck your 'pal' showed you in the compound and not some wreck he keeps out of sight at the back of his lot. Of course, you may protest: 'I trust him, we went to the same school'. Indeed, he could be your best friend, etc.

Fair enough, but many a member of the down-and-out fraternity begins the story of their road to ruin with: 'I went into business with my closest friend and a loan from an awfully nice bank manager'. If you are the owner in a 'one-truck' contract you have no assurance that it will be returned in the condition that it left you.

When (if) it comes back it might have to be parked behind your lot because it is too dangerous to park in the compound. Then you will have to off-load it onto the first fool to walk into your office looking for a 'one-truck' deal!

There is more than enough room in a 'one-truck' contract for disagreement about the condition of the truck, when it is to be returned, who is responsible for insuring it and who pays the parking tickets it collects while out of your sight.

How then do you avoid 'one-truck' contracts? Easy. The only

thing you have to do is ask lots of questions that begin with two simple words, and to keep asking questions until you are perfectly satisfied that you have covered everything. The words to put in front of every question are:

WHAT IF?

Applying this to the hire of a Range Rover for an up-country mission in the bleak wastes of Oman, you could ask, or need to be ready to answer:

What if *the truck breaks down up country for a reason unconnected with my usage or unrelated to parts for which there are spares?*

Agree on warranty and responsibility for delivery of replacement parts or a new truck.

What if *the truck breaks down after being improperly driven?*

Insist on a 'no claims for improper usage condition, and the return of the truck to your premises at the hirer's expense.

What if *it is stolen and I cannot complete my sales trip within the month?*

Agree an insurance premium that covers immediate replacement of the truck but avoid any acknowledgment of liability for his estimates of his loss of sales (no salesperson ever reckoned somebody else was responsible for them losing a *small* sale – they're worse than anglers with the 'fish that got away').

What if *your carelessness about parking causes it to be stolen?*

Have a waiver clause inserted that absolves you of liability in these cases – try to get your brother as sole and final arbitrator of any decision about the extent of 'carelessness'.

What if *it is repossessed by one of your creditors and I cannot complete my sales trip?*

Get this covered by the insurance premium for immediate replacement and insist that this is paid for by the truck owner.

What if *your creditor damages it out of both our sights?*

Shove in another waiver claim but insist that the hirer gets a signed statement as to the truck's condition before he parts with it.

What if *you socially misbehave and the locals smash up the truck in revenge – or shoot at it if a camel is involved?*

Insert a high 'returnable' deposit condition that is withheld in these cases (again, try to get your brother nominated as arbitrator).

What if *you knock down a camel and the locals hold the truck in ransom?*

The 'returnable' deposit isn't.

What if *the truck is unlicensed for cross-border journeys and I accidently make one?*

Commit the hirer to usage within the territory and liable for all breaches of local emigration laws. Charge him a 'lieu of export deposit' and also *sell* him a map of the territory.

What if *we dispute the amount of damage or the extent of the seriousness of minor scratches?*

Clearly covered by the appointment of your brother in the arbitration clause.

What if *I find you are not the legal owner of the truck and it is repossessed by the authorities?*

Demand legal proof of ownership or, in the absence of the relevant documents, get a *large* discount off the hire charge and the insurance premium.

What if *you fail to return on time at the end of the rental period?*

Insert an excess-hire charge at a steeply rising *per diem* rate and, of course, loss of the 'returnable' deposit.

What if *you use the truck for some illegal purpose and it is impounded by the police?*

Require legal usage on pain of forfeit of the 'returnable' deposit.

(And, **What if** *we don't settle the 'what ifs' before it is time for me to return to Britain?*)

(Clearly the Hussle Close tactic. Tell him if he agrees to your terms he can have the truck now. Otherwise later.)

* * *

These **What ifs** are somewhat tongue-in-cheek but they have a serious message for all negotiators.

Look at the following summary of an Omani hire contract and compare it with the 'one-truck' contract above:

One 1988 model Range Rover, as new, 12,020 miles certified on the clock, with all parts in working order, serviced at 12,000 miles, complete with spare tires, fan belts, exhaust system, plugs, a new battery, a wheel, chain and tackle and 25 gallons of fuel. Delivery to your hotel by 6 a.m. Tuesday next. $1000 COD – cash only. Insurance for month's use and all legal penalties for traffic and other offences to be borne by hirer. Any defects in bodywork to be notified at delivery, otherwise as is. Rental fee covers one month's hire and unlimited mileage from Tuesday next to 2 November next only. At the end of the rental period the hirer must return vehicle by 6 a.m. fuelled and in sound condition to the company and pay (cash only) for any damage, defects or missing parts on return.

Now I freely concede that even this contract is not *legally* cast-iron but it is certainly better than the original 'one-truck' deal offered by a 'pal' in Muscat. You can see this by looking at your last car rental form. The big rental companies are experts at avoiding 'one-truck' deals – their rivals who didn't are no longer in business.

However, car-rental companies are not quite as cautious as the airlines who have exclusion clauses on their tickets (which by the act of buying you are deemed to agree to) such that even if a 747 knocks you down on the runway and reverses over you twice, you, or more likely your widow, will find that they are absolved from all liability by something called the 'Warsaw Convention'.

That is why people of a nervous disposition about their chances ought *never* to read the small print of their airline tickets – they could die of shock and still not have a claim on the airline!

In a large deal there could be numerous *what if* questions that need to be asked and answered if the parties are to protect their interests. In a *new* deal, or strange country, it is even more necessary to do your preparation with a list of *what ifs*.

Negotiators face a big problem when a previously prepared

What if they are covered against cock-ups?

In any 12-month period over 400 claims for faulty design, inaccurate calculation and inadequate checking of work are made against consultant engineers by their clients from all corners of the globe.

Insurers are convinced that the cause is 'weak supervision' or 'inadequacy of the site engineers'. The insurance association recommends that consultants refrain 'from accepting contractual responsibility that performance criteria would be met'!

It is also adamant that consultants must not disclose, even casually, that they have professional indemnity cover for their actions. The most common cause of this disclosure is for the consultant to include in his contract the limitations of his indemnity, which only encourages the litigious client to try to recoup something from a contract that does not meet his expectations.

Apparently they only sue those they know have some cover, irrespective of the justice of their claims.

It is a fact that many construction companies open a file for claims the instant they receive a contract and set to work to make claims even before they start work on site. Some companies are rumoured to have larger claims departments than they have estimating departments.

contract that suits the interests of the other party is presented to them – that's why it's previously prepared! – and do not know where to start opening it up for discussion.

The asking of questions, and particularly the act of thinking them through *before* the negotiation, will suggest terms for negotiation. In every deal, there are dozens of *what ifs* and consideration of them is a useful way of creating negotiable variables for you to trade against the liabilities you are being asked to accept.

Of course, in some parts of the world in times of disorder a 'one-truck' contract is all that you can get. On these, thankfully few, occasions you may have no choice but to take it.

In the mélée for the last plane from Phnom Penh, you are not advised to negotiate a seat in the 'no smoking' section using *what if* type questions, nor to demand that the 'one-truck' liabilities be amended before you remove yourself from the tarmac and get on board.

However, you could still try to negotiate a deal on the price if you've run out of dollars and the pilot is being difficult. Ask him if he accepts payment by American Express – you never know, he just might have a 'pal' in Muscat who has an Amex account (too bad if he only accepts Diners Club) and you *might* be able to negotiate the surcharge!

Answers to self-assessment test 3

1 *(a)* A very risky decision on your part (and his).

   (b) If you had time but you haven't.

   (c) Oh dear!

   (d) Yes. Get more details. Ask *what if* questions.

2 *(a)* 'Sell cheap, get famous' is no way to riches.

   (b) Assumptions are dangerous until tested.

   (c) This leaves it open for you to go in high.

   (d) OK but it leaves out of account how badly they want your services, nor does it distinguish between high and low profits.

3 *(a)* He eats people like you for breakfast. His intimidation has obviously worked and he knows what you can do!

   (b) If you concede at your first (short) meeting, what will he achieve at a longer meeting in a month's time?

   (c) A trifle better – you have resisted this bullying tactic but still not your best move.

   (d) Yes. Tell him to call you when he gets back and say that meanwhile you will talk with his technical people about what exactly it is that they need. They may need your pumps more desperately than he wants you to know about and he can worry about that all the way to Australia – and back!

Self-assessment test 4

1   You are arranging to visit a number of Arab countries in order to promote your company's products and to secure local agencies to distribute them in local markets. How many days do you allow for your itinerary which is to include Egypt, Saudi Arabia, Oman, Kuwait, Iraq and Libya?
    (a) 7
    (b) 14
    (c) 18
    (d) 21
    (e) 28
    (f) 31

2   You have been given an interview with a leading local Arab agent and have spent several hours socializing and drinking coffee. No business has been discussed and you are anxious to get the discussion of your proposals under way. Do you:
    (a) Raise the subject in a lull in the conversation?
    (b) Wait until your host raises the matter?

3   You have decided to wait until your host raises the subject, and it is time for you to leave. Do you:
    (a) Ask him when you can return to see him?
    (b) Leave a set of materials about your products?
    (c) Ask him for a definite date for an interview to discuss your business?

Chapter Four

Negotiating with the Arabs
or how to take your time

Whereas with the communists the state is the dominating influence in their business lives, with the Arabs it is the extended family (father, brothers, uncles, in-laws and cousins). Obligations to one's family and friends are not treated lightly; they create, and are created by, mutual expectations of help, assistance, support and succour. Warm-hearted nepotism rules, or at least holds great sway.

Your problem as a foreign negotiator can be summed up simply: you are not related to any Arab family and therefore you are an outsider, a true foreigner in their land. To the extent that you compound your lack of familial ties by being ignorant of Arab customs, manners and outlooks (or, worse, disrespectful of them), you will find it very difficult to make much headway in your business relationships with Arabs.

The Arab nation consists of 160 million people in twenty-two states spread across Northern Africa and the Middle-East, from the Atlantic Ocean to the Gulf of Oman. While there are vast variations in outlook, practice and economic capacity between the Arab states, there are certain unifying forces of their societies that keep the spirit of Arab unity alive, and which occasionally blow a little life into its practical application.

The Arabic language is among the most prominent of the unifying forces in the region. Dialects and accents there may be, but the written language and its classical roots reign supreme from one end of the Arab nation to the other. Those who would hope to do a lot of business with Arabs would do well to learn their language – if only to a rudimentary level. In the meantime, many Arab businessmen speak English (and sometimes French), and have degrees and diplomas from Western universities.

The other main unifying force is Islam, for though Islam is now a religious way of life for many beyond the Arab nation, it remains, for the majority of Arabs, a living memory of their history. It pervades all their social structures, and in many of their states it has a grip on the secular that recognizes no separation of church and state.

Some countries, such as Saudi Arabia, Sudan, or Libya, are more Islamic in their secular laws than others, such as Egypt or Bahrain, though the differences are often more of degree than of kind. The availability of, or punishment for having, booze is a reliable, if crude, guide to the Islamic temperature of a country.

While it is not necessary to convert to Islam to do business, it is sensible for you to learn something about Islam, its history and its creeds, and to treat its modern manifestations with respect.

You must not mock by word or grimace whatever you find usual in their behaviour and you must make no derogatory, or joking, remarks about their beliefs and customs, especially as much of what passes for knowledge of Islam in Western countries is grotesquely inaccurate.

If it is Ramadan, your Arab host will not be eating or drinking until sunset, and, no matter how hungry or thirsty you are, you should try to avoid both food and tea, unless your host has it brought for you into his *diwan* (a room for receiving guests) and where to refuse might give offence. But even then, acknowledge that you know it is Ramadan for him, and nibble or sip unenthusiastically at it, rather than wolf it down like it was your last supper.

If you are insensitive to this type of situation it might very well *be* your last supper as far as business with him is concerned, in which case you will eat, drink and go home empty-handed.

Negotiations with Arabs can never be divorced from their environment, and it is for this environment that you must be prepared. By environment, I don't just mean that sand will be blown into your every orifice (though that is a distinct possibility up-country), nor that it gets very hot during the day and perishing cold at night. The environment I refer to has more to do with the social environment that influences their behaviour as negotiators.

Take their 'open door' policy, for instance. You may well be deep into discussion with an Arab contractor when some of his friends or family arrive at his office. They certainly will not be kept waiting outside the room but will be invited in for tea and talk. Your negotiations will be suspended until they leave, and they will recontinue only for as long as it takes for some more of his friends to arrive. And so it could go on all during your visit to his office (though there are some signs that the traditional open door policy is being curbed by the more commercially minded of the Arabs).

The Arab will not refuse traditional hospitality to those who come to see him, and he can be diverted for many hours a day by social interruptions. You must accept this, no matter how important you might feel you are and how crucial your timetable is to you. It is not rudeness on his part – quite the contrary, it is simply the continuation of the courtesies of the bedouin desert tradition, every bit as necessary for his functioning as a respected person in his society, as it is for you to turn up to work in your trousers and not your pyjamas.

This open door habit infuriates some Western negotiators. If you show signs of impatience to your host, you will be finished. I know one Harvard law graduate who swore to me he would never return to Egypt, no matter what the fee, because he could not stand having his day prolonged by constant interruptions in his discussion with Arab civil servants, who operate the open door policy within government departments for absolutely anybody, their lowest clerks included, even though they (or, rather their fathers and grandfathers) long ago left the imperatives of desert hospitality behind them.

In one respect I had to concur with his draconian decision: if you can't accept Arab ways, don't waste your time trying to do business with them.

The Arab attitude to time can give an entirely wrong impression to those brought up closer to the clock than is probably good for them. Americans are often obsessed with time, while Arabs can appear to be totally devoid of any consciousness of it.

Many Arabs know that time is more important than they or their colleagues acknowledge by their behaviour, and attitudes are gradually changing. No doubt a compromise somewhere between the two extremes would do everybody a little good, but the low value placed on time has environmental roots which cannot be ignored just because it is inconvenient to Western attitudes.

The Arabs are not the only nation to place a low value on time: the Italians, Spanish, Portuguese and Mexicans, among others, are notorious for adherence to the *mañana*, *mañana* school of decision-making. It reflects the non-urban life-style of a pre-industrial society, and it withers only so fast as the effects of urbanization and industrialization spread through the generations.

Hoping for quick decisions from Arabs can be a frustrating experience. On the other hand, they can make quick decisions on occasion (and deciding not to trust you could be one of them!).

Taking a long time to come to a decision about a proposition may not just be an example of muddle and inefficiency – though this can be a singular explanation in some cases. It might indicate that they are displeased with something in your proposition and that, though they have hinted at what is displeasing them, you have not picked up their signals and have not responded to them positively.

If you feel harassed by what you regard as time-wasting, you certainly will not hear nor note the signals, while, if you slowed down to their pace of doing business, and listened carefully to what they were saying, you would learn to spot the problem, and react by amending your proposition in some way (much the same advice applies to negotiating with the Japanese).

In a sense, a negotiation with an Arab is partly a consultation with him. If you are doing well in your negotiations, you will hear yourself saying: 'Here is what I was thinking of suggesting, what do you think of it?' far more than confronting him with: 'That's my final offer, take it or leave it.'

If you do not reformulate aspects of a proposition you have put to them, rather than say 'no' to your face they will not make a decision at all. They hope time will allow them to get their way, or will permit the issue to die naturally by neglect.

As you brood over your dilemma – 'Why are they avoiding me?' –you might, just might, go over what they said about your proposition and identify, by luck or by judgment, what the problem is and, in re-presenting the issue, assuming you have got it right this time, you might be surprised by the sudden change in pace as you both move on towards agreement.

If you don't see the problem at all, you will return home, cursing the inefficiency of a nation 'that was still riding around on camels while we were in High School' (as my Harvard friend somewhat impudently put it).

Arabs do not like face-to-face confrontations and quarrels with foreigners. They have a tradition of hospitality and politeness. The door that is open to the cousin or the neighbour is also open to you. You have come a long way to see them, and they respect that, and they will go out of their way to make you welcome, no matter what other urgent business is at hand.

Providing you do not upset them with your arrogance and haughtiness (the two qualities Arab negotiators identify in Westerners – especially, I am sorry to say, in the English, though not, I am glad to confirm, in the Scots – as the ones they find most unacceptable), you will eventually get round to talking about business.

They do not like rushing into business subjects as soon as they meet with you. It is bad manners to do so and they will expect you to talk with them about social and other matters for some time – perhaps fifteen minutes or more on most occasions, sometimes several hours, or, on other special occasions, through several meetings.

Your best guide is to leave to the Arab negotiator the decision of when to talk business, and do not under any circumstance be the first to raise the subject.

This can be very off-putting, especially when you have met the Arab for the first time and, as far as you know, he does not know why you have come to see him. In your mind is the thought that unless you tell him that you are looking for a local agent to market your binoculars and range finders, he might think that you are a tourist just passing through the Gulf on your way to play polo in Delhi.

If you are tempted to raise the matter of business first, in one word, don't!

If the interview is clearly at an end, very politely thank him for his generous hospitality and ask if you can come and see him on another day. He will certainly not refuse to see you again (here the open door works for you!) and you can try again.

The Arab businessman may behave generously to a fault, and sometimes appears to have an other-worldly naïveté about him, but he is not at all as stupid as an ignorant Westerner might think – indeed, there are more Arab graduates of Western universities sitting across the carpet negotiating with Western businessmen than there are Western graduates sitting across the carpet negotiating with Arab businessmen!

By showing that you understand the social mores of the Arab peoples you will be more likely to get a chance to talk business with him when you meet again. If, however, he is away when you next return to see him, or is in and meets with you but does not discuss business, it suggests either that you must keep trying on another occasion, or he is telling you, without being rude, that he does not want to be an agent for binoculars and range finders (he will have found out why you are in Doha or Bahrain without you knowing about it).

Another word of caution is due here: if he does ask you why you have come to see him, do not start off a sales pitch along the lines of 'the great opportunity I am about to offer you is to get rich as an agent for my company's products', which is an OK line in Garry, Indiana or Walthamstow, London, but totally out of place in the Middle East.

It is far better to pitch it along the lines of you wanting his help in a business proposition. He is unlikely to need to get richer and will resent the implication that you think he wants to, but he cannot resist 'helping' someone he has learned to respect.

Most Arab governments insist that you do business through a local agent, whether you are negotiating with a private business or with a government department. This policy has ensured lucrative careers and incomes to Arab nationals, and siphoned back some of the profits to the lands that generated them. It is a sound and sensible policy, very much in the national interests of the Arab countries.

You will not get far without a good Arab go-between. On a big deal, he can help you make the right contacts in the government and those you will need to get a decision to go ahead with the project. He will speed you through the paperwork (taking 'speed' in a relative sense, of course!), arrange for labour, materials, transport, storage and accommodiation, and, most importantly, expedite (less slowly than otherwise!) payments to you for your work.

A good local agent is more than somebody working for you, he is a partner in the venture and should be treated as such. He gets his income from commission (a percentage of the gross value of the deal) and he will expect to be consulted about everything, perhaps far more than you normally disclose to your own employees, including, for example, your pricing policy.

Just how you handle this aspect of your relationship could influence greatly the energy with which he represents your interests in negotiations with other Arab nationals and government departments. It may appear that he is not doing a great deal for his commission (and the sum you pay to him can appear horrendous when said slowly, especially in comparison with your own earnings for creating the business), but without him you might find out just how bad Arab agents can be when they don't try very hard.

You will have to negotiate with him first about the level of his commission, and this can range from four to nine per cent. On a multi-million dollar deal he is going to be very rich in no time. Sure, you should still haggle for each percentage point, or fraction of a percentage point, that he gets in commission. He will expect you to do so, and might get suspicious if you don't.

You will find him accommodating in a negotiation with him and it will follow the same pace as the deals you will do with him as a partner with other nationals. 'What will you be doing for our money?' is a useful question to keep on the table as you negotiate his commission, as is: 'What other major projects have you been agent for?'

Finding out what you are getting for your money is always a good idea in any negotiation. If you are not impressed with what is on offer you can lower his expectations of the price he will get for his services or you can increase his commitments in return for what he gets.

Previous experience is another useful line of attack. If he was the go-between for a Japanese steel works or an American downstream processing plant, you can have some assurance that he is worth what he is asking (also you have somewhere to go to check on his performance). If yours is his first big project, this is surely going to be reflected in his commission rate?

The worst thing you can say about your Arab go-between, even if he is half decent at his job, is that he takes a long time to do it. On the surface this looks to be a sign of inefficiency – of which you will no doubt get lots of other examples while you stay in hotels or travel around Arab countries.

On the other hand, it may be that you are pacing the deal too fast for the local community. He will spend not a little time socializing while engaged on your behalf in business with other Arabs. The delays that appear to be inflicted upon you will be inflicted upon him, with the difference that he will not be so acutely embarrassed by them as you might be.

The people he deals with have a different set of values from you. For instance, they will regard efficiency with less awe than you do, perhaps considering that loyalty from and to their Arab staff is more important.

Again, psychologically, the Arab is out in the desert, alone with the people upon whom he depends for his very life. Loyalty when there is a water shortage is more important than efficiency – if you doubt this then you have never depended absolutely upon anybody for much that mattered.

The bedouin is loyal and he is learning about efficiency rather than practising it. You should remember this in your dealing with your agent – show loyalty to him and you will get it back with interest .

Another carry-over from this earlier age (not all that long past – thirty years ago the bedouin knew the true worth of a camel) is the sense of fatalism. This is a direct consequence of living on the edge of survival where not much changes in the lifestyle of successive generations. The cycle of life is not often interrupted by anything that man does – nature holds dictatorial sway.

The rural societies of those who live close to nature tend to have a fatalistic view of the universe. 'God wills' is an acknowledgment of man's weakness before the natural order of things. Once science is allied to man's needs, nature submits and with it the idea of fatalism.

When Westerners witness Arabs in a fatalistic mood they conclude that this is an essential characteristic of the Arab outlook on life. It is not, and a moment's reflection on the rural societies of Europe in previous centuries, or the indigenous societies of North America, would show this 'fatalism' to be on a par with the superstition and myth of our own pasts (how many Westerners read their 'stars' each day?).

The modern Arab – the one you are likely to be negotiating with – is unlikely to leave his share of the deal to fate! You may take it for granted he will work for the best deal for himself and leave nothing at all to chance.

The more perceptive reader will have noticed that this entire chapter has been written in the male gender, as if the female did no exist. This might have antagonized feminists. It has been, however, a deliberate policy on my part to exclude from this chapter any reference until now to Arab women.

It is not that the Arab woman does not count; of course she does in her society. But unless you are mixing business with cultural reform (a short-term activity in the Middle East), the position, and the future, of Arab women is, to be pretty blunt about it, none of your damn business!

Old hands in the Middle East always advise outsiders to steer well clear of even the notion of Arab women while visiting Arab countries. And they do so, for good reason. Arabs do not like interference in their private affairs by foreigners, especially those who know little of what they are talking about.

If you want to join the League for Stirring Up Trouble in Arab

No agents here!

Not all Arab countries insist on a foreign firm having an agent. In Iraq, for example, the government has decided on a deliberate policy of discouraging foreigners from dealing with government agencies through agents. The reasons have much to do with the proclivity that the agent system has for encouraging corruption and the abuse of influence. Also, under socialist influences, the role of agents in enriching themselves runs counter to prevailing ethical standards, even if they are acting as honest go-betweens and in no way corrupting anybody (in Egypt the government encourages agents but requires them to disclose their commission earnings and prohibits them being paid via accounts kept overseas).

It is an offence to use the services of an agent who is not formally registered with the public authorities. To do so risks being black-listed by the government from future business with Iraq. Moreover, even registered agents can be refused access to negotiations on your behalf in some state agencies.

In this atmosphere it is best to avoid dealing with anybody who claims to be able to put a contract your way because of their alleged influence with somebody in the government service. You are unlikely to be given a contract as a result of such a person's activities and are more likely to end up with yourself, or officers from you company, in a local (unpleasant) jail.

In Saudi Arabia, in contrast, while local agents must register with the Ministry of Commerce, their role in acting as intermediaries between the Saudi purchasers (government or private) and the foreign supplier is directly encouraged. But care is needed in selecting an agent in most Arab countries, for once an agreement has been reached with a local national it is extremely difficult to disengage from an agency relationship that has proven to be less than satisfactory (the local courts are not models of objectivity in disputes between locals and foreigners).

countries, you may go ahead and state your views to whosoever will listen to you. You will not, however, be able to combine such activity with doing business with Arabs.

I was once saved at a dinner party in London from an indiscretion in talking about the subject of Arab women in their homelands. My guests were an Egyptian Arab and his wife, and during the evening I raised the subject of the Arab attitude to women in conversation.

The reply I got came not from the man but from his wife, an articulate educated woman, who spoke better English than I did Arabic, and who knew both Western and Arab societies from having lived in both since she was a schoolgirl. Her defence of her status within her Arab family left me realizing I knew nothing at all about the issues involved and I resolved never to raise the subject again. I suggest you make a similar resolve.

In some countries, Arab women play an increasingly important and public role in government, business and political affairs. In others, there is a long way to go before they achieve even limited recognition outside their immediate families. That may or may not be enough to encourage you to accept that other people live the way they do because it suits them or, if it doesn't suit them, that only they can change it.

In all countries you would do well to concern yourself with what you came to do, namely to negotiate with your Arab counterpart, which means, in the main everywhere, and exclusively in some countries, that you will do business with a man. If you resent this, or can't accept it, you are unlikely to do business at all.

Hence, in Arab countries do not even think about women, let alone attempt to importune them, innocently or otherwise, and, if you must look at a camel, as I was advised in Muscat 'make sure it is a male one'!

Answers to self-assessment test 4

1 You must arrange to take as much time as is available to you if you intend to conduct business with Arabs. If your time is short (seven days) only go to one country. If you must visit them all, take at least 31 days and, if possible, another two weeks.

2 *(a)* Never! Do not introduce a business subject with an Arab under any circumstance. Even if he is visiting you, wait for the

subject to be raised by him. If he is visiting you in your own country, wait for some considerable time before raising the subject, and only then after you have exhausted your 'small talk'. Never appear in a hurry to talk business and never ever appear irritated by the lack of progress in this area.

(b) Yes!

3 *(a)* Yes. A sign of your respect for him.

(b) No. It's too obvious an attempt on your part to hustle him into discussing business with you before he is ready.

(c) Absolutely not! This suggests that you are annoyed and that he is a poor host. Stick to *(a)* and let business take its own course.

Self-assessment test 5

1 You are looking at a car in a showroom and it is priced at £9,000. You decide to buy. Do you:
   (a) Ask what is included in the sale price?
   (b) Offer them £8,500?
   (c) Tell them you'll think about it?

2 You are a management consultant and receive a telex from Sydney asking you to quote for a sales seminar for the Chamber of Commerce. Do you reply:
   (a) How many and who is to be there?
   (b) Tell them that your standard daily fee is £1,500 a day plus expenses?
   (c) Ask for £2,000 for the seminar plus expenses and £500 per day for travel?

3 If after two weeks you have not heard from Sydney do you:
   (a) Telephone or telex them asking for information?
   (b) Wait?

4 Suppose they reply to a request for £1,500 a day plus expenses that you are asking too much for the fee, though they agree to meet your expenses. Do you telex back and:
   (a) Reduce your price because you want to go on an expenses-paid trip to Sydney?
   (b) Confirm your price but offer to travel Economy?
   (c) Confirm your price but assure them you are worth it?

Chapter Five

The negotiator's dilemma
or how to stop worrying and love the haggle

People up to their necks in negotiations every day of their business life don't have a great deal of time to sit about and contemplate what they are doing.

They just get on with it, and sink or swim.

Periodically, some people are troubled by having to act without thinking through why they move the way their business nose leads them and, occasionally, in retrospect, their bank balance suggests they shouldn't have. I am referring here, of course, to the very successful, not nature's natural losers.

These people get where they are going by being good – very good –at what they do, and they are good because they know their business better than their rivals – for if they don't their rivals surely will teach them. However, no matter how good they are at what they do, as negotiators they still have to face the same problems as everybody else.

This is a revelation to junior staff who as yet have little experience of negotiating, *and* to those who think that the problems they face across the table are personal to them. Not realizing just how common their condition is can make them act like a first-time-young-mother-to-be who believes *her* pregnancy has the historic significance of the immaculate conception.

New people in the team take what happens in their negotiations very personally and in consequence get quite emotional when they discuss the perverse pleasure they believe their opponents experience from making life exceedingly difficult for them.

Sadly, a few entrants are soon lost to their company because nobody explained to them the causes of the very real problems of negotiating and, eventually, these problems prove overwhelming.

That we lose such people for a while is perfectly understandable once you contrast the fragility of human nature with the problems of the negotiating process. Identifying the source of these problems is fairly easy. Wishing them away is hopeless.

Every negotiation creates the pressures of its own dilemmas. If you claim that it doesn't you are either exceedingly thick-skinned (in which case the sex life of a rhinoceros should fascinate you) or you ain't doing much negotiating.

Top negotiators, when questioned about the dilemmas of negotiating, admit to experiencing them. A few confess that they remain baffled by the negotiating process and that thinking about their bafflement worries them. Hence they don't.

However, if they did they would soon realize that what they think is a personal problem is in fact the very essence of the process of making decisions by negotiation, and that once recognized as such it soon diminishes in importance.

I will illustrate what I mean by reference to the experience of a successful negotiator I know 'down under'. In 1981, I was walking along Macquarrie Street, Sydney, looking for a bookshop, and had stopped at the traffic lights for one of the many minor irritations that the Australians have copied from the Americans (along with armed police, appalling television and a zest for living as though they enjoy it), namely, the 'walk-don't walk' sign.

I was hailed – yes, hailed! – by a man across at the other light. I took him for a nutter on the look-out for a lonesome 'pom'. However, when I got closer I recognized an old friend whom I had not seen for 22 years. Being British, I lied and told him he hadn't changed a bit, and being Australian, he confessed he couldn't say the same about me!

Bob, for such is his name, was on his way to eat and naturally we teamed up. We walked back a few blocks and passed the Inter-Continental (where I was staying, as it happened, but I did not disclose this fact in case his destiny had been all it had promised to be when I last saw him). Eventually we found an all-hours diner.

We had been close friends in our teens and had been through several adventures in those halcyon yesterdays that get more halcyon only because time passes. Our last fiasco had left us flat broke and we kipped at a church hostel in Melbourne. The stench of sweat, urine and vomit, all washed down the floor by a powerful hose at 7 a.m. (we were warned to keep our shoes on the shelf) shocked us to the quick.

Also, the 'holy' warden knew about bargaining power: 'If you want my hot soup you'll have to sing my hymns' was how he put it.

Naturally, we sang. After that we parted at Flinders Street Station. Bob went back to Sydney to write the Great Australian Novel, and I to London to change the world.

Our conversation that afternoon was intense, as you would expect. Eventually the subject of what we were doing now came up.

Blandly I told him I was in Sydney for a week conducting clinics on negotiating. As blandly, he told me he was into property development.

Obviously the Great Australian Novel had been left to be written by somebody else! (To be fair, the world is much the same as it was in 1959.)

Over the next few days I went up the coast to his beach house (magnificent views and privacy), flew over one of his developments in a light aircraft and sampled suburban affluence with his wife – a professor – and his teenage kids.

All this background is by the way of ensuring that nobody gets the notion that Bob is one of society's losers when it comes to the negotiating business.

We bantered on a lot with occasional serious interludes. During one such I asked him about *his* negotiations and to my astonishment he told me that it was one side of his work he did not enjoy.

Now this was curious because if there is one business that is all negotiating it must be the property business.

'But you negotiate constantly,' I insisted.

He agreed, but insisted that he often hated it when he had to negotiate with anybody. He coped, he said, by gritting his teeth and getting on with it.

'Tell you what,' he said, in the manner of someone about to make a proposition, 'if you can explain to me how to cope with my aversion to negotiation, I'll come to one of your clinics.'

Now there is nothing more dangerous in my field than for a generalist to attempt a specialist's problem: the road to grief among consultants is strewn with 'experts' who rush into assignments faster than they can complete them.

'OK', I said 'I'll have a go at your problem if you tell me how you came to be a millionaire from being a broke libertarian, but it will still cost you $200 for a place at my clinic.'

The deal being struck, Bob insisted on talking it through at once. Bob's real problem, it emerged, was that he thought of himself as the only negotiator who experienced 'his' problem! He couldn't talk to his own people about it because such a confidence could undermine his reputation as a hard-nosed negotiator. And losing a reputation for hardness in Australia could be terminal in his business.

What did Bob think was his problem?

It was really several closely related dilemmas.

In negotiating we do not know for sure what the other person will accept – sometimes we are not too sure about our own limits – and not knowing what the other person is thinking creates a dilemma.

The three dilemmas mentioned by Bob were:

1 Where to open?
2 When and how far to move?
3 How long to hang on?

The root problem here is that of *uncertainty*, and decision-making under uncertainty is one of the most perplexing of all activities.

A brief summary of the workings of a market economy should enable us to see why the first dilemma arises. A mass consumer society has the singular advantage over its rivals that it enables people to make informed judgments about what they want to do with their money.

Their wants lead them to look at the price tags on the (abundantly) available goods and they mentally compare the benefits of those goods with the benefits of holding onto their money. If they prefer the goods more than they prefer to keep their money (bearing in mind how little, or how much, they have) they exchange their money for the goods. If they prefer to keep their money they may do so, but then they must do without the goods.

The problem with this (admittedly idealistic) picture of consumer markets is that on a very large number of goods and services in our economies there is *no* price tag: you can't simply look at a price tag and make a choice.

You and the person who owns the goods have to fill in the price tag before you can decide whether to buy or he can decide whether to sell. The process by which the tag is written out is called negotiating.

Prices in markets for goods without price tags aren't fixed by law – they are decided by what somebody is prepared to pay and what the owners will accept. These two prices – what you are prepared to pay and what they are prepared to accept – need not start out the same or even similar. Nor need they move closer in the course of the negotiation. They only have to be identical if and when a deal is struck.

What's it worth?

Australia has a lot of sandy acres. How much an acre? Some of those sandy acres were worth next to nothing until they discovered they were high-grade bauxite.

A downtown Sydney site with a two-storey 'colonial style' pub on it has one price. Get planning permission to clear the site to build a 40-storey office block on it, and the same site has another price.

An American film studio's library of thousands of old black and white movies cluttered up its warehouses. What were they worth in cash, not sentiment? The new management sold them for $9 million cash to an agent and then sold off the acres of warehouse land for redevelopment for $15 million, making $24 million in all. Meanwhile the agent resold the old films individually to the world's television companies and has so far grossed over five times what he paid for them, i.e. $45 million. Which was worth more – the films or the land?

If the price has to be settled by negotiation, the first decision 'crisis' (as Bob put it) is which price to open our bids at? If we pitch our opening price too low we could blow the deal, with a request that we 'offski' for being impertinent.

Alternatively, the other person could say 'yes' out of relief at the generosity of our offer compared with his expectations of his goods' worth (clearly, he hasn't read Chapter 1!).

Hence, are we too cheap or too dear?

This is a dilemma felt by all negotiators – including the most experienced – and causes them to hesitate before declaring an opening price, just in case they open too far from where they might be able to settle.

As Bob expressed it, there never is a price he would gladly accept for a building that he wouldn't abandon at the first hint that he might get somebody to give him more for it. Nor, presumably, is there a price for somebody else's property that he wouldn't drop to if he thought they would accept less for it.

In the business of buying and selling, where there are no pre-set price tags, we are torn between our need and our greed, though what is daylight robbery at one moment can look cheap at the next if the buyers know something about the market that we don't – yet!

Not knowing for sure where to open in each individual case, we suffer the mild stress associated with making any decision under uncertainty. I told Bob that we can never avoid the dilemma of deciding what price to open at in negotiations and, contrary to some views, experience does not totally eliminate the problem.

Experience helps though to reduce the stress of uncertainty. Also, the existence of competition acts as a restraint on wildly erratic pricing behaviour. But reduction in stress and restraints on behaviour are not enough to *eliminate* the dilemma.

Why? Because as we become more conscious of the consequences of missed opportunities, experience only pushes it into the background, while in the foreground we reflect privately that we do not like the 'ritual' tensions of negotiating. This leads us to ask: when and how far should we move in a negotiation?

Inside every negotiator there is a person wanting to make a deal.

We just don't like 'losing' an order nor do we like starting over after we've lost. If you have gone into a negotiation wrong-footed you search for a means of getting back from the dead, *if you can*.

If your company policy does not allow an adjustment in price to something below the 'bottom line' you will try to invent an exception that covers your retreat from the high ground. You know you shouldn't but you do anyway. Salespeople the world over are always inclined to cross a bottom line in hot pursuit of an order.

In the cases cited by Bob it was not the bottom-line price that he was concerned with. He wanted to know how to handle a situation when the deal he was offering was unacceptable to the other side and he did not know how far he might have to go to get an agreement. He need not be anywhere near his bottom price when this happens.

That precisely is the dilemma: we do not know for certain what the other person is up to when he refuses our offers. Is he laying it on thick just to get us to concede more or is he testing our resolve to stick to our offer as it stands?

If we make a movement – because we believe that it is necessary to do so to save the deal – we could incite them to continue haggling. If we don't respond, or respond too late with too little, we might provoke a deadlock.

Getting it right and minimizing the chances of our movement – or lack of movement – being misunderstood by the other person is by no means easy. They face the same dilemma as we do (this at least is of some comfort). They don't know whether we are bluffing or being candid, when we resist their pressures to move from our positions.

Some negotiators have tried to resolve the movement dilemma by making a unilateral pre-emptive offer and refusing to budge from it come what may. This tactic has the singular advantage that it removes the indecision about how far to move: you don't!

However, it has a number of drawbacks that make it unsuitable as a 'negotiating' policy on most occasions. Not least is the necessity that you have overwhelming bargaining power and a credible willingness to use it.

Among the consequences of using naked power is the retaliation it provokes among its victims – nobody likes to be pushed around.

Normally, movement is required in negotiation but there is no predetermined 'rule' that can tell you how far you may have to move or if you have to move at all. Would that there was! We could then compare the extent of the move we have to make and decide whether we prefer to move that far or accept deadlock.

Where does this leave the negotiator?

59

One thing is certain: the dilemmas cannot be avoided. Every negotiator faces them and realizing this alone should help you cope.

'Well', asked Bob, 'how long should I hang on for a better price?'.

'We are back with another dilemma,' I told him.

As we don't know for certain what is going on in the other person's mind we do not know whether his reluctance to settle on our (by now amended) terms is not just another test of our resolve to stick to them. Remember, it is his job to keep pushing us on the current offer. He must try to nibble away at the edges, or try to take us with a frontal assault on some core principle. He wouldn't be worth a bowl of cold porridge if he didn't! Nor are you if you don't resist every step of the way.

The problem this causes us is to think about the time spent in the negotiation with one guy that might be better spent in negotiation with another guy. Negotiations take time which has valuable alternative uses.

Instead of chasing a better deal with Fred by holding out for more, by settling for the terms that are on offer (or breaking off at a deadlock), we might be able to get over to Bill's office to spend the time negotiating an even better deal with him.

Alternatively, we can hang on at Fred's and perhaps secure a deal that justifies our foregoing the opportunity to open up a negotiation with Bill.

How much time to spend on a particular negotiation is never obvious until after the time has been spent. But it's not hindsight we are short of!

Every man knows the feeling when he is trying to read a woman's mind: is she saying 'no' to test his devotion and intentions, or is he wasting his time trying to change what is for her (and therefore for him) an irreversible decision to have nothing to do with him?

Eventually, he gets the message and perhaps looks elsewhere – though she can never be sure that this is not a ruse on *his* part to test her resolve!

Time is a great pressure on negotiators. It is always the case that there is no point spending time negotiating if it doesn't matter *when* we reach agreement, for if it doesn't matter when we agree we might as well do something else meantime.

Though time pressure is present in every negotiation, it is not necessary that every negotiation reaches a decision within its allotted time – deadlines, like the seasons, come and go. Judging

Pre-emptive final offers

In Britain in the 1970s many volume car plants were strike- prone – if it wasn't the assembly workers it was the electricians or the engine fitters, or even the tea ladies. Two major companies, Ford and the then-named British Leyland, tried a similar tactic to force through a non-negotiable wage rate. They told the unions what they intended to pay the employees for the coming year and firmly refused to negotiate any amendments.

In Ford's case it provoked a bitter strike – even though the actual wage offer was at the upper end of the union's expectations. Deprived of a role as negotiators, the unions won the support of the employees by claiming that Ford's tactic was an attack on the principle of trade unions, but they won even more support by asserting that if Ford offered so much in the opening round there must be lot more to follow if management was pressed hard by union solidarity.

British Leyland's experience was slightly different. Initially the management, led by Mr (later Sir) Michael Edwardes, were successful in the pre-emptive non-negotiable offer. The company was bankrupt and Edwardes made the credible threat to close the business down for good if the employees went on strike. His reputation as a no-nonsense boss who said what he meant and meant what he said had preceded him.

On the second occasion he tried the same tactic – some plants went on strike in immediate protest. In the eventual vote on the deal there was a narrow victory for the management. However, no sooner were the plants back at work than local disputes broke out – stirred up by shop stewards playing to a resentful workforce. It took some weeks of local strikes and much lost output before everything settled down again.

Unilaterally short-cutting the negotiating process seldom pays when the expectation is present in at least one of the parties that decisions are going to be made by the process of negotiation.

Time and circumstances change, of course, and what does not work on one occasion might on another. In the 1980s, trade union militancy collapsed in the UK, largely under a new phenomenon known since as Thatcherism. Whether the 1990s will see another change or it will be more of the same is one of the factors which make life as a negotiator so interesting.

whether to hang on for a better deal or to try elsewhere is the inescapable dilemma for every negotiator.

Some people can never reconcile themselves to the negotiator's dilemmas and they avoid, wherever possible, overt negotiating situations. Upon such people every fixed-price store builds its business. Others face up to the dilemmas and make the best deals they can.

If the dilemmas are difficult when you are dealing with money prices for goods that you are familiar with, it is a great deal more complicated when you are confronted with barter deals, and these have been getting a lot more common in international trade recently.

Barter was the norm in trade negotiations about four centuries ago and it was replaced by cash deals only as the international trading system found a common currency – gold. As paper currencies became 'as good as gold', i.e. they could be switched into real goods when presented to the country concerned, the international trading system moved from barter to cash transactions.

The world trading system, however, has long been divided into those countries that have 'hard currencies', i.e. currencies generally convertible in any other country into real goods on demand, and those that have 'soft' currencies, i.e. currencies which nobody would accept in a lucky dip. Trade between 'hard' and 'soft' currency countries often has to be conducted in some form of barter, or its more complicated version known as 'countertrade'. Increasingly, however, countertrade has become an acceptable mode of trade between hard currency countries. For example, the USA has swapped 747s for Saudi oil, and many off-set agreements between Europe and the USA are a form of countertrade. In fact, countertrade is rapidly becoming a major instrument of international trade, and new negotiating opportunities (and not a few examples of dilemmas) have opened up as a result.

Whereas the negotiators can be reasonably sure of the monetary value of the goods they supply for countertrade, they may be slightly less than sure of the value of the goods they are offered in exchange.

Some surprises can be experienced in this business. A Swedish office equipment firm agreed to give typewriters to the Soviet Union in exchange for ladies' watches. Upon inspection these watches were found to have a Western market value greatly in excess (because of their quality) of the nominal 'price' of their typewriters. Indeed, the Swedish firm disposed of them to a Dutch importer at a considerable premium and was most happy with the deal.

However, not all barter deals are as successful. In order to dispose of the barter goods, the negotiator may have to sell them to a third party. In one such deal, a Belgian exporter of chemicals swapped them for Polish cement which it sold on to an African country (of 'Marxist' persuasion). In the view of the Belgian negotiator, the cement was of such low quality that water mixed with corn flakes would produce a better bond than the cement, and he considered himself lucky to have got out from under the disastrous deal (he got cocoa for his cement which he sold for US dollars).

In many countertrade deals, the negotiator does not know the realizable value of the goods that are offered, and he must remain perpetually vigilant about their quality – at least until he has off-loaded whatever he has been lumbered with. He still has to face the dilemma of where to open, or whether to reject the deal altogether. Many traders open with a demand for a countertrade deal – they used to be less candid about mentioning countertrade until they had sucked the other negotiator well into much expense and trouble in the preliminaries in a bid to force him to accept some form of barter to recover his costs of searching for business.

Should the negotiator settle for his losses or press for better terms, or even payment in hard currency? How hard and how long should he push for a better deal than the one they open with? At what point does he conclude that the only deal on offer is the one they last mentioned? If so, does he take it or shove it?

The dilemmas in countertrade are the same in any other negotiations. The negotiator's dilemmas are universal. Nobody doing serious (or even frivolous) business ever avoided the negotiator's dilemmas. Fortunately, whatever the dilemmas, every negotiator opens somewhere, moves so far and stops moving somewhere. The dilemmas are resolved by what negotiators do, not by formulas invented by mystics (whose mysticism is as deep as their pockets).

Answers to self-assessment test 5

1   (a) A good move with cars as the window price is usually the base line upon which they build lots of extras (delivery, number plates, etc.).

(b) Much better if this move follows *(a)* as they might agree and then build the price back towards £5,000.

(c) Car salespeople hear this several times a day and generally it means a polite withdrawal. How do you get back into a good position when you return?

2 *(a)* Always a good move as it gives you information.

(b) Pricing depends on how badly you want to make a 29-hour air flight to Sydney and how much you think they will pay. You certainly must not go for less.

(c) A much more impressive move but as you don't know what they have in mind you may be pricing yourself out of the running. It's the opening dilemma!

3 *(a)* This weakens your negotiating position. If you are worth your fee, you should be so busy with other clients that you haven't noticed their delay in replying!

(b) Yes.

4 *(a)* You probably will if you are more interested in long-distance travel than in making profits. However, they ought to worry whether you are worth any fee if you drop your prices so easily. What exactly are you going to teach their negotiators if this is how you behave?

(b) Not as bad as answer *(a)* but still subject to the same criticism that it undermines your credibility. If you are earning £1,500 a day in Europe why suffer the trauma of a 29-hour flight to Sydney for the same money?

(c) Much better. You may not get the job (this time) but you are obviously setting high standards as a negotiator which shows you are worth your fee. If they agree to the fee it will be because they realize you are more likely to make an impact on the conference participants than your rival cheapies. (You could put it that way in your reply!)

Self-assessment test 6

1   You are in Tokyo negotiating for a long-term contract with a Japanese producer of conduit, and the negotiations have stalled for several days. It feels like you are going round in circles. Do you:
    (a) Wait for them to make the first move?
    (b) Make a small concession to shove the boat out?
    (c) Change the subject entirely?
    (d) Adjourn?

2   You are negotiating with a video publisher in New York who has offered to market your series on management education. They offer you an advance against royalties of $50,000 – $25,000 on signature of contract and $25,000 on delivery of the video tapes. They rejected your demand for $60,000 split similarly. Do you:
    (a) Accept their offer?
    (b) Tell them it is not good enough?
    (c) Offer them a repackaged proposal?
    (d) Walk out?

3   The buyer for a large chemical company responds to your price for parafin by telling you: 'The competition is very strong and you'll have to do better than that.' Do you:
    (a) Offer to cut your price in exchange for the order?
    (b) Ask him by how much your price is above the others?
    (c) Suggest that he accepts the other offers?
    (d) Ask to see the other offers?
    (e) Ask him what he likes about your proposal?

Chapter Six

The myth of goodwill-conceding
or how to teach wolves to chase sledges

It is paradoxical that the handling of concessions is probably the most difficult task facing the negotiator, despite the fact that the rule for above-average performance is fairly simple:

In negotiating, be more like Scrooge than St Francis of Assisi.

Why should you accept this somewhat uncharitable advice? Because in negotiating, generosity is *not* contagious. Would that it was.

Indeed, experience suggests that liberality in concession-making is the worst thing you can do if you want to get concessions from the other person. If you concede why should he do likewise? Surely, by remaining where he is, he might induce you to concede yet more?

In this chapter I discuss the 'goodwill' theory of concession-making, hopefully to eradicate it from your repertoire. Where does this goodwill-concession theory come from?

Its origins are obscure but I have traced it back as far as the unlikely named Bjorn McKenzie, who was a travelling salesman for a short while in the 1890s in the Hudson Bay area of Northern Canada.

Whether further research could throw new light on the origins of goodwill-conceding is, perhaps, less important than the fact that it appears now to have a widespread grip in all walks of business. You have only to ask negotiators if they practise goodwill-conceding to realize just how prevalent it is.

Strange as it may seem, those people who wax lyrical about goodwill-conceding cannot understand criticism of it. This has led to some stormy sessions at the negotiating workshops. Two of the most common defences of goodwill-conceding take the form:

1 I concede a couple of little things early on, just to soften them up.
2 Somebody has to push the boat out or we'd never get the negotiations underway.

Both of these defences, in a triumph of delusion over experience, indicate utter confusion as to the tactics that produce better deals.

Naturally, at the workshops, when I put it so bluntly, I do so in order to ruffle the feathers of the afflicted negotiators and to get them thinking about the consequences of their beliefs.

Consider the first defence. What is the evidence for this?

I won't go so far as to say *all* research findings – in case I have missed some – but certainly all I have seen suggest the very opposite is the case:

Goodwill concessions by one party do not 'soften up' the other side, they make them tougher!

True, the research I referred to is mainly conducted in the hallowed halls of Academe and therefore is vulnerable to being loudly dismissed to the sound of raspberries by 'practical' people.

I too have laughed loud and long at some of the research projects conducted in our universities: not so long ago, someone was researching the phenomenon of 'deviance' (i.e. criminality) among *left-handed* immigrants into the Orkney Islands', and another, this time an anthropologist from the London School of Economics, was studying 'gossip in a Highland village'.

But these are totally atypical of the serious academic research into negotiating behaviour conducted all over the world during the past 40 years. Incidentally, much of this research is also largely confirmed by the practical experience of those negotiators who are free from the curse of goodwill-conceding. You have only to consider what the goodwill-believer is suggesting to see that they must be wrong.

The idea that concessions 'soften up' opponents suggests that negotiators are provoked by evidence of your generosity into being generous themselves.

Now why should your 'early' concessions have that effect?

Consider it from your opponent's view. In seeing you make a concession, he can interpret what you are doing in one of two ways: either: *you are displaying goodwill*, or, *you are displaying your weakness*.

Goodwill is a precedent

A supplier of electrical switch gear was asked to quote a contractor for a job in the Middle East. They went in with their list price and ran into serious resistance from the contractor who flatly refused to pay the list price for anything.

An exasperated sales negotiator eventually pressed the question: 'Why are you so adamant about getting a reduction from our list pricces?'

'Because you gave a subsidiary of ours a ten per cent discount off your prices last year,' replied the contractor.

'But that was a once-only introductory discount for a special job in anticipation of future work', the negotiator replied.

'Well, this contract I am offering you is part of the "other work" and as far as I am concerned I want to be "introduced" to your below-list prices too!

Even if he accepted the first interpretation, there is no compelling need for him to react with reciprocated goodwill and be generous in return. He still has the tempting option of taking a less compromising stance himself.

And if he makes the second interpretation of your conceding behaviour, he will be even more inclined to take a tougher stance.

Certainly, the likelihood of him reacting with goodwill must be very small, unless both of you are imbued with an overwhelming desire to be generous despite your perceptions of each other's relative strengths.

If both of you are compulsive 'goodwill' negotiators, may you always *only* negotiate with each other! But what happens if your next negotiation is with an opponent who is not a believer in goodwill-conceding, either by conviction, from practical experience, or on the evidence of academic research?

Your goodwill strategy then relies entirely on him being 'converted' to goodwill-conceding by your example.

How do you 'convert' him? Do you tell him that the purpose of your concession is to 'soften him up' (which will go down like a lead Zeppelin), or are you going to be less than candid (farewell St Francis!) about your motives and merely hope that his defences are down?

What is the most likely consequence of your attempt to 'soften him up'? You don't need a PhD in human nature to suppose that he is most likely to read your concession as a sign of weakness and act accordingly by getting tougher.

Turning to the second defence of goodwill-conceding ('to push the boat out' and 'get things underway'), you should note the sense of desperation in the tone of this line of defence. As a tactic it is as vulnerable to the same response as the other one: it is more likely to provoke a tougher stance in your opponent, rather than an outbrreak of goodwill, because he will interpret your concession as a sign of your weakness. But there is a more fundamental criticism of it.

Presumably, if you are feeling a need to get the negotiation under way, so is the other person. If this is the case, why is a goodwill concession your *best* move?

Far from getting the negotiation under way, you only succeed in moving your own negotiating position towards the other person's. In effect you have moved onto the slippery slope to surrender. If you concede when I press you, my best bet is to keep pressing until I am convinced that you are not going to move any further.

Up in the Northern Tundra the people are smarter than your average goodwill-conceder. They know about the fallacies of conceding as a negotiating style. They learned it the hard way.

Indeed, drop into any little town inside the Arctic Circle, up in Northern Norway, or Canada, or Alaska, and announce over your beer that you are a devotee of goodwill-conceding and they will throw you out into the snow (even at 40 below).

Some trading posts have Local Ordnances against the practice of goodwill-conceding, and Sheriff Courts up there show no mercy to city folks brought before them charged with the offence. In fact, goodwill-conceding in the Tundra is positively anti-social.

Why?

Well years ago, when the first travelling salesmen went up there to sell them the benefits of civilization – refrigerators, suntan lotion and icecold beer – they were welcomed in the warm and generous spirit that snow people are renowned for the world over.

The salesmen went from outpost to outpost carrying their wares on sledges pulled by dogs. (I refer to sales*men* rather than sales*persons* because the disaster was entirely the fault of smart-assed males from down south, and in those days the only women in the Tundra were born there and were too sensible to ride around on sledges selling suntan lotion.)

The trouble was that some of these salesmen brought with them their 'civilized' vices, one of which was the filthy practice of goodwill-conceding.

At first, the locals didn't realize the poison that had been brought into their midst by their new friends and life carried on as normal. The trouble began when the locals taught the salesmen how to hunt for meat to eat on the long sledge journeys between outposts. The practice that led to disaster was slow to gather momentum, but once it got going drastic measures were needed to stop it.

It seems that Bjorn McKenzie, a cold-beer salesman, presumably of Swedish and Scottish extraction (the accounts vary and are probably mixed up anyway), found himself, one afternoon, being stalked by a wolf, some miles up the track. He had just shot a large elk and had struggled might and main to get it onto his jumbo-sized sledge. The piercing howl of the wolf made Bjorn jump, as it seemed to be very near.

Fear forced him quickly to evacuate his camp and he set off, as fast as the dogs could pull him, down the track to the nearest outpost. The wolf followed just out of rifle range. Bjorn increased the dogs' pace and the sledge lurched forward, groaning with the heavy weight of him, his cold-beer samples, and the dead elk.

As the wolf closed in – he swore he could hear it panting behind him – he searched desperately for a solution to his predicament.

It was then that Bjorn had a blinding flash: of course, the wolf was hungry and wanted some of his elk! 'What better way to get the sledge moving faster than to cut off some of the elk meat and throw it behind to the wolf?', Bjorn asked himself, and immediately congratulated his mother for having such a brilliant son.

The hungry wolf, Bjorn reasoned, would be satisfied and stop hounding him if he was given *some* meat to eat, and, meanwhile, Bjorn could give it the slip and reach the safety of the outpost.

Hence, Bjorn cut off a small slice of meat – a difficult task as the sledge was moving fairly fast at the time – and threw it behind him. He had plenty of meat left and he thought that a small slice would not matter much to himself but would likely help to lower the wolf's hostility towards him.

Everything went according to plan for the next two miles. The dogs strained away and the sledge fairly skidded along over the icy track. Bjorn was already composing the story of his brilliant escape for his pals at the outpost.

But suddenly he heard the howl of the wolf again.

And this time he thought he could hear two of them – perhaps three!

Bjorn's heart thumped away and it was all he could do to remain in a state one degree short of panic. Thinking quickly, he concluded that he had not given the wolf enough meat – he did not bother to ask himself where the other two had come from – and so, he cut off some more meat and threw it behind him.

This time he threw out three portions, just in case one wasn't enough, which still left Bjorn with lots more for himself. He swore later to his pals that he had only gone a few hundred yards when he heard the howl of wolves again. There must have been more than three behind him this time and he could see several more coming through the trees alongside the track, all racing like crazy for the sledge.

Bjorn whipped the dogs harder, and croaked out 'mush!, mush!' (as they do in the movies), and also began to cut meat off the elk at a furious rate, throwing out great chunks of it in all directions.

And still the wolves came on.

Dozens of them.

From every direction they raced after the sledge. Yelping for more.

And more.

And yet more.

They howled in what Bjorn was convinced at the time sounded like derision when they got a chunk of his meat at their feet. Nothing, apparently, would satisfy the wolves and they appeared to have gone crazy (they were already wild, of course, but now they were furious too).

Bjorn started throwing meat to specific wolves, hoping that by pleasing them they would recognize a friend if it came to the final supper with him as the main dish.

Before long Bjorn was running out of elk but he didn't run out of wolves: now there were hundreds of them!

He threw the last of the elk to the wolves just as he reached the safety of the outpost.

It was a close-run thing.

Bjorn felt lucky to escape with his life. True, he had thrown away all of the elk, though he had intended only to throw a few small bits away. But he was alive and able to tell the locals and his fellow salesmen of his brilliant ploy to get the better of the wolves.

The locals had never heard the like of his tale in all the years they

71

had run sledges in the Tundra. No wolves ever came near their sledges and certainly no packs of wolves ever bothered them in the slightest. They shook their heads and put it down to the city slicker's imagination.

In contrast, the salesmen, who had no experience of wolves or what they were really like, immediately made preparations to load up their sledges with elk steaks; they were not going to be caught in the Tundra without a defence against ravenous wolves!

And that was the source of the disaster.

For the next six months Bjorn, and the other salesmen, raced around the Tundra, plying their refrigerators, suntan lotion and cold beer, and throwing meat to any wolves that chased after them. They considered Bjorn's discovery of how to handle wolves the most brilliant idea that they had since their companies had sent them to the Tundra to make their fortunes.

True, none of them had made a fortune yet, but neither were any of them eaten by a wolf.

They were absolutely shocked beyond belief when the local people ganged together and sent them packing down river at gunpoint. 'Haven't we brought you the prizes of civilization?', they asked as the locals herded them with menacing looks into makeshift canoes.

'Yes', the suntanned locals replied, as they distributed more cold beer from the outpost's refrigerators to the armed guards. 'But what about the wolves?', they demanded, much to the astonishment of Bjorn and his pals.

'Wolves? What about the wolves?', Bjorn asked. 'My fellow salesmen and I have done nothing to any wolves. In fact', he added, 'we've been following my infallible system for keeping ravenous wolves at bay.'

At this, the locals almost lynched Bjorn there and then on the spot.

'You haven't kept the ravenous wolves at bay, you idiot', shouted the locals. 'You've simply taught wolves that if they want food they should chase sledges!'

Now what happened to the good folk of the Tundra is a poignant lesson for the rest of us. They managed to eradicate the source of their trouble – wolves being taught to chase sledges to get fed – by deporting the salesmen who introduced the practice of goodwill-conceding into their territory. Eventually, as the wolves tired of chasing sledges, getting nothing but empty cold-beer cans thrown at them, they went back to getting fed nature's way and left the sledges alone.

Unfortunately, though Bjorn and his pals are long gone from this life, and the Tundra is free of the filthy practice of goodwill-conceding, no such remedial action was taken in the big cities of the world.

Negotiators still go around throwing out concessions to their opponents, sometimes out of fear of not getting the negotiations started and sometimes in the hope that the other person will recognize a friend and be nice to them.

The disease is widespread, and, for those afflicted with it for more than a short time, it can become terminal – they get done so often by other (tougher) negotiators that they are fit only for a job in sales training, where they will teach tomorrow's bright young sales-persons Bjorn's infallible system for dealing with ravenous wolves.

Answers to self-assessment test 6

1 *(a)* With the Japanese you could wait a long time!

(b) Free-gift concessions do not push the boat out, they encourage the opposition to sit tight and wait for your next free gift.

(c) Yes. The Japanese will get the message.

(d) Weak. It shows your impatience.

2 *(a)* Not if it's their first one!

(b) Invites them to bid blind. They won't.

(c) Much better. You could try an offer such as: either a two-third advance of their $50,000, i.e. $33,000, or a half advance of your $60,000, i.e. $30,000. This gives you more of the money they are offering sooner.

(d) Almost always a foolish move, unless other video companies are fighting for an appointment!

3 *(a)* You are bidding blind and he will tell you your cut is not enough.

(b) He might bluff you on the difference.

(c) A risky call of his bluff.

(d) Good if you believe there are other bids but could be bad if you catch him out in a bluff.

(e) This is a positive move and could lead to a discussion of the differences between your offer and the others. Price is not the only determining variable in a buying decision.

Self-assessment test 7

1   You are interested in opening up business in the United States and are planning your first sales visit. You have decided to visit California first. How long do you allow yourself to meet, and make presentations to, potential clients.
   (a)   7 days?
   (b)   10 days?
   (c)   21 days?
   (d)   30 days?

2   You have been granted an interview with the president of a local corporation who might be interested in your product. The conversation after five minutes is still concentrated on small talk. What does this tell you?
   (a)   That you are getting on fine with the other guy?
   (b)   That you should raise the subject of your visit?
   (c)   That you should wait for him to open the business discussion first?

3   Your (expensive and well-produced) sales literature has been prepared in the UK and does you very proud in your normal negotiations. Should you:
   (a)   Get it entirely re-done for your US trip?
   (b)   Add in a supplement with prices quoted in US dollars?
   (c)   Leave it as it is and use it as you normally do?

Chapter Seven

Have a good day
in the US of A
or wham, bam, it's a deal Sam

Nobody in the United States of America wants to take a long time to get a deal. They tend to make up their minds quickly. If they can't sell to you, they move off and try to sell to somebody else. They don't waste much time on the preliminaries. In fact, Americans (or more correctly, citizens of the United States – for though Uncle Sam's children are normally known as Americans, we should acknowledge that this can irritate those millions of other Americans who live south of the Rio Grande!) are probably the world's fastest dealers. They operate as if there was no tomorrow and very little left of today. They rush in (and out) where angels have not even thought about fearing to tread. It's flavour of the minute rather than of the month.

This makes for a major adjustment crisis when a negotiator from Chicago meets a negotiator from almost anywhere else. The American at any one moment is likely to want to be ten moves ahead of where the negotiations have got to and, if uninitated into the ways of those whose lives have been untouched by the Great American Reality, will probably grow impatient at the other's 'sloth'.

The pace of a deal is determined by the pace of the dominant party. You cannot rush people whose instincts or bureaucratic systems require them to move crabwise or tortoise-like rather than in a full frontal assault at hare-like speed. If you want to do business with the Arabs, the Japanese, the Chinese, the South Americans, the Soviets and others, you must slow down to their pace (or speed up to it if you are even slower!).

In dealings with Americans you most certainly must speed up, if only a little – much depends on which of you wants the deal the most. Two Americans making a deal are a picture of haste – zap, zoom, woosh, wham, bam, let's Go Go Go! Their language colours their moves: 'Make it snappy', 'Jump to it', 'What are we waiting for?', 'Have we gotta deal, or have we gotta deal?', 'OK!, let's step on the gas!'.

The time-hustled American business executive is a model of success. Seen to be in a hurry from New York to Los Angeles is no bad thing for anybody wanting to impress his or her peers. Where the sight of the over-extended executive would worry the Japanese sick, the more over-extended he is the higher his status in downtown USA where success is synonymous with pace. To conspicuously have too little to do is a symptom of failure, even if the American is busy doing very little.

Contrast the gentle two or three day pace of English cricket with American football. Note how North American games (ice hockey, basketball and football are prime examples) divide the match into sessions where every second, including the last, counts. If, for any reason, play stops, so does the clock; American spectators watch clocks with the same obsession that most people watch players. The entire nation is time-conscious and the ticks of passing seconds are heard right across the country. Wasting time is wasting life itself – it's unAmerican!

Haste leads to a dynamism of a special kind in America. The entire business world is dominated by high-energy activity. They think big and solve problems in big ways. No river is too wide for them to find a way of crossing it. Where most people would make do with a single bridge, they think nothing of having a dozen. They let competition sort out the appropriate level of a service. Their economy is on a grand scale – the world's largest at several trillion dollars a year.

They use up and spew out resources at a rate that is truly astonishing. They have created vast cities with urban and suburban sprawls that dwarf, on all indicators (good and bad), those of the rest of the world. Their prairies are larger than entire countries and their natural resources are the envy of the world. They feed themselves and much of the world too. By their economic strength they can afford to buy up the greater proportion of the natural resources that they don't have from those parts of the world that do. In short, the US of A is an El Dorado. It knows it, and much of the world resents it; yet all the world wants to emulate it!

Go into any up-country village and you will find ordinary people who describe their desires in terms common to the (somewhat dated and often phoney) image of the USA that they get from TV or the movies. Whereas political leaders may aspire to economic development, measured in terms of steel tonnage or national airlines, the ordinary people think in terms of coca-cola, consumer goods and large cars.

The very size of the US market means that their international negotiators usually are interested only in the very largest of contracts (Bechtel's contracts, for instance, are very big). For this reason, US international negotiators tend to deal with national governments – for whom, incidentally, the annual value of the output of the companies they negotiate with is quite awesome when set against their own country's GNP.

This is not to say that the US negotiators get it all their own way. Many is the tale told by experienced US negotiators that lists the irritations they have suffered at the obfuscation, delay, bureaucratic ineptitude, sheer bloody-mindedness and, in their view, ultimately self-defeating obstruction of a national government agency, when they have tried to put together a mega (or super-mega) deal. Their frustration is enhanced when they consider the project to be of mutual benefit to the US company and the (often) poorer country. Whereas profits motivate a US company, the politics of resentment and suspicion (naturally) dominate a government's negotiating policy. These differing objectives can conflict in ways that inhibit successful negotiation – and the world as a whole is poorer for it.

Doing quick deals has several drawbacks. The most obvious is that it is easier to make mistakes, especially ones that in due course you will regret. This adds another dimension to negotiating with US companies: they are more than a trifle litigious. At the drop of a subpoena they will have you in court, and never for trivial damages!

You miss a delivery which costs a client $10,000 and he will sue you for $10 million. Fail to shape up to a partnership or agency agreement and you will be chased for half of your country's GNP. This makes the US of A a haven for smart lawyers (not to mention doctors, psychiatrists and marketing specialists). Fortunately, lawyers are not prejudiced – they will sue other lawyers, even for malpractice.

But the business atmosphere is one of constant upheaval. They do quick deals quicker than anybody else, then they engage in further deals to get out from under the deals they have done. Promises are extravagant before the sale (marketing and advertising are true US art forms) and negotiators work hard (and fast) to get the deal set up. In other places that would be the end of the matter but in the US of A a whole world of after-sales negotiating exists because of the risks arising from the before-the-sale deal. Only in the US of A is the threat that a politician could be a used car salesman a serious warning that you ought not to vote for him!

Indeed, look at any American text on negotiating (they call it 'self-improvement') and you will see much attention paid to negotiating your grievances with the people with whom you have recently done business. It's not just 'how to get a discount' but 'how to get it fixed when it (inevitably) breaks down'.

Handling grievances, complaining, getting refunds, suing the suppliers and generally fighting for your corner are all par for the course in American negotiating. The expectation is that sooner or later deals will go wrong in some way, because making deals faster means making more deals.

Instead of slowing down the process of getting into a deal they recommend that the parties indulge in 'self-assertion' therapy. To assert oneself in a noisy marketplace means, at the end of the day, becoming noisier oneself. Instead of meekly accepting the deal that you made, you are encouraged to assert your rights in no uncertain way.

Most US citizens interpret firmness and certainty as being synonymous with shouting and talking quickly. Hence, they repeat the behaviour – only more exaggerated – that got them into the lousy deal in the first place: they talk and shout quickly. Of course, the other guy shouts back and we have a typical North American version of a Mediterranean street row.

There is no point complaining about the 'quick kill' school of negotiating. The US of A is not going to change its behaviour merely because you think it ought to do so. The American way is, for better or worse, the way it is and you must adjust to it. The American negotiator is not as subtle as, say, the Japanese. Being in a hurry, the American has to try to bring things to a head in the shortest possible time and he (or she) will do this by a combination of apparent confidence, to persuade you of their integrity (hence the significance of their question: 'Would you buy a used car from this man?'), and early use of whatever power, or, as they call it, leverage, that they have in the relationship to compel you to accept what they are proposing.

They love to impress upon you just how powerful they are. They can do this by emphasizing the sheer size of their company – 'the

Love me, load my dog

I saw a man at O'Hare airport, Chicago, shouting like a barrack room sergeant at a new recruit, and complaining vividly, complete with gesticulations of a kind that would have made Mussolini envious, at the damage done to a dog crate by somebody loading or unloading the plane. The dog was slumped in one corner (presumably having heard his master in full throttle more than once) and, to put it mildly, the crate stank (suggesting, perhaps, that it had been dropped when the loaders carrying it had fainted!).

The airport official, a quiet lady in uniform, stood there listening to the tirade but otherwise appeared unperturbed by it, and kept calling calmly on her personal radio for the supervisor.

When the supervisor arrived, she told the loaders to move the crate from the area, at which the irate man blew his top even more. Nothing, apparently, was to be moved until his lawyer got there and the airline boss arrived and paid compensation ('the damn dog cost me six thousand bucks and the crate is evidence that you've tried to kill it').

Having not much to do, I (and about a hundred others) watched the scene with interest. The man had a point but his manner seemed a trifle absurd to me – even counterproductive – and I thought he should be concentrating on his proposed remedy (compensation) rather than competing for an Oscar for dramatic acting.

You will not, however, negotiate in the US of A for long before you come across a version of the dog owner at O'Hare. You will also learn not to take the dog owner type too seriously, or too personally. To the uninitiated, the dog owner's behaviour is pure intimidation. It is the verbal equivalent of the massive damages claim put in by his lawyers to scare the timid into a quick settlement. Courts do it too. They set you up for ninety-nine years in jail and then let you plea-bargain it down to six months suspended! .

biggest in Texas' – in terms of market share, billion dollar sales, or number of employees. When you are in the presence of a US executive from a multi-billion dollar company you are not likely to be left unaware that doing business with him is in your best interest.

The United States contains many of the world's largest corporations. Indeed, to be large is regarded as being very American, and they identify their corporate interests very closely with the interests of their country: 'What's good for America is good for General Motors'.

Large corporations do not lose their competitive edge in the US environment (though it has to be said that the largest US firms are a long way from being competitive in the literal sense). The giant corporations play a very hard game, with little quarter shown or expected between rivals. The government has curtailed some of the worst excesses of the abuse of corporate power by regulation and recently has resorted to exposing US corporations to more competition.

Being large they have room for some market failures and can ride out a disaster or two. Big deals are set up by teams of managers who work extremely hard and very thoroughly to develop a negotiating position. They will decide on a policy that suits their own best interests and then push hard for it.

If you are selling, they will go strong on the size of the market in the United States and, therefore, why you should do business with them, emphasizing gross sales and revenues. If you are buying, they will go strong on the sheer size of their worldwide sales and, therefore, why you should do business with them, emphasizing their total service and how much profit you can make.

This approach will also hint at whether you think you are big enough (macho?) to do business on a scale and at a high enough standard that their operation requires. You can even get the feeling that they are doing you a favour!

The US negotiator operates in a world of prepared contracts or 'established' systems of doing business. Because they have one eye on what happens if the deal goes sour, they protect themselves with legal ploys. They also tend to have a monopolistic attitude to doing business: they believe, and get you to believe, that you need them more than they need you. To some extent this is true, because with a three trillion dollar economy to play with there is always somebody else available who could do the job you want to do, if the price is right.

Car hire firms insist that you sign their pre-printed hire forms; repair and maintenance services make you sign standard contracts; you sign forms to get on a plane (less now since the shuttle and deregulation), to book a room in a hotel, or to place an order for anything.

A whole mountain of pre-printed forms exists that require your signature to get a lot of things done. It's a protective device to ensure that you have signed away your rights (or at least had them severely curtailed). For this reason you must read the paperwork very carefully – and take your time about it too! If you disagree with anything, tell them and refuse to sign until it is changed. The impression that you cannot change a printed form is a form of intimidation (that's why it is pre-printed).

They will tell you that this or that 'rule' applies to delivery, minimum orders, payments and so on. If you find these 'rules' onerous, challenge them. If there is one country in the world where they make a meal out of legal issues it is the United States (they have a large – and prosperous – legal system of which they are proud and they think it is very patriotic to use it).

Americans have an aversion to 'one truck contracts' and prefer to ask themselves hundreds of 'what if?' type questions beforehand. According to their answers, they develop fairly tight working contracts and attempt to foist these onto you at every negotiation. Such contracts can protect you too, but you can never be sure that the other person had your interests uppermost in his mind while preparing the standard contract.

Operating under the permanent threat of litigation (or, as it seems sometimes, the threat of permanent litigation!) and also at great speed, the US negotiator has developed a special form of semi-insurance, that is, the full blown testimonial. They do this more than anybody else and it is a feature of the US business scene.

From the day they graduate from High School (and then again from College or University), the US business executive has a place somewhere on the wall for the Diploma, complete with a class picture. This identifies the executive as a regular guy.

If service in the armed forces was required then some sign of that achievement will also feature somewhere in the room (preferably a picture signed by a famous General or Admiral). Again, if the executive served under or has known a top politician – the Governor of the state, the Congressman or even the Senator – a picture of the two of them together is a kosher testimonial. (Naturally, acquaintance with a President is the highest accolade, worth at least three photos of the executive with a Vice-President!)

The wall displays are there to establish the executive in the subtle

Never mind the width, feel the quality

The US of A triumphs in one area above all others: technological excellence. They are world leaders in the application of technology and have enough economic strength to buy in what they do not discover themselves. With the world's richest market available to exploit any innovation, they can afford to try out almost anything, and often do (California, for instance, institutionalizes new 'crazes' – it is also the home of the original silicon valley).

Hence, the US of A buys in a lot of semi-manufactured components. Its computer manufacturers, for instance, buy in circuit boards from places as disparate as Taiwan, Scotland, Singapore, Germany and Yugoslavia (open up the back of yours and check where the bits on the boards come from – it's a veritable lesson in geography).

To negotiate a trade deal with a large US company you must have two things going for you: first, you have to have a sensible price policy, for if you don't they will manufacture your parts themselves with their very expensive but highly productive labour; second, you must reach and maintain a high consistency in quality and you had better believe they want high quality in actual performance and not just in your promises.

If you satisfy these two conditions you can negotiate a profitable deal with a US company. But that is just the beginning of their requirements of you. They will always be looking for volume – the US of A is no place for a backyard business – for they operate on a scale almost inconceivable abroad (with the possible exception of the more enlightened of the multinational companies – often US – operating in the EEC).

Next, but by no means least, they will expect you to seek to reduce unit costs, to improve the product, to be in the forefront, without prompting, of making suggestions for alternative ways of doing whatever it is that you do best. Hence you do not just sell to the US customer, you must learn to market your product as well.

hierarchy of established US society. There are also the more mobile testimonials in the form of letters of commendation for the executive or for the products of his corporation from the top executives of client companies. No presentation to a US company from somebody who wants to do business with them is complete without a sheaf of testimonials written by other major users of the product.

This, of course, can create a problem for a new company trying to break into the US market. Most of us have known the Catch-22 situation of trying to sell a new product for a new company, when the client says: 'Who have you sold this to before?' and you have to admit that he is (nearly) the first customer. It sure weakens your negotiating position when you cannot show that everybody but everybody has bought your product before. Unless you get clients you cannot establish a track record for your product, but you cannot get clients unless you have a track record.

You will also find it worthwhile to carry with you in the USA a master copy of your *cv* for clients to photocopy. They like to know with whom they are dealing.

The overseas negotiator about to visit the US on a selling trip would be well advised to prepare a bundle of testimonials from the highest levels of the clients that are already on his books in Europe. And do not weary of collecting them after the first half dozen – there is no limit to the appetite of US customers for reading testimonials from 'names' that they recognize.

The reason is quite simple: the testimonial of a company president that your product is first class and that doing business with you is good for his business is evidence (though not conclusive) that a deal with you is not going to end in ruinous litigation. The absence of testimonials is evidence that you are a large risk.

The entire US economy is dominated by a freer market than is found anywhere else in the world. True, the US government, and the state governments, account for immense expenditures of billions of dollars, and these expenditures are major inputs into the economy. But the driving force behind the US economy is the competitive urge that motivates millions of people to take risks and seek their fortunes.

Whereas the average communist state official is notoriously risk-averse (for, it should be said, the best possible of motivations – self-preservation!), the average US commercial buyer or seller is inclined to accept risk in return for the prospect of material reward.

And the rewards are substantial. Already experiencing high living standards, represented by astonishing buying power, the US citizen functions in an atmophere of self-improvement by effort and opportunity to reach even higher living standards.

If one thing does not work, they will try something else. Americans are highly mobile with regard to business propositions. Below the huge corporations, which are huge because they do something that works, there are literally millions of people seeking to break through to the big money. This makes the US market the most exciting, and the most ruthless, in the world.

An entire range of behaviour exists purporting to guide the US citizen who is on the make. Much of this sounds quite vulgar and not a little crude to European ears. The litany includes the kind of tough-talking advice that Hollywood scriptwriters (themselves on highly tenuous work contracts that probably influence their view of American values) have made famous in their one-liners in a thousand movies: 'Nice guys come second'; 'When the going gets tough, the tough get going'; 'Shape up or ship out'; 'You get what you pay for'; 'There ain't no such thing as a free lunch'; 'If you have to ask how much it costs, you can't afford it!'; 'If you're so smart, why ain't you rich?' and so on.

Even in their approach to negotiating Americans are obsessed with 'winning'. A well-known seminar series in the US is entitled 'Winning and Negotiation', and even my own work has not been immune to this treatment. When a US firm published *Managing Negotiations* (1981; written with my co-authors, John Benson and John McMillan) they subtitled it: 'a guide for managers, labor leaders, politicans and *everyone else who wants to win*'.

The US of A is the land of winners and losers. For the winners there is nothing too good for them; for the losers there is nothing. And there is certainly nothing like the sweet smell of success, and for a sniff of this sweet smell, US citizens give it their 'best shot'.

Now it would be grievously unfair to leave the impression that the US of A was peopled by several million psychopaths who cared little for each other and even less for you. Nothing could be further from the truth. The US manner, outlined above, is by no means as serious as it sounds when you first come across it. US citizens are often misunderstood – by and large they are a very warm and generous people who establish enduring relationships in business and life that will match anything this side of Shangri-la.

The tough language, the winner-takes-all outlook, the 'get off

Attention to detail

The US economy is competitive. This has produced an entirely professional approach to how US companies view proposals from overseas negotiators. If what you are offering is available from any of a hundred other companies you will have a hard time convincing them to do business with you.

A British real estate partnership, which had developed some business with clients moving to and from New York, decided to tackle the US market direct.

The US real estate business is saturated with sizeable operations of high professional standards, and it is also flooded with low quality brokers who give real estate selling a sour name.

Clearly, to break into the lucrative market the UK company had to establish its professional credentials and rise above the pack. It did this by an example of professionalism that matched the best available in the New York market.

For five months, day in day out, the new team trudged the streets of Manhattan, up and down *every* office building in the city, making a register of all office lets. True they could have bought this information from an agency but they wanted their people to have an unrivalled knowledge of the city's buildings and the facilities. They also accumulated a mass of information from janitors, security staff and employees on who was moving soon, which floors were empty and what the neighbourhoods were really like.

Every bit of useful information was put onto a computer. Scores of hours were spent digesting potential moves and vacancies. As the information built up, the search for clients commenced. People who had complained of being too crowded, etc., where they were, had information supplied at no charge on where something more suitable was located.

Slowly the business built up until they were established as leading negotiators for anybody who had an interest in New York property. Within two years they were the most successful overseas partnership in the company, firmly established in the toughest, and richest, market in the world. They got big by being better.

your ass and get going' philosophy, are all modes of expression for the competitive urge in their lives. They are by no means a final statement of their morality or ethics.

If you bring professionalism to your presentation, sheer excellence in your quality control and realistic prices that suit their market philosophy (high initial prices with room for discounts and frequent 'special offers', sales and such-like), and can deliver what you promise in quantities that will make you gasp, then you will get the business you deserve.

The US negotiator expects to get to the point quickly. A real estate broker I know in New York tells his sales staff that when they get an interview with a potential client they have forty-five seconds to make a hit or blow it. In comparison, the approach of the Arab or Japanese negotiator is distinctly soporific. But the rewards of getting it right in the US of A are truly tremendous. So watch your first forty-five seconds – you may not have the person's attention for the rest of your first and only minute!

Answers to self-assessment test 7

1 (a) Far too short given the huge distances that you will have to fly/drive around California (there is no public transport worth mentioning). It's not the time they take to negotiate (usually much shorter than anybody else) but the sheer size of the USA that determines the time you should make available.

(b) Still too short to see enough people to justify your trip. You are bound to want/need to return and a ten-day trip will only tease the market.

(c) Much better. You can see several clients in twenty-one days spread across the state or even across Los Angeles.

(d) Ideal (and possibly longer if you can). The more time you can spend examining this market the better. It is huge and there are so many people trying to get on to the road to riches that you need time to check them out, and to count your fingers every time you shake hands with a person who is going 'to make your dreams come true'.

2 (a) If you are still stuck in small talk anything beyond a minute,

either he is a long lost relative or you and your deal are dead. He is bound to be wondering how he is going to get you out of his office and his sight.

(b) Absolutely. You had better get on with it. The fact that you are still there talking to him about nothing in particular suggests that the buzzer under his desk that he has been pressing for his security gorillas to come and chuck you out is not working. Tell him what you want. NOW!

(c) If you wait much longer he will throw you out himself, so you had better not wait for him to raise the subject of business. Go for *(b)* NOW.

3 *(a)* Absolutely correct. Even if it costs you everything you have already paid for the UK version, get a new set done for the US market, preferably through an agency that knows the US market. Their standards are higher.

(b) A poor alternative to *(a)* but much better than *(c)*. US citizens are totally incapable of understanding anybody else's currency but their own and on their own ground they will not even attempt to do so. If you quote in sterling pounds you might as well stay at home and save the airfare.

(c) You are about to waste your airfare.

Self-assessment test 8

1 You want to buy a house that has an asking price of £192,000. Which opening offer would you consider making to the owner:
   (a) £190,000?
   (b) £192,000?
   (c) £182,000?
   (d) £194,000?

2 You have decided to replace your word processor with a more powerful model and have been quoted a list price of £5,000 by a supplier. What size of discount do you expect?
   (a) 5%
   (b) None
   (c) 15%
   (d) 20%

3 You see a used Jaguar car for sale and have seen similar makes and models advertised recently for £5,000. You make a once-only cash offer to the amount of £2,250. Do you expect the owner to:
   (a) Haggle but take it?
   (b) Haggle but refuse it?
   (c) Refuse to consider it?

4 You are a fax machine sales representative and make an invited sales call at the local home for unmarried mothers. The social worker in charge indicates that she wants to purchase one of your machines which has a list price of £2,200. However, her budget from the Council fixes an absolute ceiling of £1,755. Do you:
   (a) Regretfully decline to do business?
   (b) Use your pricing discretion and make a sale?
   (c) Suggest that she considers a cheaper model?

Chapter Eight

In praise of Mother Hubbard
or how to make them cut their prices

Jack lives in California. He is an economist, and, as a hobby, collects old model (circa 1960s) Jaguar cars. Every couple of years he decamps from Berkeley to visit his wife's family in Edinburgh. While in Scotland he tries to buy old Jaguar cars, or bits of them, for export to the United States.

Apparently old Jaguars, or their parts, feature in the life styles of some of the affluent folk in California, who, having everything, also want the best, when, that is, they are not after the weirdest.

On his return to Berkeley, Jack lovingly refurbishes his own collection of 'vintage' cars with the worn-out parts from the assorted stock he brings back with him.

Occasionally, out of neighbourly compassion – rather then vulgar avarice – he sells a car (or just some bits of one) from his personal collection to desperate Jaguar fanatics (who 'crowd his space' when news gets round that he's back) providing that his beloved Jaguars go to a 'good home'.

I have been able to watch him negotiating the purchase of a Jaguar, mainly from his habit of requiring me to pull over and stop if he sees a Jaguar of early vintage parked on the road. (This habit of Jack's makes no concessions to where we are heading or what time we are supposed to be there.)

And unlike Bob in Sydney, Jack loves every minute of a negotiation. If you're there to listen to him on his way back from a deal, he relives the moves with you (and if you're not, I'm sure he recounts them aloud to himself!). And when he gets back to his wife, his enjoyment is by no means diminished, for he tells her in detail how he got the deal.

I have never seen anybody so wrapped up in his negotiations and so good tempered about them.

If a deal doesn't come off, it joins the list of amusing anecdotes he has on buying used cars. Jack insists that a deal that failed did so almost always because he didn't use his cardinal rule for negotiating:

SHOCK 'EM WITH YOUR OPENING OFFER

Jack swears that this principle has served him well over the years.

How does it work? Simple. When you open make sure it is very low (if you're buying), or very high (if you're selling). Jack doesn't believe in opening with a price close to where he might be prepared to settle. He likes to leave himself lots of negotiating room.

If you do choose to open close to your expected settlement price Jack argues, you might indeed settle at it (in which case you are no better off), or you might have to go above/below it considerably (in which case you could be worse off).

Opening is a risky business and if you open modestly you give the other person false ideas about how much room there is for you to move. If he believes you have a lot of room to move he must follow his best interests and haggle hard, perhaps forcing you to move a lot. As he does not know what your 'best' price (for him) is, he need not accept your protestations nor treat them other than as a bluff.

Whichever way you look at it, a deal on terms considerably worse than your intended terms is not a good way to do business. You might be able to convince yourself that you are 'happy' with the deal 'in the circumstances', and the contribution of such delusions to your self-esteem ought not to be discounted, but if by your opening behaviour you can avoid the need for rationalizing your defeats, it seems sensible for you to do so.

This has all the more relevance when you observe that, by using his shock opening tactics, Jack finds that he settles many of his deals a long way short (on the better side) of his 'best' price.

Why is this so?

Because his shock opening price compels the other person to reconsider his expectations about the current value of his property.

Jack loses some deals because his offer is too far away from the other person's 'basement' price, but Jack claims that on average he will get most of his deals closer to his opening price than to his 'rooftop' best price.

And even if he has to go up close to his top price, he is no worse off than if he had opened close to it in the first place, except that by opening low, Jack increases the distance he will have to travel if the other person's expectations are for a price *above* Jack's (undisclosed) top price.

Out of the mouths of children

A used-car dealer in Aberdeen had a 1962 Jaguar for sale, priced £1,850. Jack saw it in the lot and went in to have a look. The owner handled the negotiations personally and, after discussion, Jack said he would give him £1,250 for it.

The negotiations stalled but they kept talking about this and that for a while. Clearly, the dealer knew he wasn't going to get £1,850 but didn't know how serious Jack was.

While they were talking another Jaguar car pulled into the lot, driven by the owner's son. Jack eyed the car and they moved over to look at it. It was slightly newer than the other model and it was in much better bodily condition. Obviously it had been looked after.

The son said the car wasn't for sale as it was his. The owner contradicted him by saying that the car belonged to his company and if he wanted to sell it he would. Jack smelled a sale here. He offered £1,000 for it.

The dealer haggled a little and then asked how Jack intended to pay.

'Cash', was the reply.

Jack had enough cash (mainly in US dollars, but since the oil boom they know about dollars, in Aberdeen).

The deal was struck at £1,100 and the son was told to get his things out of the car, which he did with a face as long as a transatlantic cable. Jack drove off quickly.

Afterwards I asked Jack why he had gone in lower for the obviously better car. He said he originally intended to get the other car back into contention but the old man was so determined to show his son who was boss of the business that he accepted a deal close to Jack's low opening offer. 'This was a slight pity as the other car had genuine leather seats in it which are worth a small fortune back home.' However, the car he had bought was worth at least double what he paid for it in Scotland, let alone its value in the States.

In other words, getting a high price out of Jack is hard work. Not surprisingly, he values what the other guy has to work hard for, far more than something that comes easy – *even if he settles at a lower price than he expected*.

The art of making somebody happy by disappointing him with a price lower than he was originally looking for is not a mystery: it lies in your ability to make him negotiate every cent of the way.

Negotiators are always unhappy if you agree too easily with their opening prices, so make them happy by haggling!

Why does the shock opening tactic work for Jack?

First, consider the position at the start of a negotiation. When you are considering negotiating for something – be it cash, a Jaguar car, a million tons of Albanian cement, a Norwegian container ship, or a straw hat in a Mexican tourist shop – you have in mind a target price, i.e. what you expect to pay for whatever you are buying, or get for whatever you are selling, assuming that you know something about your business. Call this your *expectation*.

How expectations form in your mind *before* the negotiation is less relevant for this discussion than the fact that they change during the negotiation.

If you arrive at the negotiation with predetermined views as to the appropriate settlement, it does not follow that you will stick to them irrespective of events; they may be changed, for instance, by what you come to believe about your prospects of achieving your expectations once the negotiation is under way.

Alternatively, if your views as to what is attainable are formed during the negotiation (you having no predetermined views before you find out what is in the other person's mind), these views can also be reshaped by subsequent events in the negotiation, or, more correctly, can be changed by your interpretations of those events.

In these cases, you have the choice of reducing your expectations or seeking a deal elsewhere. It could also be the case that you have the choice of sticking to your expectations or revising them upwards if the negotiations reveal encouraging aspects of your opponent's intentions or perceptions.

Expectations in negotiation are entirely *subjective*. They do not have a life of their own independent of how you (and the other person) read the situation once you are in contact with each other.

It is Jack's belief that the most decisive moment in the negotiation to influence expectations is at the opening contact, when neither of you is too sure of what can be achieved. Hence, his belief that it pays to go in hard with a tough opening stance. This move has the immediate effect of undermining the original confidence of the other guy in any high expectations he has formed, or, if he has not yet formed his views, it severely limits the price he can realistically hope for from Jack.

In Jack's view, the greater the shock of the opening price the more effective the tactic.

If you are buying, go in low – really low – *if your opening is credible in some way*, and you will undermine even the toughest negotiator's confidence in his starting position. The same is true for going in high – really high – if you are selling.

Now neither I nor Jack claim that this move will *automatically* assure you of a successful deal. Audacity is essential but it is not enough. The main target of the shocking opening move is your opponent's beliefs about his position – you are trying to structure his expectations of the likely outcome of the negotiation.

To the extent that you reduce his expectations – even by a little amount – it has to be good for you as a negotiator. If he arrives thinking he is going to buy your business for £11 million and you open with a demand for £22 million, he is bound to have some problems with your opening: do you really mean what you say, is *your* price realistic, is *his* price realistic, has *he* done his sums correctly, are *you* in as weak a bargaining position as *his* accountants reported, and so on?

He may not roll over and play dead but it will certainly stop him in his tracks while he thinks it over.

You walk into a store to get a discount of 15 per cent and the clerk tells you that the company only makes seven per cent gross.

What do yo do?

If you even half believe him you know you have no chance of getting 15 per cent. So either you lower your expectation or try another store.

You decide to get your company products advertised on television and allocate a budget of £7,000 to the project. At your first meeting with the producer he tells you it costs £2,000 a minute to shoot 20 minutes of film which will be cut down to a 40-second commercial. Anything cheaper would get you a wooden Oscar.

What do you do?

Either you increase your budget or you forget about TV.

You pitch for a 20 per cent share of the gross income and your partners show that they only make ten per cent and then only if they sell 1,000 sets a month.

What do you do?

93

A shocking tender

A city council called for tenders to demolish an old abattoir and clear the site. Several demolition firms submitted tenders ranging from £10,000 to £25,000. One company sent in a £1 tender. This was accepted (after checking it was not an unfortunate typing error).

Why did they only want £1 to do such a large job?

Because their survey showed them that there were about 500 tons of iron girders and iron piping in the building plus a hundred tons of other metals, with a scrap value in excess of £70,000.

Give up dreams of a Hollywood lifestyle or get new partners?

You ask a lady to accompany you to a convention in Acapulco and she tells you she might consider a dinner date in a month's time.

What do you do? Lower your sights or try dating her sister?

These cameos illustrate the impact that a shocking opening can have on the negotiators. Their sights must be lowered in the negotiation whatever else they do (such as try their luck elsewhere).

Moving someone from an opening that is a long way from your original expectations is like climbing the Eiger in the buff. If you aim for the stars and the other person intends to start with the trees, you have a long way to go to get him airborne.

It is a fact of negotiating life that the majority of us will not persist with what we come to *believe* are unrealistic demands. We will sooner back off than persist.

Generalizing from Jack's insight into negotiating behaviour, we can see that the best opening is the *toughest* opening. All else weakens your influence on the eventual outcome. The tough opening has, however, to be *credible* in some way. The shock opening tactic is of little use (in the sense of getting a good deal) if you believe that *any* crazy price will do. There is no point trying to buy the Empire State Building with an opening bid of $200 – though if you wait long enough the City might one day pay you to demolish it.

The difference between a shock opening and a silly one is not easy to define because the boundary between a negotiating move that pays off and one that doesn't is not always obvious. The only

A shocking typing error

A union official submitted a written pay claim for his distillery members and a week later met the management to negotiate the new contract.

He was surprised to be given details of company sales and costs. He also listened to a long presentation from the management on the financial prospects of the next year.

Perplexed by this unusual behaviour, the official scanned the papers across the table. On top of them he could see his written claim, and he read it upside down.

He spotted the cause of the problem. His secretary had typed the figures incorrectly: instead of a claim for a 12 per cent wage rise (with an expectation of settling at about seven per cent) she had typed 21 per cent. No wonder the company was making such an extraordinary fuss!

He said nothing and waited to hear what they would offer after their heart-rending presentation of how poor the company was at present. They opened with an offer of 12 per cent and eventually they settled at 15 per cent: eight per cent more than he expected to settle at before the meeting. This taught him about the modesty of his previous claims.

important difference between one and the other is that the shock opening is *credible* and the silly one is not.

If you can defend credibly your opening you can make what, in some circumstances, would plainly be a silly opening into a winning one. Credible reasons for an opening position give it a lot of mileage. And remember the reasons you give for your opening only have to be credible to the person listening, not a panel of neutral judges.

Jack, for instance, has one disadvantage when he opens his mouth to negotiate in Scotland – he sounds just like what he is: an American, and, as every canny Scot knows, Americans abroad (unless they are in the Navy) have more money than sense.

Jack would be stretching credulity if he was to plead poverty as a reason for his low offer. So naturally he doesn't bother. However, he does have a credible line: he has to ship the vehicle all the way to California and this, he tells the sellers, 'doubles' his costs.

He always adds that his deal is a cash deal, the mention of which is often a strong incentive to settle where a used-car negotiation is concerned. Also, the fact that Jack is taking the car to California – thus removing him from the vicinity where the seller lives and therefore from comebacks if the car is not all it is cracked up to be by the seller's pitch – does not escape the seller.

These circumstances make Jack's negotiating position fairly strong.

Of course, the real issue that ought to concern the sellers is not what the car is worth to them in Scotland, or what it costs Jack to ship it home, but what the car is worth to Jack *in* California when he gets it there. By all accounts, the value of Jaguars in Berkeley exceeds by a long way the price Jack pays for them in Scotland.

In general, if your shocking or tough opening is credible it has a good chance of forming the basis of the negotiation, so open with the toughest credible opening you can think of.

One way to gain confidence in using the tough opening is to use the Mother Hubbard (of the 'cupboard is bare' fame) line. In this tactic you must convince the seller of two interconnected points:

1 That you genuinely want to buy the seller's product.
2 That you do not have the resources to reach the seller's opening price.

In effect you tell the seller that the cupboard is bare.

How close you pitch Mother Hubbard to the seller's opening price is a matter of judgment. Perhaps it will be best if you try it out first on prices close to theirs and gradually widen the gap in subsequent negotiations as you get more confident in its use.

You must decide just how bare you are going to make your cupboard and which stance is credible in the circumstances.

The seller is bound to ask you (if he has bitten the bait): 'How much can you afford to pay?' At this point you must be wary of being sidetracked into a 'deposit with a loan' deal or some such way of undermining your play (including the 'running two budgets together' move). You must establish that the *total* amount you have available for the purchase is *all* that will ever be available.

Let me illustrate the use of the Mother Hubbard by a barrister friend, Nelson, in London. We were having lunch in the Groucho Club in Dean Street, Soho when he asked my advice about a computer that his partners had charged him with purchasing. At the time I was working as a sales consultant to a computer company and was familiar with the market.

My friend's problem was that he knew which machine he wanted but was £2,500 short of the total price the computer sales negotiator had quoted him. There was also the important question of doing well in this negotiation as he had only just joined the practice at Lincoln's Inn as a partner and as their first black barrister he wanted to do well.

I suggested that he raise more cash but he explained he could not do this as he was already running two office-equipment budgets together by making the purchase at the end of one financial year and the beginning of the other.

So I suggested he use the Mother Hubbard, and was 'persuaded' to explain it in detail for the price of the lunch and a bottle of Chianti Classico. After lunch, Nelson returned to his office to meet with the computer negotiator (incidently, they were rivals of my client so I was delighted to put them under the squeeze).

Being imaginative (and slightly inebriated, for the Chianti was followed by several sambuccos) he contrived a very convincing 'script' and used it at the negotiation.

Nelson started (correctly) by making the computer seller go over the machine's virtues once again and he also booked a demonstration of the machine for his partners in the office later that week.

The seller really got to work on what he now considered to be a 'prospect' (sales jargon for someone likely to buy) and (correctly) he kept plugging away at the deal. However, he also disclosed (incorrectly) that he was anxious to get the machine into a legal practice as a basis for making sales to other partnerships among the Inns.

Nelson did not pretend to have the gift of those sales at his disposal but he hinted vaguely (correctly) that if the machine was as good as it was claimed, it was bound to have some effect on sales in the profession.

A week later, after the office demonstration, the Mother Hubbard was sprung.

The seller was told that the partners had approved the purchase of *a* computer in principle, but they had imposed a budget ceiling on the acquisition of £11,500.

'Not a penny more to be spent', Nelson reported, and to underline this point he read the decision out from the minutes of the weekly partnership meeting. He placed the minutes across the desk in full view of the seller.

This was a correct (almost inspired) move on Nelson's part. Why?

Because, since Moses brought the tablets down from the mountain, the written word has an authority over the mere spoken word. People appear to accept almost anything as true if it is written rather than spoken, which is why sellers have their prices printed in lists to give them an altogether undeserved authority!

Regretfully, Nelson, told the seller that as his machine was priced at £11,500, to which was added a £500 training charge, an annual maintenance fee of £1,900 and a tax of £2,000 giving a gross price of £15,900, the partners had instructed him to look elsewhere for a more realistically-priced machine.

He regretted this move as he thought the machine on offer would meet their needs and he pointed out that the partners were less keen on modernizing than he was, but wanted to see some more demonstrations of other machines in the coming week.

The seller was visibly put out by this news (though it was a mistake to display his emotions) and, predictably, he tried several lines of attack on the ceiling price of £11,500. He offered (incorrectly) several concessions in the form of additional software free of charge, a reduced training package and an extended payment period.

His mistake was that none of these tackled the central problem of the £11,500 budget ceiling, though Nelson (correctly) made a note of the concessions for later use.

But on the gross price of £11,500 Nelson could not budge. As his shocking opening was credible – the written minutes 'proved' it – his regret was genuine. He accepted that searching for a cheaper machine was a 'drag' but he would have to do this as the price of £15,900 was way above his budget.

The seller was boxed in and he knew that if he wanted to make this sale he would have to come down in price. But £4,000 was some drop and he needed a good reason for arranging anything like that. As he didn't have a good reason to hand he agreed to get back to Nelson after he had 'consulted his head office'.

It would have been better for him to have said he would get back 'after he had thought it over' rather than disclose his lack of authority in the negotiation. Also, it was a risky decision to leave his 'prospect' in case the competition came in while he was away and introduced Nelson to a 'cheaper' machine (in computers there is always a cheaper machine available or on its way).

'At that price I'd rather scrap it'

Getting mechanical things repaired can cost a small fortune. This is especially true of cars, boat engines and light aircraft.

Harry Smith had engine trouble with his small weekend boat. He took it to the repair yard and asked them to diagnose the trouble. A week later the yard rang Harry and told him that he needed a new engine as the shaft had gone on his old one and it would not last another 20 hours. A new engine would cost him £900, and naturally the yard was willing to fit one for another £150.

There was no way that Harry was prepared to fork out £1,050 for a new engine on a boat he used only occasionally.

He tried a version of the Mother Hubbard.

He told the yard that he had decided to sell the boat for 'whatever it would bring' (probably about £800 in its current condition) and that he would 'collect it next Tuesday'.

On Monday, Harry turned up at the yard to collect his boat, implying that he had found a customer. He told the manager that with the money he got from selling the boat he would buy a dinghy. The money he saved by not buying an engine would go towards his holidays.

The manager was not keen to see a lost engine but could also see that Harry was determined to sell his boat. He asked Harry how much he was able to pay to replace his engine. Harry (springing the Mother Hubbard) told him that he was only prepared to stay with power boating if it cost him no more than £350, but that he was quite happy to go back to dinghy sailing as engines 'cost money to fit, to maintain and to fuel'.

The manager went for the £350 ceiling.

If Harry was interested, he could have a reconditioned engine from stock for £400 – 'a customer had left it three years ago and had not been heard of since' – plus £85 for fitting, if he could take the old engine off his hands for spare parts.

Harry agreed (eventually) after getting a warranty on the 'new' engine and a free fitting, all for £390.

Three days later, Nelson received a call saying that the computer company would make a 'special offer' of a machine at £9,500 which would reduce the tax bill to £1,425.

And there was more. The seller announced that his company would 'show their faith in their computer by postponing for 12 months the annual maintenance fee of £1,900'.

This 'never to be repeated' offer gave a gross purchase price of £11,425 'which is £75 inside your budget' (confirming the credibility of Nelson's Mother Hubbard).

The offer was conditional on the partners being willing to allow the computer company to quote them as clients to other partnerships but 'for obvious reasons' the special price they had been given was to remain 'confidential'.

I congratulated Nelson on his success and remarked that his deal might have been improved if he had tried to press them on the training charge of £500 – a wholly ludicrous proposition, in my view, that requires the customer to pay a computer firm for training its people how to use their machines. It is regarded as a 'give away' by many computer negotiators but you have to press them.

However, Nelson's first attempt at the Mother Hubbard saved his partnership £4,000 – less the cost of lunch, Chianti and sambucco at the Groucho Club!

Answers to self-assessment test 8

1 (a) This is so close to his asking price that he must conclude he has a chance of getting £192,000.

   (b) You are not trying very hard are you?

   (c) A tough opening indeed – you risk not getting the house but if you do you're going to get it cheap.

   (d) You have been hustled or have more money than sense and know something about the house that I don't!

2 (a) A modest expectation.

   (b) Oh dear!

   (c) Good.

   (d) Very good.

3 *(a)* You're optimistic.

   (b) You're pessimistic.

   (c) You're selling yourself short.

4 *(a)* A close-out move, try *(c)* first.

   (b) She's done the Mother Hubbard on you.

   (c) Correct.

Self-assessment test 9

1 You want to sell your car privately to finance a new-car purchase. You think it is worth £5,500 and you know of its (to you) minor defects. Do you advertise it:
   (a) At £5,500 ONO?
   (b) £5,700?
   (c) At £6,000 ONO?
   (d) Without a price?
   (b) At £5,500?

2 You are quoting for the installation of a new kitchen in a house. Do you:
   (a) Give a detailed cost breakdown of every item in the quotation?
   (b) Give a rough breakdown of the costing?
   (c) Avoid giving a cost breakdown, only the total figure?

3 Your spouse complains loudly to you that the old trailer you no longer use is blocking the side-drive of the house and you are required to get rid of it. As the weeks go by the complaints get more strident and eventually you sit down to compose an advertisement to sell it. You think it is worth about £500, given its condition and the likely market for used trailers. What do you say about price in your advertisement:
   (a) £510?
   (b) £525?
   (c) £500 ONO?
   (d) Make me an offer?
   (e) First offer of £500 secures?
   (f) Nothing?

Chapter Nine

Why ONO is a NO NO
or how to get a better price

The used-household-goods market is small beer compared to the world of multinational business but it has some potent lessons for negotiators. This chapter is about some of them.

In Britain, schoolboys sell old toys and conkers to each other (in America, I understand, they sell flick knives and horror comics) and all children, everywhere, soon learn to trade with their pals. Their parents are no different. Alongside the official markets of everyday business and commerce, there is a flourishing, almost underground, market for household goods.

In communist countries too, the ordinary people engage in trade, whatever the official laws say to the contrary. Walk down any main street in a communist country and somebody is bound furtively to offer to buy something from you – even your clothes!

In 1965, at the main railway station in Warsaw, for instance, the government money changer in his office offered me a Zloty rate for my Sterling pounds, which I refused, and a totally different – much more favourable to me – rate five minutes later as I walked through the tunnel to the train track (apparently he had closed his office for a few minutes in the interests of a little private enterprise).

Hungary, too, was run by economic lunatics in the 1960s. At Budapest airport, no money changer would give you Polish Zloty for Hungarian Dinars, even though both were 'brother socialist' economies (and each presumably had plenty of Zloty or Dinars). They would, however, give you *unlimited* amounts of US dollars (which officially they were desperately short of) for your Dinars!

However, I don't want to give the impression that private deals are confined to those living in the 'workers' paradises'. In Washington DC, I was once caught off balance in a bookstore by the clerk offering to buy the red striped shirt I was wearing for $20 cash. I admired his taste almost as much as I regretted his timing, as I was on my way to lunch at the International Monetary Fund two blocks along, and the thought of appearing there shirtless ruined the deal.

In fact, everybody at some time or another has sold something – a used car, some furniture, a box of old books or such like. The deal could have been made with a friend, a neighbour, a member of the family, or a complete stranger. They hear of our intentions of selling by word of mouth or from an advertisement of some kind.

For example, many people in Britain sell their cars by placing a notice in a window with a contact telephone number. Often they include the price they are looking for:

For Sale
This Car
£3,200

As often, almost by the compulsion of convention, they also include the message:

ONO

meaning 'or nearest offer'.

Why do they add ONO after their price?

Answers vary.

Some say it stops a potential customer being put off by the price: if they believe the price is negotiable they are more likely to ask to see the car, etc. Others say they do it because they do not want to lose the chance of a sale even if they must drop their price a little. Still others do it because they have seen other people's ads use ONO in them and they presume that it is part of the 'rules' for used goods selling.

In my view writing ONO is a mistake.

In fact, I believe that ONO is a 'NO NO'.

Why?

Ask yourself what a buyer thinks when he sees ONO? It tells him that you are willing to accept *less* than £3,200 *before even hearing what he has got to say*.

This weakens your position. Instead of the buyer thinking he has to compete against others for the right to buy at a price *above* £3,200, he starts off knowing that the seller is worried about the possibility that he will not get a sale.

And who does that help?

The potential buyer of course!

It is generally true that in writing ONO you almost always weaken your bargaining position by disclosing your keenness to sell. You open the negotiations at an implied price below your opening

£3,200, without having found out anything about the extent of the buyer's keenness to buy.

That way you start off with a handicap – like opening at love-40 in tennis. For all you know, the buyer, because of a family commitment, may desperately need to purchase a car that very day – yours may be the fifth car he has looked at – and he has run out of time. This could make £3,200, or even more, for it a bargain for him (and for you!),

In negotiating you don't know what is in the other person's mind or the extent of the pressures upon him – and you certainly don't know anything about this before you meet him. Once you are in contact with him you *might* get a clearer picture of his real position by what he says, but by using ONO, you forego that opportunity to find out his real position. Meanwhile, he knows something about your position as soon as he reads your sale notice, i.e. before he has met you. There is an asymmetry in bargaining information – in his favour!

If he knows something about your attitude to the asking price, namely, that you have so little confidence in it that you are willing to accept less before the negotiating begins, and you do not know anything about his attitude, namely, whether he thinks £3,200 a good or a lousy price, it follows that to the extent that bargaining strength may be determined by relative keenness to trade, the eventual price must be more to the buyer's advantage than to yours.

I believe that the use of ONO-type messages is a mistake on the seller's part, *and* that a failure to take advantage of them on the buyer's part is a mistake of equal seriousness. Experience shows that buyers often ignore the ONO invitation to make a 'near offer' and actually pay the asking price! In other words, buyers do not always get the message implied by ONO, and they let the seller off the hook he put himself on in the first place. Unfortunately, we cannot rely on our errors always being rectified by the errors of others, useful as they are as an excuse for our behaviour!

Why buyers fail to take advantage of the seller's ONO-type invitation could be a source of employment for an out-of-work sociologist or student of abnormal behaviour; it ought not to be the kind of mistake you make in future.

If you see something for sale with an ONO price tag, you must assume immediately that the *maximum* price he is expecting is certainly *less* than the asking ONO price. And you also know that his rock-bottom price will be lower still because the *minimum* price he will accept will be *lower* than his maximum expectation. You don't know what he will take until you try him out with some low (and I mean *low*) opening offers. Follow Jack's rule!

You might be the fifth potential buyer he has seen and he may be desperate not to lose you like he lost the others. Sooner or later, time runs out in every deal, and his time might have run out for him.

The fact that he has used an ONO price indicates an amateur approach to selling, and you need not be shy about taking advantage of this. Indeed, you do him and the wider community a great service by teaching him how to conduct his business. The extra discount on the price in your reward and the gratuitous experience is his.

Could there be a fairer way of educating the ONO seller?

If you ask people (as I do at my Negotiating Clinics) why they include ONO in their advertisements (not just for cars) they often rationalize it by claiming that their prime aim is to sell the used item because:

I needed the space and it was in the way.
I needed the money for a trade-in deal.
I just wanted rid of it and any price was a bonus.

In other words they felt under pressure of some kind to make the sale – the money was a secondary consideration as long as it was 'around the asking price'. But remember, being under pressure to make a deal is not unique to you. Nor should you assume that the other person is not under even greater pressure. To do so is to make concessions before the negotiations begin, and, in making opening concessions without receiving anything in return, you are in danger of sliding down the slippery slope to surrender.

Self-induced delusions that the other person has all the power (commonly heard from trade union negotiators about the management, and from the management about the union men, and from buyers about sellers and *vice versa*) can be a costly mistake.

The price you set for your surplus household items is often purely arbitrary – the price you would *like* to get, rather than the price you know for certain it will fetch.

Fortunately, you will soon learn if the market thinks your price is totally unrealistic. The notion that the world will beat a path to your door to negotiate a deal for a pile of old junk dies rapidly with every outbreak of seller's naivety in the suburbs.

It is not altogether different in business, despite treatises written by economists to show that price setting is a science rather than a hunch.

You are unlikely to know what the market value of used personal property is at any one moment, and, anyway, you are likely to be prejudiced about its value.

You might think the old table is worth a small fortune just because your granny got it as a wedding present – the market may see it as more fit for firewood – but good luck to you – at least you are not under-selling yourself.

I once raced across Edinburgh to see what was described in the advertisement as an 'antique desk', priced at £70. (At that price I should have known better.)

The desk in question was Clerical (i.e. the very bottom grade Civil Service, circa 1950). It had been bought by its redundant owner out of his own office when the Government had a clearance sale. For some reason he thought it antique because he had sat at it for 20 years!

You know what you paid for your household property, perhaps but you cannot know what other people are prepared to pay for it today until you attempt to sell it.

Not knowing what the price should be, you are tempted to use an ONO price tag as an encouragement to potential buyers to come and look at the item. But it is also an invitation to them to correct your assessment of what it is worth, and having taken the trouble to oblige you on the former, they are more than likely to help you with the latter.

Naturally, getting someone to your front door to look at your car, or old washing machine, or box of books, is an essential first step to selling them. If nobody calls to see what you are selling, then certainly nobody is going to buy them. Hence, the temptation to set a price low enough to attract customers but high enough to make it worthwhile for your trouble.

Choosing the 'right' price is a difficult task – how 'high' is high and how 'low' is low? But having set a price, why choose to qualify it with ONO? By doing so, you undermine your decision on the price.

You know that anybody taking the trouble to see your goods is half way to buying them – searching around the second-hand market for a sofa can be a time-consuming business.

After a while the buyer is inclined to lower his sights if the price for something, not quite what he is looking for, appears to look like a 'bargain'.

You can define a 'bargain' any way you want to. You can compare the price for the used machine with its new list price; you can compare it with what you expected to pay, or with the price a friend paid the week before. The range is limitless – which is why we can rationalize our 'bargains' at least to our own satisfaction.

The buyer's strength is that he knows that the cost of newspaper advertising for low-priced household items can be a relatively high proportion of the selling price, particularly if the advertisements have to be repeated several times before a sale is made.

You must consider the consequences of a prospective customer hesitating over buying your car. This automatically produces prospects of additional costs (such as advertising *and* waiting) to attract alternative buyers.

If you are tempted to avoid these costs, you can only do so by being prepared to reduce the asking price from £3,200 to something near it. Hence, the mistaken reason for ONO: you want to make it clear that a 'near offer' will be accepted.

My point is that you ought to bear in mind that the buyer also faces search costs and that he can only avoid these if he settles with you on your offer. The pressure on him to settle is just as relentless as the pressure on you, but he has no way of knowing what pressure you are under unless you tell him or indicate it to him in some way, e.g. appearing very anxious to close the deal.

There's a right time and a wrong time

Graham is a farmer and he knows about the importance of the seasons. He also knows that there is a right and a wrong time to buy or sell almost anything.

He argues that most people forget the elementary rule of business: if you want to sell, avoid a buyer's market (and *vice versa*).

How do you avoid a market when the advantage is with the other person? For one thing, Graham argues, you can deliberately choose not to enter a negotiation when a moment's thought should warn you off.

He gives the following advice for timing negotiations:

The best time to buy a boat (Graham has three) is at the end of the season when the owner faces harbour fees for the winter if he doesn't sell; conversely, the best time to sell is at the start of the season when the buyer is itching to sail his new boat.

The best time to buy a house (Graham has three) is when the owner has to sell it irrespective of the season, hence enter the market in the winter if you're buying, avoid it if you are selling.

The best time to get cash, use of the car, and a late night at a party is when father is about to watch the big match on TV or mother is talking avidly to a girl friend.

The worst time to negotiate about anything is when you are in a hurry, you're tired, you've just been fighting, you're sexually aroused, you've something important on your mind, you're bored stiff, or you want to be somewhere else.

The best time to buy Christmas presents is right after Christmas in the New Year sales. Buy your Christmas cards in the Spring, Mother's Day cards near Father's Day, winter coats in the summer, summer clothes in the winter (especially if it is snowing), vegetables near closing time, food in the market or the cash-and-carry, booze at the brewery, travel at off-peak times, hotel rooms at the weekend, and property during a war.

If a reduction in your asking price is necessary to clinch the deal it is up to you to decide how far to move downwards, if at all (but make sure that any such moves are small and infrequent).

But what is not necessary at all is for you to signal at the *start* that the price is negotiable. If he wants to haggle, he will. You are no worse off by leaving that opening move to him. Indeed, you are better off because if you leave it to him to start haggling with you, he has to overcome any inhibitions he has about haggling in order to do so.

And lots of people find it very difficult to open up a haggle. They cannot bring themselves to do so without a great deal of stress and effort. They are inclined either to accept the deal as it stands or back off. If they accept the deal because of their shyness about haggling then you are home free.

If they need encouragement to negotiate you might have to provide that *but only in the negotiation*.

Ask questions, such as what they like about the item, is it what they were looking for, in what way does it suit their needs, etc.? The answer will reveal their inhibitions about price. If you can coax out of them an offer you can decide how you want to handle it – offer them a 'deal' or go to deadlock.

This is by far a much stronger line to follow than ONO.

Answers to self-assessment test 9

1   *(a)* ONO is a NO NO! You are telling the buyer that your price of £5,500 will be reduced.

   (b) A strong move as it gives you room to come down if you need to and is in touch with your target price.

   (c) Out of touch with your target and weakened by ONO.

   (d) Could be OK depending on the state of the market.

   (e) Not good – any concessions bring you below target.

2   *(a)* Never offer to give breakdowns (always ask for them!) as they encourage buyers to squeeze your price.

   (b) Ditto – not even rough ones!

(c) Correct: a total figure helps repackaging.

3   *(a)* Competent buyers offer less than what you ask for, so you leave yourself some negotiating room.

(b) Good. This leaves you room to move and scope to argue about the trailer's worth and condition.

(c) No, because you encourage a buyer to pay less than £500 *before* he sees the trailer.

(d) A sure hostage to fortune – what happens if he opens at £450 and your spouse is glaring at you?

(e) Better than *(c)*, if you mean it.

(f) If anybody turns up you will be too euphoric to hold your price, especially when they note the trailer's defects.

Self-assessment test 10

1 You are the key accounts negotiator for a soft-drinks firm
   and have just been told by the chief buyer of the country's
   largest hypermarket chain that you must cut your prices by a
   penny a case or they will drop your brand. They sell a
   million dozen cans of your Cola Pop a year. Do you:
   (a) Smile and say 'no'?
   (b) Agree?
   (c) Suggest a compromise?

2 Your next negotiation is with the rival hypermarket chain
   whose chief buyer expresses his delight at seeing you so
   fortuitously as your main rival has stopped deliveries
   because of a strike. He asks if you can fill the gap with an
   emergency order of 50,000 dozen cans of Cola Pop,
   delivery immediate. Do you:
   (a) Smile and say 'yes'?
   (b) Say yes, but offer no discount because of the additional
         costs of emergency delivery?
   (c) Smile and say it isn't possible at such short notice?
   (d) Tell him it's his 'lucky day' because not only can you
         deliver what he needs but you can also give him the
         bulk-purchase discount that is being offered this month?

3 You have been working only three weeks in a new job as a
   shipping agent in Baltimore and had planned to get married
   on Friday 18 August (which you did not disclose at the job
   interview). Your 'intended' has demanded a proper honeymoon vacation of at least a week in Miami. It's now 16
   August and you ask your boss for leave both for the wedding
   day and for the honeymoon. He is visibly put out by the
   request and asks stiffly how long you were 'thinking of being
   absent'. Do you say:
   (a) The wedding day only?
   (b) Two weeks?
   (c) Three weeks?
   (d) One week?

Chapter Ten

The Law of the Yukon
or how to toughen up your negotiating style

Toughness in negotiating, in my view, does not attract enough attention from practitioners. As with the great classics of literature, which are more often quoted than read, toughness as a negotiating style is more often spoken of than practised.

In this chapter a case is made for toughness in your negotiating behaviour which, hopefully, will succeed in moving you along the tough-soft spectrum *towards* the toughness end.

Toughness is not a simple concept. There are many facets to toughness and it takes as many forms as there are people willing to use it as a negotiating style.

A *tough* negotiator generally:

- Is not easily intimidated.
- Sticks to (or close to) his demand.
- Trades a few, small, concessions.
- Gives ever smaller concessions as the negotiations continue.
- Is undisturbed by threats of deadlock.

In contrast, a *soft* negotiator generally:

- Is easily intimidated.
- Moves considerably away from his opening position.
- Frequently makes large unilateral concessions.
- Is terrified by the prospect of deadlock.

Which are you at the moment?

Consider Joe, a key account manager for a firm of soft-drink manufacturers. He negotiates with major food store chains and has the authority to close his deals on whatever he judges to be the 'best price'.

He sells cans of fizzy drink in quantities of up to a million dozen at a time. His company is in heavy competition with others and he is under constant pressure from the buyers he deals with to shave a penny off here and penny off there. He is constantly told that his rivals are making these concessions and that if he doesn't match them his products will disappear from prime shelf positions.

Watching him negotiate under these conditions is an education in professionalism. He never betrays the slightest reaction to bad news of any kind, or to threats, or to shock-horror tales about what his clients have done or might do about his product lines.

He speaks very softly and manages to combine a nodding head at what he hears from the buyer with a smile as he says a clear 'no' to the latest outrageous proposal.

Obviously, for the buyers their tactics of squeezing until the pips squeak must work against the majority of sellers they see.

They don't hold their jobs at the top of the buying tree by failing to get it right more often than they get it wrong. It's just that with Joe they get it wrong when they try the squeeze on him.

Joe knows that once he starts competing with his rivals to shave his prices he will be as ordinary as they are, and, perhaps more seriously, he and they will start a slide downwards to the extinction of some of them.

Fortunately, Joe's company believes in sustaining a high-profile advertising presence in the media and is not dependent on the goodwill of particular food-store buyers. In this way it maintains public demand for its products and where there is demand there has to be supply. If one chain does not stock these goods others will – moreover, the local store managers don't like losing sales of popular products that Head Office refuses to stock to their rivals who are not so inhibited, and they are easily encouraged to put pressure on Head Office to ensure them of supplies.

Joe does not act as if he is at the mercy of the buyers. He may be alone in the buyer's office for a negotiation but he does not forget that he represents a large operation and that his products have a loyal support among the customers in the buyer's stores.

When buyers try to hussle him into thinking that pennies off his price are absolutely critical (after all that's their job isn't it?) he does not forget that the customer who buys a can of fizzy pop for thirsty kids to drink is not aiming to save a fraction of a penny per can (assuming the store passes on the discount instead of banking it as a profit, which is more likely in the retail grocery business). The truth is that kids like his company's fizzy drink enough to badger their parents into buying it.

While Joe's perception of the realities of why customers purchase his company's fizzy drink gives him enough confidence not to crumble at the bark of aggressive buyers, it is in no way sufficient to permit him to dictate terms. However, it is just enough not to lead him into the negotiations entirely naked.

Hence, Joe adopts a tough position on his prices, and his concessions are miserly. If a buyer wants a penny off a case he is going to have to give Joe something in return to get it. Joe has established his style over the years and most of his buyers know he doesn't frighten easily – not that this stops them trying every now and again.

What do you do when the buyer hits you with 'you'll have to do better than that!'?

Do you cave in or do you refuse to panic?

The answer is to some extent a matter of personal concern to you alone – on it may depend your career progress, your material affluence and, indeed, your personal happiness. It is also of interest to your company because a lot of other people in the organisation – whose welfare is every bit as important to them as your welfare is to you – depend on the negotiating abilities of you people in the front seats.

No matter what else those back at the office think of you as a person, you can bet your last pay cheque that they prefer you to get big orders for the company's products rather than small ones and they also prefer you to be unintimidated by aggressive buyers.

Every penny off the case you give away too easily is money taken away from their next pay increase – perhaps, even, from what is available to keep them on the payroll. Nobody profits from a company that makes losses and every step you take down in price is a step nearer to bankruptcy.

It is no comfort to argue that a penny cut by you is trivial. Despatch may concede a penny on vehicle repairs, the works may concede a penny, or more, on the wages, accounts a penny on bad debts, and administration a penny on carbon paper. And so it goes on.

Nobody thinks their behaviour counts because on its own it doesn't. But taken together, this habit of cutting and running could put your company out of business.

Well, what of the evidence on toughness in response to a tough demand from the other negotiator? Surprisingly it is extremely consistent.

The shifting Chinese middle

A European firm, world-renowned in the oil industry, was asked by the Chinese to enter into negotiations to supply its services to the small but growing domestic Chinese off-shore oil industry.

The Chinese, who are anxious to develop their oil resources and are using Western technology to do so, went hard at the prices quoted by the European firm.

First, they got a price quotation for the company supplying its services for three years, then they demanded, inclusive in the quoted price, a lot of extras.

Among these extras were some very expensive add-ons, such as free training for Chinese nationals, free manuals for operating the specialized equipment, masses of spares and stores, and domestic charges for accommodating the company's technical staff. This last was a trifle ambitious on the part of the Chinese who insisted that the foreign staff be charged at the same *per diem* rate for subsistence that they were charged for their staff visiting Europe where prices and living standards are, of course, much higher.

The European negotiators fought hard to avoid pricing themselves into unprofitability and regularly complained that when they made a concession the result was not a reciprocal move on the part of the Chinese. Far from it. The Chinese regarded 'split the difference' moves as invitations to put pressure on the Europeans to move even closer to the Chinese opening position.

The remedy was in the Europeans' hands: pad their prices before they opened negotiations; never make a single concession without getting something back from the Chinese; avoid any 'fair play' illusions about 'split the difference' gambits; totally resist the 'add-on' ploys; and, lastly, sit it out, for the Chinese need oil technology far more than oil technologists need to work in China.

Briefly, it pays! Negotiators form their opinions about the realism of their expectations in contact with their opponents. They cannot act in this matter independent of the other party. What is, or is not, realistic is not decided by a court of Socratean Sages who sit in judgment and pass the results of their deliberations to we mortals below. It is decided by our beliefs about what is possible and those beliefs are influenced by what the other person says and does.

If the other person acts contrary to the way we expect, this must influence our judgment about the likely outcome of the negotiation. For instance, in the unlikely event that a buyer greeted Joe with: 'Am I glad to see you!' and then pleaded with him for an emergency delivery of a million dozen cans of sodapop that night (when Joe was expecting a big fight to get a small order), it is unlikely that Joe would respond by offering a discount and free delivery.

The buyer's disclosure of his predicament is Joe's opportunity. Would Joe take it? You bet he would! If the other guy goes in real hard on you, how do you rate the chances of an order? High, middling, low or none at all?

You would be less than real if you associated a tough stance in an opponent as an indication of his generosity. You would be an eternal optimist to conclude that it is going to be easy to settle on your best terms in such circumstances.

What is true for you is true for them.

Ironically, many negotiators react to the appearance of a tough stance and the absence of generosity by playing the role they sought for the other person: they go soft and demonstrate their own generosity.

In effect, they reward the tough stances with softness on their part, for observation shows that toughness often generates the opposite response from an opponent.

If you take a tough stance he is *more likely* (and the evidence is that he is *much* more likely) to take a soft stance than a tough one, either by modifying his original tougher opening position or by cranking down his tough position to a much softer plateau.

The converse is probably more obvious: if an opponent opens up with an unexpectedly soft demand, it is most likely that you will revise your expectations upwards rather than downwards.

If you don't then you are in the wrong business!

This is precisely the basic weakness of the theory and practice of goodwill-conceding – if you are soft, he responds by being tough. If he doesn't you're dealing with as dangerous a threat to his company as you are to yours.

Negotiators in between drinks at Thank-God-it's-Friday 'seminars' will warn you that taking a tough stance increases the chance of a deadlock. That this may be true appeals to intuition.

The question that ought to be put is: just *how much* more likely is it that a deal will fold because I take a tougher stance? It would take a very wise negotiator to answer that question with any confidence because nobody knows before an event what is the precise likelihood of a deal folding for a given degree of toughness. (If you think you can predict this likelihood accurately there is a Nobel Prize – with $186,000 – waiting for you!)

In the real world it is impossible to be certain about the likelihood of a deadlock in a negotiation because you take a specific stance in it. That deadlock is more likely is not disputed but if the likelihood of deadlock is only *marginally* more likely if you take a tough stance, and the rewards of doing so are much higher if you are successful, then clearly it might pay you to be tougher rather than softer.

Observation and experimental evidence around the world suggest that the likelihood of deadlock is only *slightly* greater if a tough stance is taken in response to intimidation from the buyer.

You may achieve slightly fewer deals but the ones you do get are so much better in value that the gross result is a much higher income stream flowing to your company.

What happens all too frequently is that young negotiators listen intently to what old hands tell them at the weekly TGIF and react out of all proportion. They reason that, if what the old hands say is true and that it is more likely that a deal will deadlock with a tough stance than a soft stance, it follows that a soft stance will be more likely to lead to a deal than a tough one.

Also, their experience before hardened buyers convinces them that the only way they will get the buyer to recognize them as part of the human race, let alone 'like' them just a little, is to please them in some way, such as by giving them concessions. It takes a heavy investment in training to eradicate this nonsense.

As to the 'wisdom' of a TGIF (Thank God It's Friday) seminar, new hands should make an allowance for the old hands' natural desire for a quiet life. They should also study the arithmetic: seven negotiations that result in five deals at £10,000 are better than seven deals at £7,000.

It could be that the number of 'hits' will be higher than five out of seven, making the arithmetic even better. It all depends on how big a difference in the *likelihood of settling* there is between a tough stance and a soft one in your product line and the *price difference* between the two stances. Certainly, you will never know until you

Remember, they have a choice!

The gambling boom in the United States led New Jersey to attempt to cream off some of the glittering prizes flowing to Las Vegas. They invited casino operators to set up shop in the State.

Some of the locals thought this a heaven-sent opportunity to cash in on the bonanza.

One house-owner went too far.

His little two-storey brick house occupied part of the site that the Penthouse group wanted to build their casino on. He asked them for $2.5 million dollars for his house and refused all entreaties to budge his price.

Negotiators always have a choice of saying 'no' and this is what happened here.

The casino group gave up negotiating and built their casino right up to the house property boundary. The casino rises seven stories above the house on three sides, completely blocking the 'view' except at the roadside.

Whatever the house was worth to the owner before the negotiations ($70,000?), it is now worth much less, except perhaps as a curiosity!

start trying a tougher stance, as nothing much was ever proven over a few beers at a TGIF seminar, except perhaps that they pass on the bad habits of each to everybody else.

The adoption of a soft stance in the face of intimidation is wrong because it starts a process of creeping limpness in the people who operate it. First, they convince themselves that by being softer (read cheaper) they get business that would otherwise go to the competition. Then, as the habit of softness gets a grip on them, their outlook and their behaviour, they develop a cringe, and even palpitations, every time they see signs of the other person dithering on the brink of deadlock.

Naturally, unintentionally they convey this attitude to the other person and he soon learns – as if programmed – to exploit their incipient fears of not getting a deal. He lays it on and before long all their deals are at or below the 'bottom line' of profitability of their company.

Tragedy at Makola

Ghana's economy went through a bad time and a collapse in economic confidence led to a military coup. The military had good intentions but remained economically illiterate. Faced with serious food shortages and rapidly rising prices they chose the age-old method of intervention.

This never works. They sought popularity by blaming the shortages on black-market stock-piling; they took stern measures against smuggling; they instituted price controls and finally they turned the mob on the market traders at Makola (Accra).

The mob destroyed the market by fire, violently dispersed the market 'mammies', and still went home hungry.

By intimidating the only people who could be mobilized to get food into Ghana – not by exhortation but by self-interest – the Government perpetuated the shortages. If it had told the market mammies that they could keep all their profits from trade, if they had repealed all laws against smuggling, and if they had abandoned price controls – in other words the exact opposite of what they did – they would now be ruling a fitter, fatter Ghana.

Why? Because it is a law of human nature that if it is worth somebody's while to put themselves out they will always do so, and if by doing so they bring in food to a starving country they will do more for the people than any other grouping. Next door to Ghana, the Ivory Coast has none of Ghana's draconian laws about food prices. It is also suffering none of Ghana's self-inflicted ailments.

If a buyer goes soft the respond borders on the paranormal; hordes of tough sellers gravitate to the buyer's office carrying hard deals by the bundle. You see, the word soon gets round. Why?

What you are you don't begat: you create your opposite type.

How does toughness manifest itself in the negotiating crucible where the 'beam me up Scotty' option is not available?

Tough negotiators have high expectations. If they meet a tough opponent they either face it out or end up at deadlock. They don't give in to toughness by becoming soft.

In the game of 'chicken' they jam the accelerator and lock the steering wheel at straight ahead. The pressure on them to modify their stance is exactly the same as on the other person and experience shows that most people respond to toughness in negotiating by becoming soft. The tough guy doesn't.

If he modifies at all, it is slowly and in small, infrequent and irregular steps that get smaller not bigger. Tough negotiators always trade smaller concessions than their opponents – they take more than they give. If they are offered a horse they respond with an egg.

Tough negotiators are less concerned with deadlock than soft negotiators. Their main concern is with the deal being close to their expectations, rather than with *a* deal for the sake of it.

If you are worried about the order, your opponent will sense it like a dog always knows who it is safe to bark at and who it is prudent to slink away from. If you can't walk away from a deal that is struck on unsatisfactory terms, you are psychologically half-way to rationalizing any terms you can get.

In negotiating you must act more like Scrooge and less like St Francis of Assisi. In other spheres of human contact perhaps the exact opposite should apply. But negotiating is unique – it is a remarkable fact that negotiators who can stand up to intimidation end up enriching a far wider set of people than themselves. Those who aim for the trees never get off the ground, and drag more than themselves down with them.

Years ago, when I was a boy, my grandfather entertained me with stories about his days as a goldminer in Canada before the First World War. He told plain unsophisticated stories, for his was a hard labouring life.

There was a proud fatalism about the North American miners in those days and he often recited a few lines of verse that captured their spirit. They are an apt inclusion in this chapter:

This is the law of the Yukon:
  that the strong shall thrive.
For surely the weak shall perish
  and only the fit survive.

Remember the *Law of the Yukons* as you prepare for a negotiation, because it can call for great toughness of spirit to hold out for your target while looking into the cold, steely eyes of an opponent who thinks he has got your measure.

Answers to self-assessment test 10

1 *(a)* Definitely your best first move. A million dozen cans suggests a lot of happy customers the chain would not want to disappoint.

(b) Not unless you want price pressure every call.

(c) A sign of weakness. Make him work for his cuts.

2 *(a)* No. Are you an 'order taker' or a negotiator?

(b) Much better. A plausible opening counter.

(c) Surely not if your company is a serious rival. Anything is possible if the price is right.

(d) You are obviously an out-of-work Kamikaze pilot. If you avoid taking advantage – even mildly – of a buyer's predicament you'll never survive when he doesn't need you.

3 *(a)* No. An abject surrender which you will spend the rest of your married life explaining to your spouse.

(b) Good. Start high and work down if you have to. Your boss will respect your courage – eventually.

(c) Weak. He'll squeeze you to a weekend in Newark.

(d) Not as good as *(b)* but showing some signs of negotiator's grit, hopefully with future potential!

Self-assessment test 11

1 You are in Kobe, Japan, discussing the possibility of business with a local company and the leader of the Japanese team hands you a colourfully wrapped box which is clearly intended as a personal gift. Do you:

(a) Thank him profusely and open the box?

(b) Thank him profusely and put the box away?

(c) Thank him profusely and hand him a gift in return?

2 On arrival at Narita airport, Tokyo, you are met by your Japanese hosts, who kindly enquire as to your return journey, offering to check your reservations for you and to handle any related matters during your stay. Do you regard this as:

(a) An example of Japanese courtesy?

(b) A means of finding out your time deadlines?

3 When you are considering doing business with a Japanese company, which of the following would you and they consider to be most important?

(a) The profitability of your company?

(b) Its market share?

(c) Its growth rate?

(d) Its labour relations?

(e) Its standards of quality?

Chapter Eleven

The land of the rising yen
or where not to take yes for an answer

Japan is different. It is also rapidly growing into the world's largest national economy. At present it is the second largest industrial power – the United States is the largest and will remain so for much of the rest of the twentieth century, but beyond that it is more likely that Japan will become number one.

Unlike the United States, which relies on only ten per cent of its multi-trillion dollar economy for international trade, with the Japanese, the proportion is more like 30 per cent. That means it is, and will remain, in the business of trading worldwide for its living. In turn, this means that it is more than likely that your own business interests are going to be influenced, directly or indirectly, by the Japanese. Either you will buy or sell with them – in which case you had better get your act together as a negotiator – or you will buy or sell in competition with them – in which case you had better get your act even more together!

The Japanese are unique because of the way they have handled the transition from a traditional and ancient society to a bustling modern one. In many ways they are a 'model' for those who would also wish to combine change with maintaining traditional values and mores more or less as they have been for centuries.

Japan's process of change began with the Meiji restoration in 1868 and, by excelling in modernization without overturning its traditional values, it has continued until the country is on the brink of overtaking the USA.

To do business with the Japanese you must make some effort to understand how they function (better still, if you have the time, you should try to appreciate *why* they function the way that they do). The shortest way to express what I mean here is to say that for the Japanese everything is managed by a strict routine of courtesy.

Courtesy is more than just being polite. In a traditional society courtesy expresses the role everybody has in the 'proper' (that is, traditional) order of things. People interact within their own group and their manners express mutual recognition of their membership of the group. People also interact outside their own group with people in other groups, and courtesy here enables them to interact in mutual recognition of each other's group role.

Hence, members of the family behave in a certain way with each other, and they behave in a certain way with members of other families. Courtesy facilitates contact between individuals in a way that does not threaten the established order, whether it be the family, the company, the government or whatever.

As a Westerner, you will have extended to you the courtesies of the group or groups to which you are properly introduced and admitted. From the moment that you hand over your own business card and find it studied by your Japanese contact – who will have handed his over in the same expectation – you will be drawn into a social system without parallel in the West.

How rapidly you build up your rapport with your Japanese opposite number will determine whether and to what extent you will do business. You cannot overestimate the role of mutual respect, friendliness and rapport in your relations with the Japanese.

Much of what passes for quaint custom and ritual in Japan is actually an expression of their need to peruse you and your company (and its propositions) for signs that there is a potential for long and fruitful business based on strong and enduring personal relationships.

If you are in a hurry, or do not consider personal relationships of any value, or cannot abide messing about with highly polite (and, to most Westerners, almost excessively polite) exchanges of conversation, gifts and kindnesses or, to the Japanese mind, are quite rude, you are unlikely to secure much interest in what you have come to sell (or buy).

The role of time in negotiating with the Japanese can easily be misunderstood (I certainly misunderstood it for some years until I got more familiar with the Japanese mode of business). For example, in the first edition of *Everything is Negotiable!* (1982) I drew the reader's attention to the potential weakness that a deadline can impose on a Western negotiator. I did this by asking a self-assessment question similar to question 2 at the start of this chapter. The question derives from the experience of several negotiators who on their arrival in Japan are met by their contacts and go through the ritual of having their air-ticket reservations scrutinized, ostensibly, I suggested, in the interests of extending a service but really with another motivation.

I implied that the real purpose behind this move was for the Japanese to discover the deadline towards which the Western negotiator will be working, in order, I asserted, to use this information to apply pressure and secure concessions.

The truth is slightly more complicated (though with some Japanese people my original implication may have some foundation). Time is needed by the Japanese to consider all the implications of a business proposal and they carry out this consultation much more thoroughly than is common in Europe or the United States.

The Japanese process of consultation (*ringi-seido*) could bring to the surface problems not appreciated or known to the senior managers negotiating on behalf of the company. This in turn will require further consultations to see what can be done to remove the problem. All of this takes time as the decision passes up and down the company structure.

Meanwhile the Western negotiator will be kept waiting. Nothing he does can hurry up the process, though impatient intervention

Sumo wrestling and negotiating

The Japanese can spend what appears to Westerners to be an unprecedented amount of time in preliminaries before discussing their business. These preliminaries have, however, an essential role to play and cannot be skipped through, if you want to get the best deal that is available.

An international banker, with many years' experience of negotiating with the Japanese on joint US-Japanese ventures, explains it as follows:

Negotiating with the Japanese goes through several phases, of which the first is probably the most crucial (for the other phases, in the main, follow internationally recognized norms).

The opening phase is like two Sumo wrestlers facing each other before the start of their contest. They make highly ritualized and absolutely expected genuflections, and go through a detailed ritual involving salt being thrown in each corner and much bowing and other demonstrations of respect.

Then they engage each other's attention and prepare themselves. They examine each other and pace their breathing, gradually increasing the tempo until they are both sure that they are ready. Then, and only then, do they lunge forward.

Neither will move towards the other until they are absolutely sure that they are in balance with each other, both physically and mentally.

during it, or signs of disapproval, could slow it down or even make it unnecessary – they could decide that you are showing disrespect and are not the sort of person with whom they want to do any business.

In part, my earlier view was based on discussions with other negotiators to whom the incident had happened and from which they derived the conclusions alluded to in my answer to the self-assessment question. From additional experience I now see that these conclusions were in error, or at least not entirely the complete picture.

Let me explain. There is no doubt that Western negotiators operate at a different pace to their Japanese counterparts. This reflects the differing decision-making systems common to well-managed companies in both cultures. The Japanese take what seems to be an inordinate amount of time to reach a decision. This is because their management system requires that a full consultation takes place with all persons in the organization who are likely to be influenced by the decision.

It is the need to get into mutual balance that distinguishes the Japanese businessman in his contact with non-Japanese negotiators. Only when they feel 'on the same wavelength' will they begin their business and all that precedes this stage is aimed at achieving an interpersonal harmony.

This contrasts with the normal Western approach of sales staff who often make commitments on behalf of their company which are not necessarily confirmed beforehand by their production counterparts. As we all know sales staff can and do promise potential clients almost anything to get the order, including performance levels, quantities and delivery dates that are not possible in practice. This causes the familiar tension between sales and production (and between sales and accounts – the former preferring that the company holds vast stocks of everything in all variations just in case a customer wants to buy one, and the latter preferring that the company has no stocks at all because stocks tie up capital, etc.).

A well-managed Japanese company (and not all Japanese companies are well-managed) will require that a commitment offered to another company is endorsed by those whose actions will determine, in practice, whether that commitment is to be met.

Failure to meet a commitment is a serious matter and the Japanese prefer to take time out before they make a commitment to make sure that everybody (and I mean everybody) in the organization understands the commitment and agrees to it being given, rather than that they be forced to spend time later on trying to sort out what to do about a commitment that should not have been given in the first place, and have to chastise those who have failed in some way to honour the commitment given in the company's name.

If a delivery date is being given, then clearly those parts of the company responsible for designing, constructing and completing the product will have to be consulted to see if they can meet that date. A Japanese company requires a formal written endorsement for each manager responsible for each activity and will expect each manager to have consulted his workforce before he gives his endorsement.

When a Western company overextends itself this creates problems for those whose job is made more difficult as a conse-

Jade pot blames red kettle

A Japanese negotiating team met their match when they spent many fruitless months trying to negotiate a business deal with the Soviet Union. They specialized in heavy machinery for open cast mineral extraction and the Soviet Government wanted to acquire their technology for use in Siberia.

The negotiating teams from the two cultures did not get on at all well. In fact, negotiations got bogged down and the Japanese returned home more than a little demoralized at their experiences.

First, the Japanese complained that their opposite numbers on the Soviet team were quite uninterested in developing personal relationships and rebuffed all Japanese attempts at conviviality. Moreover, the Soviet team changed personnel several times during the six months the Japanese were in Prestoplavsk.

Second, the Soviets took an excessively long time to make a decision, which will cause a wry smile among those who negotiate with Japanese companies and indicate just how long the Soviets must have been taking if it was so long that the Japanese felt they had cause to complain about it!

Third, the Japanese felt that the Soviets, because of their monopoly position as the sole customer for Japanese products in Siberia, were using unfair tactics by having several Japanese companies competing for the same business and by keeping them apart from each other in case they compared notes.

Fourth, the Japanese were appalled at the amount of detail the Soviet negotiators wanted (implying that the Japanese were not capable of producing world-class machinery) and they were apprehensive about the extent of the proposed contract that the Soviets wanted the Japanese to sign (implying a lack of trust in Japanese commitments).

Lastly, the Japanese complained that Prestoplavsk was an awful place to spend much time in and that their Soviet 'hosts' left them to their own devices for social entertainment, often for days on end. Also, they only got decisions to go ahead on important details just as the Japanese had to leave to get transport home.

quence. The usual message from the top of a Western company that has overextended itself to those who feel overwhelmed in consequence of this situation is often a single instruction: 'Cope!'. A Japanese company avoids this situation by in-depth consultation and agreement beforehand. But detailed consultation takes time. The Japanese regard this as time well spent. So should you.

From the point of view of an uninformed negotiator who makes a short visit to Japan in order to sign an agreement, the details of which he plans to negotiate face-to-face with his Japanese contacts, the delays in getting a decision look quite different. We always assume the worst when we contemplate the source of our inconvenience.

You assume that the delay is aimed at putting on negotiating pressure as your deadline to return home approaches. ('Did they not make a point of enquiring when I had to leave?' 'Is it not the case that we have spent several weeks in socializing, with short bursts of negotiating activity lasting a day or so, and now, just as I have two days left before departing, are they not presenting me with amended proposals?')

The answers convince you that you are dealing with tactics aimed at using your deadlines to pressurize you into making concessions. When you add to your suspicions the fact that you did make concessions in those last hurried meetings before walking on to your departing aircraft, you complete your belief in the scenario that deadline hustling is a peculiarly Japanese tactic.

It might look that way but it almost certainly is not (though no one can blame the Japanese if they accept the concessions offered to them by a time-pressurized Western negotiator). Delays during a negotiation are a consequence of a necessary part of their management system. The amended proposals they present to you on their return to the negotiations will have arisen out of their consultations and represent the consensus of their management team. The fact that you are now in a hurry to return from whence you came is not their fault; their earlier interest in your departure deadline is purely one of ascertaining what time they have available for doing business with you.

The counter to deadline pressure – from whatever source you experience it – is, of course, not to have deadlines in the first place. If you go to Japan to do business in a hurry it is your sense of time that is wrong, not theirs. If you went to Japan with an intention of spending a month or more, thus giving them time to consult their people, you would not be under the self-inflicted pressure of your own deadlines. There is nothing to stop you taking longer to conduct your business with the Japanese (if there is, then perhaps you should try selling to the US of A rather than to Japan). You can just as easily visit them and leave your proposals on the table while they think about them and arrange to get their own management's agreement. You can always use the time available to visit other companies or other parts of the same company, or you can return in a month or two when they are ready to reply with their considered response.

If you insist on everything being settled in a week or ten days you are going to be as disappointed as you are suspicious. Hence, the time pressure that many Western negotiators feel they are the victims of is just as often the result of their own attempt to pressurize the Japanese into an earlier settlement than they are ready for. Think of your behaviour from their point of view: why is this person in such a hurry? Is there something in his proposals that we have not noticed; perhaps we should re-examine them?

International negotiators have to accept that the pace of a negotiation will always be determined by the pace of the dominant party. If this is clearly understood by the negotiator visiting Japan it will produce a lot of respect from the Japanese, and, in Japan, business goes to those whom the other party respects the most.

Like the Soviets, the Japanese are avaricious when it comes to acquiring technical details of your products, though the motivation in the Japanese's case is somewhat more honourable. The Soviet negotiator seeks to protect himself from accepting something that is not quite kosher and at the same time engages in some *en passant* technological 'espionsage'. The Japanese are more likely to be establishing through their technical queries the technical soundness of the product and your own suitability as a person with whom to entrust their business future.

If they are going to acquire a licence to manufacture your product, they must, of course, know everything there is to know about your product. Likewise, if they are going to act as agents in Japan to sell your product, at the very least their own sales agents and service people will need to know everything they can about your product.

The meetings that take place between your team and theirs in Japan will involve considerable portions of time spent interrogating (there is no other word for it) you and your team, and not just on the technical qualities of what you produce. They will expect you to know the finest details of the financial arrangements of your business, including market share, growth rates and the intricacies of your company's place in the wider context of the industry you are in and, where applicable, in your company's structure if you are a subsidiary of a larger organization.

Western business negotiators tend to be more concerned with profitability than with growth rates. The difference is interesting, though its basis is not entirely a cultural one. It reflects the entrepreneurial psychology more common in expanding Japan than in the more recession-obsessed West. Several Western entrepreneurs are more 'Japanese' in their attitudes to growth than their contemporaries and this suggests that the difference in outlook is not entirely culture-based.

The Japanese business leader will study the relative market shares of his own and rival companies in all of the product lines they handle. He will be interested in growth rates of sales and the steady drive to domination in each sector of the market. His judgments about how well a company is managed will be influenced greatly by what he sees in these figures.

Whether a plant is profitable or, more correctly (because some level of profit is required if a business is to be sustained), how profitable the business is, will be of less interest to him, and, indeed, could actually cause him to worry if the profit levels are (by Japanese standards) exceptionally high, for this indicates they are concentrating on short-term profits rather than market penetration.

The Japanese will always opt for increasing their outlays on sales (both by direct marketing and by aggressive prices) rather than for accummulating high profit levels. They live their business lives on the edge of constant growth rather than in safe consolidation of previously successful products. The entrepreneurial Western businessman behaves in much the same fashion, with the difference that he is more likely to be an exception in his own country rather than, as in Japan, the rule.

A few very large companies dominate the domestic Japanese market. They also dominate the import business. They rely heavily on bank-financed loans for their operations and their expansion. They do not worry too much about the ratio of debt interest to profits, as long as they are expanding, and to expand they must invest in extending their capacity to produce more.

The contrast with a Western (especially UK business) is stark. A British firm will see investment as a means of reducing labour while maintaining output. This leads to lower unit costs and therefore, at least in theory, to increased or maintained unit profits from doing much as they did the previous year.

A Japanese company will see investment in equipment as a means of expanding output with the same workforce, and regard the job of selling the additional output as a challenge to its philosophy of growth. Nowhere is the consequence of this different approach seen more clearly than in the attitude of the respective labour forces to the role of investment: in the UK, new technology is equated with job losses (and therefore resisted); in Japan new technology is equated with preserving employment (and therefore accepted).

These differences in outlook explain some of the differences in the preparation negotiators in each country will undertake prior to meeting to discuss potential business opportunities. The Western firm will study (assuming it studies anything at all!) the Japanese firm's financial soundness and its profitability. The Japanese firm will study the Western firm's relative position in its markets, its suppliers, its customers, and its organizational connections (if relevant) with associate companies in the holding group.

In early meetings the Japanese will expect the Western negotiators to know in minute detail everything about their company's financial structure and the financial structure of any company (including rivals, suppliers and customers) with which they compete.

When it comes to price negotiations the Japanese will tend towards aggressive price policies that will maximize sales, not maximize profits. To get into a market they will expect to take losses and will not bother too much about so doing. This puts a lot of pressure on Western companies that follow a different pricing policy, assuming that they want to do business with or in Japan.

Another area where there might be a difference in approach, and because of this a danger to good relations and harmony, is in the question of contracts between the parties. The Japanese are at the other end of the spectrum in the matter of contracts to the Soviets, who normally require the most detailed specification of mutual obligations, including penalty clauses, incorporated into the contract before agreement is reached. With the Japanese the exact opposite tends to be the case.

Business relations with the Japanese are not separated from the mutual respect each party has for the other. In fact, they are an integral part of the same experience. A tightly drawn-up contract in the usual legal language common to Western business practice ('party of the first part' and 'party of the second part' etc.) is anathema to the Japanese approach.

First, English legal language is mind-boggling even to the English and, one suspects, few English lawyers fully understand it themselves (they certainly charge enough for giving conflicting interpretations of the same document!). This presents an enormous problem when translated into Japanese (it's bad enough trying to translate an English contract into plain English).

Second, the implication of a heavily documented legal contract written in formal legal language is that the parties need to cover themselves for every eventuality. Now some eventualities are of a sensitive nature (what happens if they run off with the loot?) and, when presented in a stark way to a Japanese negotiator at the start of what is intended to be a mutually beneficial relationship, you run the risk of causing great offence. If you need to cover yourself against the prospect of them being dishonest, or of them failing to meet their obligations in some way, they are likely to think that you do not trust or respect them.

In short they prefer not to do business with people who do not treat them with respect. What might need to be taken for granted in Europe – the need to avoid 'one truck contracts' (that is, a contract that leaves both parties at the mercy of 'Murphy's Law') can, if handled carelessly, be deeply offensive in Japan.

Now this is not an unsurmountable problem. My advice is to keep your legal people at arm's length and to require of them that they explain in straightforward English what their legal mumbo jumbo means in language that can be translated into Japanese with the least chance of causing misunderstanding. Better still, work from a Japanese contract and add in only what is absolutely necessary.

Japanese businesses do not engage in deliberate malpractice, nor will they cheat those with whom they share their business. You can relax a little more than you normally would.

Nothing I have said here should be interpreted as suggesting that the Japanese do not participate in negotiating a contract. They will do so, and they will insist on being very specific in terms of quality, performance, quantity, delivery and specifications. They will also hold to the terms of the contract, but what they find difficult to accept is a multi-clause contract drawn up in legalistic language that suggests from the start that their intentions are suspect or that the worst must be prepared for or insured against.

The Japanese hold very strongly to the role of personal relationships in their business dealings. They like to get to know the people with whom they intend to do business and they like to deal with the same people over and over again. Here they are not unlike the Chinese, who reserve a special place in their negotiations for 'old friends' (that is, foreigners they have dealt with before or who are introduced to them by somebody they revere or trust – usually another 'old friend'). Similarly with negotiators in South America. They too like to 'relate' to the people who want to do business with them. If this proves impossible – the 'chemistry' is wrong, for example – it is unlikely that business will be contracted.

The domination of interpersonal relations in the outlook and approach of Japanese negotiators finds its populist expression in the almost total inability of the Japanese to utter the word 'no', even when they wish to do so, and their substitution of a complicated, though unintentional, prevarication when put into a situation where to a Westerner 'no' is the appropriate answer to a question.

Almost being unable to say 'no', they can be misunderstood when they say 'yes' ('Hai!'). If you have asked a question that requires them to say 'no', it is your fault for asking the question in that way if you end up disappointed by their inability to deliver on the 'yes'. (A similar problem is found among the Arabs – saying 'no' implies that they do not want to help, so they say 'yes' even if they have no means of fulfilling that sort of commitment.)

This can be very off-putting when you hear a stream of 'Hai! Hai!' sounds and think he is saying 'yes' to your prosposals. He might just be letting you know that he is listening to what you have to say. This leads to the indirect approach in conversation. To tell you that your proposition is unacceptable by saying 'no' would give offence so he will say words to the effect that your proposal 'could be better if it took in this or that'. How many 'this's' or 'thats' will tell you just how unacceptable your proposition is!

Listening for signals from a Japanese negotiator is even more essential than when dealing with your own colleagues. They will try to nudge you towards what they want rather than go at you with a direct proposition, particularly if it contradicts something for which you have expressed a preference or where it could indicate that they have not been paying attention (hence, avoid asking them if they have understood your proposition as they will say 'Hai', even if you were totally incomprehensible!).

In the land of the rising yen (and there's nothing to suggest that it won't continue to rise for many a year yet) it is best if you are exceptionally polite, completely relaxed about time, and know that you must never take 'yes' for an answer!

Answers to self-assessment test 11

1   (a) Always thank your Japanese hosts for anything they do for you, even well beyond the point at which your thanks would be a cause for comment in the UK. But do not open any wrapped gift in these circumstances, unless expressly urged to do so by the person who gives it to you. There is a danger that he or she might lose face by offering to you a gift that is too expensive (compared to the one you intended to give) or too cheap.

(b) Yes. In putting it away do so carefully and tell the person who gave it to you how unworthy you are to receive such generous treatment.

(c) Even better. A small gift, neatly wrapped in traditional Japanese design paper and tied with a nice bow is always welcome. The value is less important than the thought. If you were unprepared for the gift exchange ritual, do not panic. A small token at the time, followed by a proper gift at the next opportunity will do fine. In this respect, if your Japanese partner requires something which you promise to send on to him, *do so*, even at the cost of extraordinary effort – it will pay you back many times over.

2   *(a)* More than likely. The Japanese are exceptionally polite and go out of their way to help you. It is best to treat this event with an open mind (and, just to make sure that it is a courtesy only, always travel to Japan with open return tickets without a deadline on them!).

(b) They could have this motivation, though much of the problem with Western negotiators is their tendency to try to rush things in Japan and the deadlines that they feel strangled by are often of their own making.

3   *(a)* Unlikely to be a decisive consideration.

(b) Yes. Your market share tells them about your market strengths (or weaknesses). If you are seeking to supply their markets they will expect large volumes from you; if you are seeking to represent them in your territory they will want you to do so if you can move large volumes for them.

(c) A high growth rate can compensate for a currently low market share. It will also tell them how entrepreneurial you and your company are and what they can expect from you.

(d) Japanese industrial relations can be stormy. Their interest in your industrial relations would reflect their estimate of your capacity to produce output or provide a service. In Japanese eyes constant strikes over 'trivial' issues suggest that there is something wrong with your management style.

(e) In Japan, quality is considered to be the supreme characteristic of a well-managed company. Total Quality Management is a Japanese way of life.

Self-assessment test 12

1 You are a package-tour operator negotiating with a Spanish hotel chain on the terms for next season's bookings. The price they are asking per person per week in their hotels is £30 higher than your current offer. They offer to 'split the difference' 50–50. Do you:
   (a) Suggest, say, 60–40 in your favour?
   (b) Say you can't afford to split the difference?
   (c) Agree to their offer?
   (d) Agree, if it is a 75–25 split in your favour?

2 Do you see negotiating as being about:
   (a) A fair and equal transaction?
   (b) Finding the most acceptable compromise?
   (c) Making a joint decision with the other person that meets as many of his and as many of *your* interests as possible?

3 You are engaged in extremely difficult negotiations with a Lebanese-based construction consortium. After much haggling over finance for a road project, they make a small unilateral concession on their demand for irrevocable lines of credit. Do you?
   (a) Note the concession but otherwise ignore it?
   (b) Reciprocate with a concession of your own?

138

Chapter Twelve

The negotiator's most useful two-letter word
or how to make your offers count

When asked what they think is their most useful two-letter word, many negotiators suggest:

NO

This answer is not surprising if the question is posed *after* they have heard the story of Bjorn Mackenzie's infallible system for coping with wolves (see Chapter Six) or about the Law of the Yukon (see Chapter Ten), as these tend to leave a somewhat negative impression of good negotiating behaviour.

However, while 'No' isn't the right answer, it isn't entirely wrong.

The question asks for the negotiator's *most useful* two-letter word and 'No' merely qualifies for the status of *being useful*.

The most useful two-letter word in the negotiator's vocabulary is:

IF

Why is *if* such an important word to a negotiator?

The answer lies at the heart of the negotiating process itself and fully explains my unrelenting hostility to unilateral conceding under any pretext whatsoever, or for any purpose.

The *Oxford English Dictionary* – that final arbiter of literacy – defines conceding as, *inter alia:* 'to *grant, yield* or *surrender*'. For this reason I begin this chapter with the quiet but firm statement that readers are not reading this book to improve their skills in commercial *conceding*.

Your only interest is to improve your performance as a *negotiator*, which has nothing to do with surrendering. If you have to surrender there is no need for the other person to negotiate: you will be told what to do by the person with the whip. On the other hand, if you choose to surrender by unilaterally conceding *when you don't have to*, you are less than suitable to be in charge of protecting anybody's interests (including your own).

How do you know when you're in a negotiation and when not?

It isn't always obvious to begin with!

It is possible for a negotiation to be almost over before you realize you're in one (that's when you'll regret those early free-gift goodwill concessions), just as it is possible to abandon hope of negotiating about something too soon (that's when you start cringing instead of cold-eyeing them).

You find out sooner or later, of course, whether you can, or should, negotiate your way to a better deal. One thing is certain, though – at the outset always test the situation before you assume anything about the relative power of the other party.

We will discuss this in more detail later, but for the moment do not assume that the sound of a whiplash is proof positive that they have the power and you don't. They may just be good at sound effects.

If you identify the elements that make negotiating different from the alternative means of making a decision, you can use that knowledge to see if the conditions for negotiation are present. Essentially, negotiation can be defined as:

A transaction in which both parties have a *veto* on the final outcome.

If you don't have a veto (which includes the right to walk away and do business with somebody else) then you will have to accept whatever is on offer.

Each party in a negotiation has to consent to the outcome if it is to be implemented and each has an interest (not necessarily an equal one) in the other agreeing to it.

Thus by negotiating we make a *joint decision*.

If you don't like the other person's proposal as to what that joint decision should be, and are unable to agree on an alternative, you have the option of *not* agreeing to what he proposes, because:

Negotiation involves the *voluntary* consent of both sides to the decision.

If you are compelled to agree *against* your will, it's *not* a negotiation (the sharp sting on your back *is* the whiplash!).

What does this view of negotiating imply?

Conceding ain't negotiating

A package-tour operator in London (Costalot Travel Ltd) had occasion to meet the sales manager of a Spanish hotel chain to discuss next year's terms for block booking the resorts. The meeting opened with a long list of changes that Costalot wanted following widespread complaints from their clients about the hotels and also several lapses in service contrary to what the hotels had agreed to provide.

The Spanish manger (Señor Paco Eminos) started through the list item by item and agreed to most of them as they stood or in a slightly modified form. Eventually, he stopped his progress through the list with the exclamation: 'Señor, I thought this was a negotiation but I am making all the concessions.'

'True', replied Mr Costalot, 'and when you stop conceding I will start negotiating!'

First, that the parties can have different preferences for which of the available outcomes is suitable as a joint decision. Naturally, you prefer the joint decision to be more rather than less favourable to yourself. If you don't, you've no business negotiating because, if you negotiate, you'll soon have no business:

If you are selling, you prefer high prices, if buying, low prices.

You prefer longer time to pay back than you do to get paid.

You prefer large simple orders to penny packets with precise specifications.

You prefer less up-front money if you are buying than you do if you are selling.

You prefer sale or return if you are buying and no-returns if you are selling.

If he wants delivery everywhere in awkward loads, you'd prefer he paid extra for it.

And so on.

It's not simply a matter that you gain what he loses. If you've negotiated successfully, the total package gives you more on the swings than you 'lose' on the roundabouts. That is what is meant by it being more favourable to you.

A trade-off in one area for something in another may give a

differential advantage to you but this is no way implies that he directly loses what you gain. His swings may be your roundabouts; his willingness to give on price may be tempered by your willingness to accelerate on payment.

On the other hand, if you lose more on the swings than you get back on the roundabouts, your negotiating moves ought to have ensured that the final package isn't even less favourable to you than it might have been if you had been less skilful.

Secondly, this view of negotiating implies that your most favourable outcomes (the ones you would choose in the absence of having to consider the other person's interests) are not often available to you because he can veto any and all of your propositions. Nor are his most favourable outcomes available to him by virtue of your veto.

Hence, you both have to choose a joint decision, from among the many that may be attainable, that meets sufficient of the interests and expectations of both sides not to provoke a veto by one of you. If you cannot reach a settlement by joint decision, you must deadlock and, excluding the possibility of arbitration, take your business elsewhere.

Part of the work of negotiating consists of the careful search for outcomes that are veto-free or can be made veto-free by one means or another (of which more later). Some of the proposals for a joint decision or settlement are more favourable to both of you, some less, and some others may not have been considered during the negotiation.

Which outcome is finally chosen depends on a lot of factors, not the least of which is your view of the prospects (including the cost in time and energy) of negotiating a better outcome than the one presently on offer and the consequences to both of you of deadlock.

If you view negotiating as surrendering – in whatever form your surrender takes, including a proclivity for unilaterally conceding in the futile search for goodwill – then it is predictable that the deal will be less favourable to you and more favourable to them. This is not to say that poor negotiators can't get deals. They can, but they tend to get lousier deals than good negotiators.

How then is a negotiation to progress if there is a prohibition on surrender? Surely, if we merely stick where we start we will never get a deal? This is a case where we must not assume that the alternative to 'no surrender' is a fight to the death.

It is not the necessity for movement that is denied here. What is most emphatically denied is that movement must take the form of unilateral concessions.

Negotiating is about *trading*.

It is when you view negotiation as a process of *exchange* that you see the importance of *never* conceding anything without getting something back for it. In effect, as a negotiator, if you have to walk towards the other person you *must* ensure that he walks towards you as well.

Better still, your aim is to get him to walk *faster* towards you than you do towards him!

Is negotiation a matter of give-and-take?

Not quite.

The idea of give-and-take is acceptable as a broad-brush concept of negotiating only as long as you do not make the mistake *of giving more than you take!* There are no 'rules' that say you have to make *equal* moves towards each other – the idea ought to be anathema to negotiators – nor is there anything that says you have to move at all just because he moves.

This leads us to the most important single principle of negotiating:

NOTHING, ABSOLUTELY NOTHING, IS GIVEN AWAY FREE

I know of *no* exceptions to this principle.

This principle is the foundation of effective negotiating behaviour. The fact that it may not be guiding the other person's moves is not relevant to your behaviour – if he wants to give you things for nothing that is his private business and you should accept them without a quibble. You are under no obligation to look after his best interests!

Thus, if you are negotiating with a unilateral conceder (should you be so lucky!) your best response to his conceding is to sit tight where you are. And when the other person requires you to move you must insist that he moves too, preferably by much more than you do.

This might be considered to be 'unfair' (why it should be considered so is one of life's minor mysteries), for you might think that in negotiating we 'ought' to aim to make equal moves and sacrifices from our opening positions.

To my mind that is a mistaken view of negotiating.

Just because you reduce your demands it does not follow that I

Impulsive conceders

The worst thing about unilateral concessions is that they weaken a negotiating position much more than the amount of the concession.

Consider the following cases:

'How much for the video player?'
'£300.'
'As much as that?'
'I could let it go for £275.'

'I see you have requested a starting salary of £25,000.'
'Yes.'
'This operation cannot afford to pay that amount – in fact it would make you the highest-paid accountant in credit control. Would you consider less?'
'I'm willing to be flexible but I must get at least £19,000.'

These concessions are got for practically no effort at all. The drop of £25 in the video negotiation after a single question tells the buyer that the owner has plucked his price out of thin air. He should (and did) push on price even harder (it eventually went for £250). The out-of-work accountant dropped her price by £6,000 almost without a whimper, and also demonstrated her total unsuitability to be employed (she wasn't) in a credit-control operation – she will never get money out of debtors if she is a compulsive conceder.

In both cases, the use of *if* conditions on the concessions would have protected the negotiating position:

'You can have it for £295 without the spare tapes.'
'If you pay me a commision on the debts I collect and you pay my petrol account I will accept a salary of £19,000.'

---

must improve my offer by the same amount. Perhaps you can afford a 20 per cent 'cut' in your price – which shows just how much you padded your opening position. I can't afford to reciprocate, and that's that! You see, I don't subscribe to the 'equity theory' of negotiating and neither should you.

'Fair exchange is no robbery', but that says nothing about a fair exchange being equal in some way. In fact, no trading exchange is an *equal* transaction.

When you buy a Mars bar from a kiosk for 20 pence there is no question of an equal transaction between you and the kiosk company. The Mars bar is not *equal* to the 20 pence. If you believe that it is, try eating the 20 pence!

When you hand over your money to the person in the kiosk for the Mars bar it is a *fair* transaction. If you believe that it isn't, take your business elsewhere. Nobody in a free society compels you to eat Mars bars.

At the moment of purchase you need the Mars bar more than you need your 20 pence – you have money but no Mars bars. For the kiosk company, they need your 20 pence more than they need the Mars bar – they have a warehouse full of Mars bars.

For the soundest of motives, i.e. profit, they prefer to fill their till with cash and empty their warehouses of Mars bars. Hence, the trade can be fair without necessarily being equal.

If the best way to conduct a negotiation is to make absolutely no concessions without getting something in return (though we can accept concessions if they are offered for nothing), how then do we avoid deadlock?

This is where the power of the negotiator's most useful two-letter word – *if* – comes into its own.

The most important guiding principle of negotiating – even if you forget everything else – is to preface *all* your propositions and concessions with the word IF:

>   *IF* you drop 20 per cent on price, I can sign an order

>   *IF* you accept liability, we will release your shipment

>   *IF* you waive on-site inspection, we can meet your schedules

>   *IF* you pay the courier, I will despatch the plans tonight

>   *IF* you place an order immediately, I can meet your price

By using the word *if* you protect the integrity of your proposals. They cannot regard a movement as a unilateral concession on your part precisely because you have tied it to your conditions. As they say: you can't have one without the other.

Get into the habit of using *IF every time* you make a proposal and the other person will get the message:

The IF part tells him the *price* of the offer.

The offer part tells him what he is *getting* for the price.

Do this in negotiating and you will also help to educate your opponents (you are doing the comunity a social service once again, for if you didn't help educate them who would?). Even the dumbest opponent will get the message, eventually.

In one of the university campuses in the United States, a psychology professor taught a pigeon to pick out the ace of spades in a deck of cards. Now your opponents are always going to have bigger brains than those belonging to pigeons – even Texan pigeons – and you can stake your last shilling on the prediction that your opponents will eventually get the message.

If they want something from you it is going to cost them.

Perhaps in future they will ask for less?

Answers to self-assessment test 12

1   *(a)* Better than *(c)* but suggests you are in a hurry to compromise.

(b) By far a negotiator's best immediate move. Why should you split 50–50 whether you can afford it or not? By making such an offer they expose that their price is padded by at least £15, and probably more. A concession of £15 on 10,000 holiday weeks costs you £150,000 – does their compromise look so 'fair' when grossed up?

(c) Never. If you show negotiators that you practise 'split the difference' compromises they will give you bigger and bigger differences to split!

(d) Better than *(c)* and tougher than *(a)*. A possible move for later (much later, when you have tested the padding in their £15).

2   *(a)* Negotiating is always fair but seldom equal.

(b) Depends on who it is 'most acceptable' to. If there are echoes of splitting the difference and equal gains, then absolutely not.

(c) Yes. It's your interests you are negotiating for – the other person is the best judge of his interests. Confusing these roles can lead to poorer deals. The fact that it is a joint decision

assures that it is at least satisfactory to you both; hopefully, it is more satisfactory to you than the available alternatives.

3 *(a)* Yes. If they make free-gift unilateral concessions you are not obliged to respond.

(b) No.

Self-assessment test 13

1   You are looking for a job and see an advertisement for out-of-work truck drivers to attend for interview at 2 p.m. on Friday at the personnel office of a local haulage company. When you get there at 1.55 p.m. you join a long queue outside the office. Do you think your chances of getting the job are:
    (a) Diminished?
    (b) Not affected?
    (c) Better?

2   You are in Accra (Ghana) and are loking for a 'Mammy Truck' that is going to Kamasi. You find one and the mammy tells you it will leave as soon as it is full. You note that there is only one seat left vacant on the truck and decide to take it. When will the truck leave:
    (a) Immediately?
    (b) Later?

3   You act as a go-between in the sale of a light aircraft. The buyer pays by cheque and the owner is willing to accept this and release the aircraft once it is cleared by the bank. When settling up your fee, do you:
    (a) Press for payment in cash?
    (b) Send in an invoice?
    (c) Accept a cheque?

4   An Arab with six camels approaches an oasis in search of water. Standing by the spring there is another Arab and a sign (in Arabic): 'Water: all you can drink – price one camel'. Who has the power:
    (a) The Arab with the camels?
    (b) The Arab with the water?
    (c) Impossible to say?

Chapter Thirteen

Who has the power?
or how to get leverage

A thousand or more years ago, Viking raiders regularly slipped out of the beautiful fjords of Norway in magnificent sailing ships bound for the coastal settlements of Europe. Today, from those same fjords, their descendants use nothing more lethal than the fax machine to run highly efficient worldwide shipping operations.

Lars is the Vice President of a shipping company operating out of Bergen. He does scores of deals a year, buying or selling ships, negotiating contracts for newbuilds in Europe and the Far East, handling repair contracts (one of the toughest sides of a tough business), bunkers, freight and charter rates, crew wages, and agency fees. He's a busy man and after 40 years in the business he still has a romantic attitude to 'his' ships.

In the matter of negotiation, Lars is anything but romantic. In fact he is downright single-minded when it comes to handling his conmpany's business.

Some of the managers – they range from clerks who learned the hard way, through graduates who learned the smart way, to 'retired' Masters who learned it anyway – occasionally discuss their negotiating problems between fax messages. If Lars happens to overhear such a conversation, while passing through the open-plan offices, he is likely to proffer the summary of his negotiating wisdom:

> In any deal, ask: Who is buying and who is selling?

To Lars, the answer tells him who has *the power* and, as far as he is concerned, having power is an asset, not having it a handicap, which is a pretty sound approach to this aspect of negotiating.

It follows that Lars believes that his managers should seek power *before* a deal in order to exercise it *during* the negotiation.

What does power consist of?

If we haven't got it, how do we get it and from where?

First you must rid yourself of any lingering illusions that power

149

doesn't matter. It does. The quaint view that power doesn't matter is often expressed in the belief that the act of negotiating somehow shelters the parties from the crudities of power.

This is altogether wrong. Negotiating merely expresses the power balance in a different form!

The understandable preference for Jaw-Jaw rather than War-War has nothing to do with the excision of power from the relationship between the two contestants; it merely expresses a preference for one form of the power balance rather than another.

Lars is absolutely right in one thing:

power is the very essence of the negotiating process

It is through our perceptions of power – ours *and* the other person's – that we conduct ourselves as negotiators. This leads us to the most important single characteristic of power in a negotiation: it is entirely *subejctive*.

In short: power is in the head.

And remember, in negotiating there are *two* heads – yours and the other person's – not one!

150

Nice one, Tokyo

In Australia they have lots of iron and coal. In Japan they have none and import the lot. Who then is in the strongest bargaining position?

Right, the Japanese?

How do they achieve this remarkable result? By making the Australian negotiators go to Japan to do the deals. Once there the Australians are negotiating at a Japanese pace while their minds remain operating at an Australian pace.

The Japanese are in no hurry – they live there!

The Aussies are in a hurry because they don't.

Australians like Australia. Hence, after a short while they like their affluent and sunny selves to be firmly planted back in Oz near the pool, the beach, the barbeque, the wife and the kids.

The Australian coal companies have not always exercised their strength as seen by the Japanese – they have most of the coal Japan needs and this ought to be reflected in the price.

Instead they have gone for their own needs, seeing Japan more as a means to their *own* ends than as a customer desperately anxious to get its hands on long-term coal supplies.

Hence, it is what happens in the heads of the parties that determines how power impacts on the outcome of their negotiation.

'How so?', you might ask, 'surely power has an objective dimension too'.

I am compelled to agree, of course, that a world surplus of tanker capacity is an objective circumstance of some relevance to the power relationship between a tanker owner and a chartering agency. That cannot be denied. But what can be, and is, asserted here is that:

The negotiator's subjective perception is *more important* than the objective circumstances in themselves.

It is what the negotiators *believe* is true that counts, not what a panel of independent assessors could tell them if they sat long enough and reviewed in minute detail all the so-called objective evidence. (And note that their review of that evidence is itself subjective, as is your interpretation of their assessment.)

Negotiators instinctively understand the importance of subjective belief – that's why they spend so much time trying to convince us that their perceptions are so much more credible than ours.

If a shipowner sees a fleet of unchartered tankers riding at anchor in the bay, it does not follow that he rolls over and plays dead when he gets a bid for a time charter. He will attempt to convince the charterer that the vessel he has for hire is somehow different from the others in the bay.

If they believe what they hear and persist with the negotiations, this will reduce their apparent negotiating advantage.

Alternatively, suppose your business requires additional computer programming staff. What will they cost you? 'That depends', you answer, 'on how many computer programmers are in the market looking for a job.'

Now in an economics class you would get a bonus point for such a brilliantly obvious conclusion – though, not surprisingly what you have alluded to is of little consequence in the real world.

How many job-seekers make it a hirer's market? We could as productively ask: how long is a piece of string? Moreover, we don't negotiate with markets. We negotiate with people.

You cannot *safely* assume that the people you negotiate with are as well informed about the 'market' as you are, or think you are. Nor can you assume that what you know about the market is correct. Even majority opinion of the state of a market is a notoriously poor guide to its actual state – as you will find if you ask anybody who has been caught short when they played the market.

In fact the way to wealth in the Stock Market is to know better than the market about its prospects: when the market believes shares will go up and you think you know better, you sell out and take your profit; when the market believes shares will fall and you think you know better, you buy-in and wait for your profit.

If you wait for the market to form an opinion you could be buying when you should be selling and selling when you should be buying. Setting aside how you know at any moment that the market has got it wrong and you've got it right, it is certainly true that if you get it right more often, and for bigger stakes, than you get it wrong you might retire owning a fortune, and if you don't, you won't.

All economists assume that something called *the* market makes decisions about prices and quantities and that they (and their students) have a bird's-eye view of the entire market mechanism.

Fly me

An oil company that operates several rigs in the Mexican Gulf hires $70 million worth of helicopter services a year. Most of the business is placed with one of the largest helicopter operators in the world. It is highly efficient, competitive in price and has an excellent safety record.

However, the oil company does not place all its business with this operator, and about 20 per cent of its goes to three other much smaller companies.

They are run by 'two-men' outfits (mainly ex-pilots for the major company who branched out on their own) and are slightly more expensive than the corporate giant.

Why does the hirer do this if it costs more? Because the oil company does not want to drive out of business the smaller suppliers in case this gives its largest supplier ideas about the power balance.

But in a negotiation you don't have a bird's-eye view because you are not a bird – you're part of the mechanism!

Suppose, as an out-of-work computer programmer, you walk into the personnel department of a company that has advertised a vacancy in its computer department and the waiting room is crammed full with other applicants.

Are you stronger or weaker as a result?

Your natural reaction would be to feel less confident of your chances – clearly there is a lot of competition for the job.

Or is there?

The answer is, and ought to be: how do you know?

How do you know what they are queuing for?

How do you know that you're not the only computer programmer they have seen all week?

You may be weaker with competition around but on the other hand it may not be competition at all. They could be queuing to be interviewed for a receptionist's job in the word-processing department.

But if you *believe* they are computer programmers you will feel weaker and are likely to end up a *cheap* programmer. It could be that the employer has hired a group of actors from Rentacrowd to intimidate you into accepting £5,000 less per year.

Times change

In 1958, a French car firm agreed to make an Arab businessman its agent in the Gulf. The Arab had approached them seeking an agency and had persuaded them that he had the acumen and the contacts to make the agency profitable.

The French negotiated an agency deal that required the Arab to pay in advance, every six months, for the cars they were about to ship out to him. They regarded this as a prudent necessity to protect themselves in case the Arab failed to meet his commitments.

The requirement to pay in advance almost busted the Arab, as it meant he had to borrow heavily from a local (foreign) bank who took a jaundiced view of lending large sums, on very little security, to local Arab nationals.

Over the years, however, the agency prospered and the Arab sold a lot of cars at a profit and had a thriving spare parts busness in support of the main operation.

After the 1973 oil price hike, when billions of dollars worth of income began to flow into the hands of the Gulf Arabs, the demand for cars rocketed and he stood ready to make a great deal from his agency and his considerable experience in this market.

First, he took on the agency for a German car firm as well as the French one, and then he used the terms the Germans were delighted to offer him, in view of projected sales figures, as a basis for re-negotiating the original deal he had with the French, who had no wish to be cut out of the lucrative Gulf market. He was able to re-negotiate the agency deal to get cars on credit. From this he expanded his agency rapidly.

The shift in market demand meant that the agency agreement, held by the Arab in the lean years, was now worth a lot more to the French car firm than it was to the now very rich Arab businessman.

He also set up his own local bank to manage the financial side of the agency, and cut out the foreign bank that had given him a hard time on credit limits before 1973.

The circle of negotiating relationships

Negotiators for Third World governments and Western mineral corporations over the past 30 years have seen a significant shift in their relationships.

The balance of power has changed since the first 'concessions', were granted during the 'colonial' period.

In the first stages of the relationship, the company was given a 'concession', i.e. an absolute right to remove from the territory primary resources for a fee or a royalty per ton removed.

Several 'revisions' have been negotiated, basically concerned with the demands from the host authority for a greater share of the income from its mineral resources. The major inhibitions on the rapid spread of these revision agreements was either technological or monetary.

The more the mineral operation concentrated on simple ('steam shovel') operations or the greater the facility for raising necessary funds from international agencies, the greater the bargaining position of the host government.

The other major barrier to host country development has been the lack of access to Western markets, without which there is not enough demand to justify a host monopoly.

But the picture is patchy across the extraction sectors in Third World countries. Some countries manage to tie their contracts to the establishment of local 'down-stream' capacity, others to local participation in the equity of the mineral companies.

In addition the government has renegotiated both royalty and taxation liabilities with the mineral companies.

The final stage has been the movement over to 'management' agreements where the corporation manages the exploration, commissioning and extractive contract for a fee from the indigenous (usually nationalized) company and arranges the marketing of the output (again for a fee).

This reverses the original relationship but the parties have found a way of living with these changes.

In general then, we cannot be sure that what we think in the situation actually pertains in practice.

If our opponents persist in seeing the situation differently, we have the classic negotiator's dilemma: we can't be sure that our opponent's apparent position reflects the true power relationship between us and is not just a tactical stance on his part to convince us to change our perceptions.

Indeed, we can conceive of all negotiating moves and tactics as attempts in one degree or another to structure how the other party views the power relationship. The more skilfully we structure our opponent's subjective views of the power relationship in our favour, the less relevant to the outcome of the negotiation the objective power balance of the market.

In other words, if you believe *they* have power then nothing more need be said: they have it (and they have you too!). For this reason, I tend to (respectfully) disagree with Lars on the importance of who is the buyer and who is the seller, if by the answer he implies an *automatic* conclusion that buying puts us in a more powerful position than selling.

It does not matter whether we are buying or selling *if* we get the power dimension to work for us rather than against us.

Consider the Arab oil states – the sellers, and the world's consumers of oil – the buyers. Up to 1973 the oil companies believed they had the power and the Arab negotiators agreed. Then they changed their minds and changed the world.

It all boils down to how you and the other person see your relationship. If you can influence his perception you get a better deal.

What factors influence our perception of the power relationship?

The answer could open up that most complex of subjects – what makes people think the way they do? – and would fill volumes rather than close off this chapter. For the moment let us confine our discussion to the perceptions we form *before* we meet the other person, for these are often the most influential on our approach, our manner, our demeanour, our confidence and, eventually, our deal.

Almost all sellers suffer from a twin obsession: the *power* of the buyers and the *extent* of the competition. Given the slightest encouragement a seller will catalogue the atrocities committed by buyers or the competition on his good self.

Any five people from sales mixing socially regale each other with ever-more incredible tales of perfidy among buyers and 'the dirty tricks of the contemptible competition'. In short, they psyche themselves into believing in their own weakness by assuming the buyers' strengths.

The market mammies of Makola

When Ernst Weinbanger went to Ghana as the marketing manager for a large Dutch oil company, his first assignment was to visit dealers, many of whom lived up country. He wanted to see as much as he could of Ghana and meet as many people as possible and he was advised by colleagues that there was no better way to learn about the 'real' Ghana than to travel by 'bus', which in Ghana means the back of an open truck.

Ernst's colleagues did not warn him about the business standards of the 'bus companies', and he made the mistake of assuming that Ghana ran its public transport with the same attention to timetables as the honest burghers of his native Amsterdam.

He innocently believed a mammy in the Makola market who said her truck's departure for Kamasi was imminent and that as soon as the truck was full it would depart. Ernst could see that every seat in the truck was full except for one and concluded that he would soon be on his way to Kumasi. So, as it was his first visit to Ghana, he paid his fare and got on board – only to see the person next to him get off!

That is how the market mammies use Rentacrowd to fill their trucks with cash customers.

Eventually, it dawned on Ernst from the number of times the mammy repeated her sales routine that he was not the *last* but the *first* fare-paying passenger to get on to her truck that morning.

If it happens to you, it's no good trying to get your money back – when a market mammy says 'no' in matters relating to business, you had better believe that she means it!

Ernst Weinbanger learned a lot on his first tour. So much in fact that for years he sent newly arrived managers, without a briefing, to see Ghana by 'bus'.

'Nobody,' he is wont to say over drinks in the bar of the Ambassador Hotel in Accra, 'warned me, so I didn't warn them, but what they learn in a month about how they do business in West Africa is worth a year at Harvard.'

Yet buyers can see things differently. For instance, I know a buyer for a large mainframe computer company who buys millions of pounds' worth of components for his company's assembly plants each quarter and who firmly believes that sellers have the power.

How did he draw that conclusion?

There was a time when he knew his company's computers inside out (he used to make them) but the technology has moved so fast in the past ten years that he feels at a disadvantage because ten years out of computer engineering is two generations too long.

He buys thousands of different components in large and small lots for the entire range of his company's computers and he claims that the manufacturers' representatives have an advantage over him as they are specialists in their own components, while he, as a buyer, knows little about any specific item.

He must rely on the seller to guide him on technical matters regarding their products.

It all comes down to perception. If you are selling and believe that the buyer has the power, you could be filling your head with the buyer's ammunition.

How do you know whether a specific buyer has more power in a negotiation than you do? Do you believe what he is saying about the competition just because he says it, or worse, do you believe you are up against tough competition before you have even met him and found out what it is he wants?

Think less about the buyer for a moment and think more about the alleged competition. In the ordinary run of events in business, people deal with more than one company. Their experience of a particular company can vary from satisfactory to absolutely hopeless. It is just not true that every other company that sells similar products or services to you is set to get the order you seek from a buyer.

The buyer may have dealt with your competitor before and been given cause to weigh his products or service in the balance and find them wanting. In which case, you are stronger than you think. Competition is only strong if every firm that is knocking at the buyer's door is equally competent in providing what the buyer wants. Experience of business suggests that it is very unusual to find firms competing on exactly the same terms (it's so unusual that in most countries they get very suspicious if it happens!)

The buyer may prefer to deal with firms that are close to his own plants or are owned by fellow Bostonians. This reduces his power if you're local or from Boston, but enhances it if you're not.

The buyer may operate a company policy that excludes certain firms – perhaps they didn't deliver what they promised, or chased too hard for their money, or antagonized the staff in some way – and this too weakens the buyer's power as long as you are not one of them.

The buyer may be buying to a departmental specification that reflects the preferences or training of the people who will operate the machinery. This also weakens the buyer's power.

You can bet your last ten pence that if the programmers were trained by IBM they will tend to specify IBM plug-compatible products. If that is what you are selling you need not collapse your margins *just because* the buyer has a Wang catalogue on his desk.

(The first car that people buy tends to be the same make as the one they learned to drive on, which must give a lot of negotiating leverage to driving schools when they buy their fleets.)

Conversely, if you're selling non-IBM products you ought not to feel weak just because the users have specified IBM, providing you sell products as good or better than IBM.

Also, the buyer may be willing to look elsewhere for other reasons and override the preferences of his engineers.

The buyer's choices can be constrained by all kinds of things – he often works to a policy set by other people (not always considerate of the economics of their decisions) and he is often at the mercy of his company's specialists who seldom consider his problems with suppliers. He may be under instructions not to give all the business to a single firm in case he gets too dependent on it – that could be your chance to get in – or he could have instructions to always buy bulk – hence you're chasing a big order.

Therefore, don't forget that buyers do not automatically have the power, unless you give it to them.

And what of sellers? Do they have the power?

Not necessarily: it depends on what they choose to believe.

If the buyer convinces them that the competition really is strong, this must weaken the seller's power. For this reason, a caution is appropriate: learn to recognize the buyer's theatre 'props' (for that is what they are) as he performs his version of the long-running off-Broadway play, *Oh, What a Lot of Competition There is Today*.

Among the props that alter your power perception are:

1 Catalogues from your competitors, preferably with page markers sticking out of them.
2 A pile of papers on his desk showing their letterheads (but not

their contents) – handy to tap when he utters the well-worn (but still devastatingly effective) seven-word-killer line:

'You'll have to do better than that.'

Buyers use these props because they work – The League of Gullible Sellers has always had a mass membership!

Sellers can fight back against these tactics.

If your price is challenged you ought at least to work hard at defending it. One thing you can do is ask, 'Why must I do better than I have proposed?'. The reply can give you information about whether it is a bluff or not – the vaguer, or the more heated, the response the more likely it is a bluff.

If you have such insufficient confidence in your price that your first thought when it is challenged is to think how you can drop it without starting a rout, then there is no reason why the buyer should have any confidence in your price either.

Buyers always challenge prices – it's in the nature of the beast! Many sellers always back off from a price challenge – hence it pays buyers to challenge their proposals with the 'killer' line.

Buyers are not entirely defenceless against sellers who are in, or feel that they are in, a strong position. Nor do they always need to stoop to deceit to alter the seller's perception of his power.

They can adopt tactics to convince the seller that they do not need his products – perhaps by showing there are other suppliers anxious to do business with them, or that they have large stocks, or that they might set up their own production facility to make it. If this is credible, the seller will lower his perception of his own power.

Buyers can hint about the longer-run benefits of the seller going easy on price just now – 'sell cheap, get famous' – and the longer-run consequences of exploiting negotiating power – 'screw us now and we'll screw you later'. This can curb the seller's use of his power. It is not always in the longer-term interest of a business for it to screw the other person to the floor with stiff demands.

Sellers know that high prices (and high profits) attract competition, and that the one great law of the market is that if you want to sell more, you have to reduce your price or raise your marketing costs, or both. This puts pressure on the seller's power.

You can strengthen your power by persuading him that there is a lot of competition for your business – certainly you will never strengthen your power if you tell him otherwise.

Don't confide that your warehouse is full and the alternative to his placing an order is for your plant to go on short time.

If he feels there is competitive pressure upon him even when none is being directly exerted, that is bound to reduce his power and raise yours.

Hence, as a buyer, you can let him see that you are aware of his competitors' products, know their special features and benefits, and show that you are in regular contact with them.

You should never explain *why* you are not doing business with the seller's competitors or *why* you want to switch from them – and above all avoid the temptation to knock those who have let you down as it merely strengthens the seller's power.

Conversely avoid telling him how much you *love* his products – it might be just enough to give him the courage to raise his price!

Even if your business relationship with a seller is secure, you should keep him unsure of it, by showing interest in switching your buying policy to rivals on any credible grounds such as:

Price ('they're cheaper').
Delivery ('they're offering CIF against your FOB').
Quantity ('they are offering bigger discounts').
Patriotism ('the boss wants to buy home produce only').
New features ('their machine bags the cement too').
Security of supply ('they guarantee all the cocoa we can take for
    three years').
Credit terms ('they offer 90 days' interest free'), etc.

This will reduce his power over you, or at least keep him from getting big ideas about his relationship with you.

Who then, has the power?

You do, if your opponent believes you have it. And if he believes that you have the power, you can extract a premium off him for your services.

On the other hand, he has the power if you believe he has it and you can be sure that your perception of the power balance will cost you something extra above what you would have paid if you had been less influenced by what you thought you knew about the other guy's position.

If you need the deal more than you can cope with the prospect of not getting it, you will be less powerful in the negotiation. The converse is true for him – if he needs to settle more than he can face a deadlock, you have power over him.

The main point to remember is that who has the power is not decided by the calculation of a formula of relative ability to do without the deal. It is your *perception* of the pressures on him to settle compared to the pressures you feel upon yourself that will influence your reading of the power balance.

If you get this wrong because you are misled by your assumptions, you will award him with a greater power than he might have in fact –that could cost you something on the final price that you needn't concede. And this is true whether you are buying or selling.

Answers to self-assessment test 13

1   *(a)* How do you know they're out-of work truck drivers?

    (b) You are not influenced by what you think you see.

    (c) Obviously 'competition' inspires you.

2   *(a)* You have a tendency to believe what a seller tells you and in some markets that is a Class A mistake. Whether the truck leaves immediately depends on whether you are the last passenger or somebody duped by Rentacrowd.

    (b) Again it depends on whether the other people on the truck are Rentacrowd or genuine passengers.

3   *(a)* Sound advice when involved in these dealings. Until the cheque is cleared the deal could fall through. Get paid while you have some influence on the seller.

    (b) A risky decision in the 'go-between' business. Sellers value your service less after you have clinched their deal for them – every hooker knows it is best to collect before rather than after!

    (c) Only if it is certified and he gives it to you in his bank for immediate payment!

4   *(a)* How many camels has the man with the water got?

    (b) Suppose the man with the camels is the only one with a loaded rifle?

    (c) Correct. There is no way of knowing who has the power without more information and even that information may be incorrect.

Chapter Fourteen

If you haven't got a principal – invent one!

or how not to have negotiating authority

Every week in Britain thousands of readers purchase *Exchange and Mart* and scan its pages for bargains. Many thousands of others look through the small ads in their local papers to see what is for sale, or what is wanted.

To indulge in this weekly search you needn't have anything other than curiosity in mind. If something strikes your fancy you can try to buy it, or, seeing the prices offered for certain items, you might be induced, if you have similar items, to try to sell them yourself.

Some papers actually draw the attention of prospective sellers to the market prospects of goods they may possess but no longer have a need for. A paper could carry a notice like the following:

TWENTY COMMODE PURCHASERS INCONVENIENCED

The gist of the pitch is that an advertisement to sell an antique commode attracted 21 buyers willing to buy at the asking price of £370 and, presumably, this left 20 buyers still without one! Clearly, by implication, any reader of the paper with a spare commode could contact the 20 disappointed buyers by paying for a similar advertisement.

Whichever way you make known your desire to sell an item you still face the problem of actually negotiating a price for it. Getting a prospect to look at your article is a big step towards a sale, but it is only a first step to actually negotiating the price.

Prices in the 'household goods' market are not always specified in the advertisements, which is one way of avoiding the ONO mistake! This creates for both the buyer and the seller the problem of what price to open at.

Alternatively, if a price is mentioned, the buyer can decide to ignore it and see what concessions he gets when the seller believes he will lose the sale if his price does not come down.

It is typical in these types of informal transactions for the buyer, with disarming innocence, to ask:

How much do you want for it?

This can embarrass a seller who has no recent experience of haggling and is unprepared for the question. The most common counter is to reply:

How much will you offer for it?

More than likely, both parties avoid eye contact during the exchange of parried questioning, and each desperately examines the sale item as if it might give them a clue as to what to say next.

This behaviour is a natural product of unfamiliarity with the market for used household goods – only professional dealers conduct similar transactions every day of every week and, consequently, have the confidence to quote a tough opening price.

Unfamiliarity with the market comes from a lack of information about the 'proper' price for a used car, a desk, a plant pot, a wheelbarrow, a commode, or whatever.

The seller wants to sell but does not know what to ask for: the buyer wants to buy but does not know what to offer; and each tries to pass responsibility for the first move onto the other.

The ritual 'sword fencing' of what-do-you-want/what-will-you-offer is as spontaneously discovered by people as it is inevitable, because, essentially, haggling consists of:

The seller trying to ascertain the maximum that the buyer is willing to pay without disclosing the minimum that the seller is prepared to accept.

All negotiating problems involve the perplexity: how to uncover the other party's upper boundary while keeping one's own well and truly camouflaged.

This chapter discusses one common solution to the problem, namely, the tactic of the 'mandate'. It is stumbled upon by gifted amateurs, as well as being the basis of a lucrative career for some professionals. After discussing its help to the former, we will look briefly at its role with the latter.

Negotiators use the mandate tactic in an attempt to build a negotiating position. It requires only that the parties refer to some absent principal as the person who, allegedly, has determined the terms they must stick to in the negotiation. By implication, these terms are mandatory.

The negotiator will say something like:

> My brother says I must not accept less than £555.

This can be countered by:

> My husband told me not to pay more than £615.

Clearly, if a deal is to be agreed one or both of the (often fictitious) mandates has to be ignored.

An entire conversation between two would-be traders could be constructed, in which the actual principal parties to the transaction shelter under alleged mandates from their relatives who, conveniently, are not present.

You should be wary of an absolute inflexibility when using the mandate tactic – after all it is a negotiation – because you could provoke the 'organ grinder' sneer: 'If you can't make your own decisions, I prefer to speak to the organ grinder and not his monkey.' (You should only tease *him* with the organ-grinder sneer when *(a)* you are in a very strong position, i.e. he needs your business; or *(b)* you don't care about deadlock, i.e. you don't need his.)

But, if you are not sure what to do next when asked about your price, and don't have enough confidence to go in tough, try the mandate tactic.

In the case of used household goods it is not normally worth hiring agents to negotiate the sale of, say, a used washing machine (though the author, on occasion, has done so for friends).

You can use the mandate of a principal not present in the negotiations as long as their influence on the outcome is credible. I was once floored by a man who exclaimed: 'What will the wife's mother think of me if I sell to you at *that* price?'

Managers, of course, use the mandate of their absent bosses all the time:

> If I shave any more off the price, *they* will go bananas upstairs

or, in a slightly different version,

> It's simply against company policy to agree to those terms.

Selling a house clearly requires the consent of your spouse to the terms, as does selling most household items. So use her mandate in the negotiations, which effectively turns you from a principal into an agent of the 'absent principal'!

An invented mandate could give you that margin of confidence you need for the moment you seek eye contact just before the other person responds – a most off-putting behaviour if he is under pressure.

The mandate tactic can be used:

1 To support your demands that the quality of the goods is of a certain standard (enabling you to draw attention to flawed features of his product).

2 To demand that the deal must include, say, the leads and spares (enabling you to back-off the sale if these are not included or to demand that the price be discounted in lieu of them). And

3 To insist that it must be *demonstrated* to be in working order (creating the prospect of a discount for anything less – given the 'time and trouble, not to say expense, of putting things right'). And so on.

There is almost no end to the issues that you can confidently raise under the protection of a real or imaginary mandate.

Or course, in return, the seller can quote 'his brother's' opinion that he must get cash only (suggestions of a discount for cash, or, perhaps, a premium for a cheque?), and that if you want spares you must pay for them separately ('it being normal in these cases').

By displacing the source of our demands onto others, it is easier (in the sense of less embarrassing) to introduce them into the negotiation, and easier to back away from buying/selling on this occasion if the terms are not right.

In this respect, never underestimate the unwillingness of non-professionals to tell you that they don't want to buy an item:

I didn't want to tell him his car was no good, so I told him I would think about it, which got me out of the house.

Professionals are no less coy about saying 'no', as in the classic:

Don't call us, we'll call you.

With an invented mandate we act *as if* we are *agents* in the transaction when, in fact, we are *principals* and, by distancing ourselves from the issues, we achieve a kind of neutrality about them. This makes us very difficult targets if things get tough.

Of course, in the used-household-goods markets we are the principals – and the other party knows this – but the *fiction* that we are only an agent of our spouse is often credible enough for it to be accepted, so:

IF YOU HAVEN'T GOT A PRINCIPAL – INVENT ONE!

Thus, we get a line of retreat if we need it, a bolster to our price defences if they are under pressure, and less chance of tension if deadlock threatens: after all, 'it is not *me* you have to convince but my wife'.

Mandates (real or imaginary) protect the negotiator from taking personal responsibility – and thereby personal hostility from the party – for the demands they make.

Union leaders are adept at using the mandate demand, as are all negotiators who are representatives of absent principals (such as lawyers who insist on referring everything back to their clients). For instance, union officials often preface their claims with remarks to the effect that the 'members have instructed me to demand' whatever it is they are formally asking for.

Mandates also give those who use them a means to limit the number and size of concessions they can make:

It's not up to me, it's in the hands of my members.

Or:

My client will never accept less than a full rebate, etc.

A mandate can also give you a first look at their price, particularly for large-value items like houses and cars, and also a note of any concessions that the other party prematurely offers.

You can see a house alone and ascertain what is in the mind of the seller, and then 'escape' politely to 'consult' your spouse. You might be able to extract the seller's best price and also get an idea of the extra items they might include in the purchase (fittings, carpets, kitchen furniture, etc.).

This leaves the way open for a joint visit, if you decide that the house is potentially suitable, and gives you an opportunity to assess the available extras you want included in the deal. Finally, you can go to a *third* round by shunting the negotiations, *plus the early concessions*, onto your estate agent!

Husbands and wives going round houses 'oohing and aahing' together is no way to buy a house. (I once got priced out of a house sale because my mother-in-law told the owner on the first visit that it was the 'most beautiful house she had ever been in', which certainly firmed up his soggy ideas about price because three weeks later he was still quoting her statements to me in the negotiations – after that she went under a strict gagging rule!)

Another Class A mistake is to be hurried into house purchase by real estate brokers who are more concerned with their take from the deal than saving you money. (I am often asked how to tell the good guys from the bad guys in brokerage. Well, one thing for sure, the bad guys don't all wear black hats!)

In general, rushing into deals is bad news for your bank balance.

One reason why house owners use agents to conduct the sale is precisely because they can shelter behind the mandate. When asked, 'What price would you accept for the house?', you can neatly sidestep with the reply, 'All that is handled by my agent.'

The mandate tactic is not just used in negotiations for household items. Some of the world's biggest deals are negotiated using a sophisticated version of the mandate tactic. Professional *agents* often negotiate the outline of the deal subject to the approval of the principals, *who are not present*.

It is common in business for advertisements to include the phrase:

PRINCIPALS ONLY

This is sometimes an attempt to save time and money.

However, giving an agent a mandate is likely to strengthen his negotiating position. He is arm's length from the deal, and you, as principal, can accept or reject what may have been put together by much haggling with the seller: you were not party to the pressures and compromises of the negotiating process and thereby can reject out-of-hand elements of the deal you don't like.

In other words, you can repudiate a deal through an agent at no emotional cost, and, as a result perhaps, get it improved as well.

Naturally, the greater the distance between you and the negotiation the easier it is for you to say 'no'. That is why if you want to say 'no', use the telephone – or a letter – and avoid personal contact if it is fatal to maintaining a tough posture.

The other party has no way of knowing the extent of your agent's authority and consequently he has no way of knowing whether a little more conceded here or there will secure the deal. This might produce bigger concessions in your favour than otherwise.

The mandate can be used by agents to secure better terms:

Ask no questions

An agent can have an important role as a facilitator, such as when, for political reasons, two parties cannot negotiate openly together. For instance, a small communist country needed to purchase grain to supplement its own supplies. For political reasons it would not deal directly with the US Government, so it used an agent.

The agent arranged the purchase of US grain FOB (Free On Board) and shipped it to Belgium. It then transhipped it CIF (Cost, Insurance and Freight) across Europe to the client's frontier showing Belgium as the country of origin.

This met the political needs of the regime – even its own customs people remained ignorant of the origin of the grain – and the agent earned a good commission on the deal.

One by one

Another communist country – less worried about the ideological delicacies of dealing with capitalists – required to ship grain from all over the world.

Its officials knew enough about market economics to know that if they simply chartered 150 ships in one go, there would be a price explosion at their expense.

Hence, they negotiated a deal with a broker that enabled him to charter the ships *individually* from a hundred other brokers, each deal to be conducted without pubicity.

The main broker knew the market for ships and asked individual brokers for specific ships that were within their areas. This prevented them racing into the world market and forcing the price up.

The successful use of the brokers saved the communist country millions of dollars in hard currency. Long after the charters were settled the world chartering market was still unaware of the bonanza it had missed.

If it was up to me, I might agree with you, but my client insists on a full penalty clause for late delivery.

Or:

I'm sorry but there is no way my client will accept that proposal.

Both these statements can be very difficult barriers to get round.

If you are negotiating with an agent, you have no control over how he reports the proceedings to his principal – or even whether he reports anything at all. This is the greatest weakness of negotiating through agents (though I strongly recommend their use when the stakes are high and the market is unfamiliar to you).

The agent, for all you know, may be working to bump up the price in order to increase his fee, while the other principal may be quite willing to settle if he only knew about the offer you've made.

Again you just don't know.

Hence, in seeking to bar agents from the negotiation, the advertisers are trying to meet face-to-face with the person who has full authority to settle and who, by his physical presence in the negotiations, must perforce be directly subject to their pressures.

However, professional agents at my Negotiating Clinics often wax eloquently on an apparently common complaint among their number. In real estate, for instance, an agent can be undermined by a principal who instructs him to accept the other party's last offer even though the agent advises him, on the basis of his experience, that the other party can be pushed to a better price. In fact, the worst instruction an agent can get is to be told:

Get the best price you can, but above all get *a* price.

This complaint is the reverse of the suspicions voiced by some principals about agents:

I believe that agents always hold out for a higher price from the other party merely to get a bigger fee.

This suspicion can be fed when the negotiations are conducted in semi-public. Competitive business takes place in a relatively small community in any one place. To lose one's commercial reputation in the City of London is as devastating as it is to lose it in Edinburgh, Hong Kong, Bahrain, Sydney, or Los Angeles.

In all serious competing businesses, everybody knows everybody worth knowing in the rival companies, and nudge-nudge-wink-wink

Getting yourself an agent

In some cases you are better off with an agent, especially if the stakes are high and the market is unknown to you. Your first problem is to get a good agent and this is a lot harder than you might imagine. True anybody can get *an* agent – there are plenty of people doing precious little for either themselves or their clients.

What you need is an agent who will work for you and not somebody who expects you to do the work for them. If they never return your calls within a reasonable time (you can't expect them to be in their offices *and* selling your film script), do not keep you informed of progress and show no evidence of making any, constantly argue with you when you ask reasonable questions, are totally conservative about what they should go for on your behalf, and prefer to haggle with you than haggle with whomsoever they are supposed to be dealing with, you ought to get out of the relationship. (Just ask for your closing account.)

The best agents are always in demand – I know one in London who only takes *five* clients at a time and if you want her you have to wait until one of them goes off her books.

Agents cannot produce miracles – at least not on a regular basis! Nor can they be left to get on with it without help from you. My rule for judging the worth of an agent is I know I need him as long as he suggests we go for a deal way beyond the very best I had hoped for. If he doesn't, then I know I know as much about the business as he does and would be better off holding onto my ten per cent!

'confidential' whispers travel round the trade like fire around a prairie; there is nothing closer to greased lightning than the tittle-tattle of business (with the possible exception of politics). Nothing is more deserving of being true than a good piece of in-the-know scandal – and, anyway, if it isn't true it's almost certain to be funny!

In negotiating through agents, the other party can seek to undermine your position by trying to contact your principal. Of course, this could be construed to be unethical, etc. (indeed, most professional bodies frown at such conduct) but there is more than one way to achieve this end without becoming an outcast.

The other party can leak 'news' to the trade press, such as by asserting that only your personal intransigence on 'minor' points is preventing the deal going through. If your clients read these press reports (and copies can be brought to their attention) they might be conned into believing them, particularly if they already half believe you are holding out for an extra commission.

This causes them to insist on an early settlement, which, presumably, is why some negotiators go semi-public in this way, hoping that it will sow doubts in the (sometimes) anonymous principal's minds about the probity of his agents.

Apart from trying to avoid time-wasting and the possibility that over-zealous (or greedy) agents are manipulating the settlement terms by provoking an unnecessary deadlock, the demand for 'principals only' can increase the bargaining advantage of the parties.

Suppose the property for sale is a large company, and the seller ends up face-to-face with a prospect who has authority to settle – it's his own money – but little experience of handling transactions of this size. If the seller has been the owner of similar properties for long enough to be less than intimidated by them, he must have an advantage over a keen and vulnerable buyer moving into the 'big league' for the first time.

It is also possible that the advertiser is himself an agent for the real owner and is fishing for 'principals only' precisely in order to smoke out would-be entrepreneurs with little professional experience of what they are doing.

More than one hotel has changed hands in recent years on terms less than favourable to the first-time buyer, who arrives at the negotiation clutching a recent legacy or a large redundancy cheque.

For these reasons, reputable agents are a good protection for an unsure and inexperienced buyer.

What constitutes a good agent is another story. In real estate there is some safeguard in the professional status of Chartered Surveyors, and in other commercial sectors many people make an honest living by acting as agents between principals (but watch out for 'Jaws' – he and his cousins swim in the smallest ponds and strike without warning).

But in the absence of an agent, or where the value of the transaction does not justify their expense, your best bet is to become one!

1 *(a)* If you're new and hungry, you will. But such an instruction is nothing but trouble because whatever you get the owner is bound to protest it is not enough.

   (b) Correct. Get the bottom limit clearly fixed.

   (c) A trifle hasty. Try *(b)* first.

2 *(a)* A toss up with *(b)*. If you're confident of your price or just anxious to clear the garage, give him your figure without hesitation and 'um ha-ing'.

   (b) A good protective ploy if you're not sure, but you will need to work hard to raise his offer if it is low.

   (c) The 'mandate' demand has credibility.It is often a good lead into *(b)* or *(a)*.

   (d) Never make a pre-judgment of his price, otherwise you will always cut yours.

3 *(a)* Possibly, if she refuses *(c)*.

   (b) Not unless you're desperate for her dinghy.

   (c) Correct.

4 *(a)* Surely a proper first demand if it's 'principals only'?

   (b) A sound lead-in move for *(a)*.

   (c) Risky because he will constantly insist on consulting the organ grinder – at your expense.

Self-assessment test 15

1 You are in Bergen (Norway) and want to buy toy trolls for your children. You enter a *very* expensive souvenir shop which sells trolls. The ones you want are priced at 65 Kroner each. You want three. Do you ask the clerk:
   (a) How much for two trolls?
   (b) How much for three trolls?
   (c) What special offers are there on trolls?

2 You are in a bookshop looking for a paperback thriller to read on your holiday. There are several copies of the title you want but one of them is a 'hurt' book. Do you:
   (a) Select a clean mint copy?
   (b) Take the damaged copy to the cash desk?
   (c) Take a mint copy and the damaged copy to the cash desk?

3 You are in a store buying a freezer and the one you want is marked at £800. You ask for a discount and the clerk tells you that it is company policy not to give discounts off the goods as they are already marked down to the lowest possible price. Do you:
   (a) Ask to see the manager?
   (b) Accept what he says as being plausible?
   (c) Press your case for a discount with the clerk?

4 In a survey of buying behaviour of customers over three months in a major European store chain, what percentage of people do you think paid the price shown on the tag:
   (a) 53?
   (b) 97?
   (c) 37?
   (d) 78?
   (e) 11?

Chapter Fifteen

There ain't no such thing as a fixed price!

or how to haggle for a lower price

Why do shops have price tags on their goods? I have heard many explanations for this phenomenon:

To save everybody asking the price of every product.
To save time in the onerous task of shopping.
To speed-up the buying decision.
To avoid mistakes at the cash desk.
To help the consumer make choices.
To treat all customers the same with the same price.
To avoid making losses on small-margin goods.

Most of them sound plausible but all miss the point. The real reason is much more subtle: the overwhelming majority of consumers are brought up from an early age believing in fairy stories, Santa Claus and fixed prices.

The first two are quite harmless and, sadly, pass with the age of innocence. But once the belief in fixed prices gets its barnacle-like grip on your brain, it hardly ever lets go. It manifests itself in the enslavement of the consumer to the price tag.

And the stores know this, which is why they use them.

In other words, they know that customers, almost totally without exception, will part with their cash for the printed price.

And what a power this gives the owners of stores! They know that most consumers would never dream of questioning a price tag – far from it, because most consumers believe that if it's on the tag then it's *gospel* – and so the stores can choose the price to put on it.

If events prove them wrong, and not enough consumers jump at the chance to buy whatever the store is selling, they hold a 'Sale' and put *another* price on the tag. One would expect consumers to be outraged at so-called 'Sales' where the evidence is as plain as can be that the stores have been padding their prices.

But no!

The belief in fixed prices appears by some weird logic to be *reinforced*, not shaken, by the visible drop in prices! Stores even leave both prices on the tag to make you think they are doing you a big favour. Instead, you ought to realize what a sucker they were taking you for before the 'Sale'.

Ironically, the greater the drop in price the greater the 'bargain' consumers feel they have achieved. But the bigger the 'bargain' the more unchallengeable is the evidence of the humbug of fixed prices.

Barnum, of Barnum and Bailey Circus fame, confessed that he made his (wholly deserved) fortune on the willingness – nay, insistence – of the great American public to pay to see his totally improbable spectacles. They were humbugged – and loved him for it.

Yet Barnum only reserved the humbug of business life. He sold tickets to dreams that could never be fulfilled – his 'products' were always a fantasy.

In retail stores the products are real – many of them are excellent –and there is little or no humbug in the claims that are made for them (give or take the 'occasional' exaggeration!). The humbug lies in the price. It claims to be real, and you believe it is real – but it is only a childhood fantasy that was reinforced with every transaction you made since you bought your first stick of candy in the corner shop.

That is why the message of this chapter is:

There ain't no such thing as a fixed price!

Gilbert Summers knows all about the fragility of fixed prices. He runs a store in Texacana, Texas, and has done so for 20 years. He never had any trouble with his prices until 1985. Up to then families loaded up the carts in his store with their weekly shopping, waited quietly while the clerks at the checkouts totalled the price tags, and then paid with cash, cheques or credit cards.

If there were any 'rows' they were over delays while a price was checked because the tag had come off, or if the clerk suspected it had been 'accidentally' changed, or a drunk had wandered in and wouldn't go home, or a couple were fighting over an incident at last night's party.

Most of the time the only noise was that of the cash registers, the

A little less for a car with a little more

An Irish luxury-car manufacturer ran into liquidity problems though their cars were technically well received. The problem was that not enough were being sold to justify continuing production.

Stocks of unsold cars began to pile up at the Irish plant and the company went into receivership.

A leading US car-hire firm approached the manufacturer with an offer to take 1,000 cars immediately and another 1,000 over a 12-month period.

The car sold at $26,000 in the US which the car-hire firm said was 'overpriced'. They told the manufacturer that if they could let the cars go at a little less, then they should have a deal.

A lot less for the same car

All UK car manufacturers maintained differential pricing policies for cars sold in the UK and cars sold on the European continent. Exactly the same cars could cost as much as 40 per cent less in Belgium than they were sold for in Britain.

Some people spotted the price differential and refused to buy their British cars from local dealers. Instead they crossed over to Belgium and bought a British right-hand-drive car there. They brought it back by ferry and saved themselves a couple of thousand pounds.

Eventually, dealers got in on the act and instead of ordering their cars from the British plants direct, they ordered them from the Belgian dealers who shipped them over from Britain first!

This forced the issue into the open. It also fully explains why imported cars from Japan could be so price-competitive and why they could sell pound-for-pound a more luxurious vehicle even with the shipping costs from Japan taken into account.

piped music wafting overhead, the kids screaming as they larked about. Nobody, but nobody, ever asked to see Gilbert Summers about a price tag.

That was until Hang Ha Dong and family moved into the neighbourhood. They are Vietnamese refugees – the survivors of a particularly harrowing boat voyage from Saigon to Thailand. Hang Ha Dong brought with him his entire family – all twelve of them, including his wife's sister and her aged mother.

He also brought with him the habits of a lifetime – one of which is a total incomprehension of the phenomenon of fixed prices. The first time the Hang family (en masse) visited Gilbert Summer's store was nearly their last.

Dutifully they loaded up their carts with their requirements, as they had seen the soldiers do in the PX on the US Army base where Hang and his wife had worked as cleaners for several years in the 1970s. They hadn't shopped in the PX themselves – they preferred the local market – but they had been in it a few times, marvelling at its stocks.

When they got to the checkout, Hang picked up a tin and asked how much the clerk wanted for it. The bored clerk checked the price and drawled '$2.25'. Hang delved into the cart and asked: 'How much for two tins?'. The clerk looked puzzled and said, irritably, '$4.50'.

It was Hang's turn to look puzzled and he spoke to his wife in Vietnamese. Whatever she replied, Hang told the clerk that he would offer him $3.98 for the two tins. This was obviously a bit much for his wife because she let forth a gale of Vietnamese at him – and her mother joined in too. The clerk wondered what was happening.

Hang next lifted out of the cart four string bags of oranges. The clerk said: '$1.30, each'.

'$1.05', said Mr Hang.

'$1.30', repeated the clerk, adding 'Can't you read? It says a dollar-thirty on the tag. Where did you get a dollar-five from?'

'$1.10 and that's my best price,' said Hang.

'$1.30,' replied the clerk.

'$1.12, if you throw in the bag of rice at $4,' said Hang.

'It's a dollar-thirty for the oranges and five-forty for the rice, as it says on the tag.'

'But how much for two bags of rice?' asked Hang.

'Jesus!' exclaimed the clerk, by this time losing his cool. 'Are you nuts or something?'

Cheap but luxurious

Travel is often a large proportion of the expense for a holiday, especially if you want to reach exotic places.

A travel agency in London specializes in rock-bottom luxury holidays. Clients can get a two-week cruise in first-class accommodation for as little as £550 all in.

Or they can safari in Kenya for ten days on the 'millionaire's circuit' for £600, first-class airfare included.

Or how about three weeks in the Caribbean in a sun-soaked paradise for £370?

How do they do it?

The agency contracts to buy up all the cancelled holidays at the top end of the market for a nominal sum and they sell the holidays at a knock-down price to their clients.

The clients state the months when they are free to travel and they must be prepared to go on holiday at 72 hours' notice.

But the deal certainly proves that even high-priced services can be consumed at rock-bottom rates – if you look for the deal!

He decided to explain in simple English (he knew no Vietnamese, having spent his army service in Colorado Springs) how the Texacana store run by Mr Summers operated, which he assured Hang was no different to every other store in the United States of America.

'*You* have to pay the price on the tag. *I* have to check it here. When you've paid, you take the goods home. Until then they stay in the store. Got it?'

Hang and his family began speaking at once. Some to each other in Vietnamese, picking up and turning over items to look at the tags, some to the clerk in English, trying to get the haggle under way again.

The din rose considerably and other shoppers crowded round to watch what was going on (watching people shouting at each other is a common trait in the West).

At this point Gilbert Summers arrived at the checkout. The clerk explained to him that he was dealing with some weird people who didn't appear to understand how the world was organized.

'What do you mean?', asked his boss.

181

Never mind the wine, what about the money?

A discount wine chain in the UK made a name for itself for many years in selling good-quality French and Italian wines at knock-down prices.

In fact the prices were so low that people wondered how they managed to make a profit.

True, the wine company bought up vast stocks of wine and sold it virtually at cost to the customer.

How did they make their money?

On a large volume for a small profit?

Not at all.

They weren't interested in making a profit on the wine – that's how they beat the competition.

They made their profits by having a constant flow of cash into their bank accounts which they loaned to the banks for 30 days until they paid their invoices. The interest of ten per cent on the money exceeded the profit they would have got if they had sold the wine at regular prices.

'They want to haggle over every goddamed tin of peas and packet of soup,' he told him. 'Christ, Gil, they're offering me deals left, right and centre, for two of this and one of that, or three of this or one of the other. I don't know what's going on. Can't they read the frigging price tags?'

'H-o-l-d-i-t,' bawled Gilbert above the row.

His whole store stopped.

The checkouts, crowded with carts and people, stopped ringing up the dollars, which in Gilbert Summers' world made it **an emergency**.

He ordered Hang to take his family out of the store and not to come back. He told the clerk to run their carts into the shelf lanes and then get back to his desk 'pronto'.

Hang didn't move. He was clearly completely bewildered by the strange behaviour of the Bossman. He knew about hard bargaining from the market square at Lang Foo, but had never had a merchant snatch away his goods and order him off!

This was clearly a time to try another tack. He put his hand in his coat to take out his wallet.

Gilbert Summers, the clerk and a half-dozen others, hit the floor as if to get through it. When they saw Hang was holding his wallet and not a Magnum revolver they got up sheepishly.

Hang shoved a piece of paper towards Gilbert. It was his honourable discharge as a cleaner from the US army back in Vietnam. (Hang was using the 'returned soldier' ploy, or rather a 'Vietnamese ex-cleaner' version of it.)

He explained to Gilbert Summers that he had always liked the Americans and had wanted to be in Texas ever since he had seen a John Wayne film where everybody in it spoke Vietnamese. He had heard that Texas was a land of opportunity where anybody could make their fortune if they worked hard and knew that 'a dollar saved was a dollar earned'.

'Damned right,' said Summers, 'as my daddy told me, you'all work hard and live like decent folks and you'all get by.'

'OK,' said a beaming Hang, happy to have resolved the misunderstanding with such a fine Texan as Gilbert Summers (though he didn't understand why he spoke no Vietnamese). 'Now about these oranges at $1.30. I'll give you $1.15 if you throw in two tins of tomato soup at 35c each . . .'.

It took many months for Gilbert Summers to get used to Hang and his family. Likewise for Hang, who found that if he waited until 5 p.m. each day he could get his fruit and vegetables from the Summers' store much cheaper than they were in the morning (giving him a unique insight into the American concept of the 'happy hour').

He also found if he bought soup by the case he got a few cents off the per tin price. Sometimes he sat outside the shop with his family for hours and made trial runs inside to see if the price of tins of soup had fallen in the past hour. Occasionally, the clerks would give in to the Hangs just to get rid of them.

Other times, Hang chose to go in when the shop was busiest and delay the checkout while he haggled over the price of three loaves of bread, or fruit cake (for which Texacana is famous), or the weekend's groceries.

Gilbert Summers and Hang Ha Dong have got on fine since 1983. Their families became related after the eldest Summers' boy began courting Hang's daughter at the 1987 Thanksgiving.

What worked for Hang Ha Dong can work for you. His advantage is that he never believed in fixed prices – they were unknown in Vietnam, until, ironically, the Communists took over.

Communist fixed prices are the final proof of the idiocy of them. No Communist state knows the *real* price of anything because their accounting 'systems' do not recognize supply and demand or the value of what is contained in any product.

The Communist state arbitrarily fixes hundreds of thousands of prices at the centre and these are used for transactions, irrespective of whether or not they correspond to the cost of producing the goods themselves or the needs of those buying them. The stores sell goods at fixed prices and if they run out of some items that's too bad. Hence, there are long queues for some goods, none for others, and masses of the population wish to emigrate at any one moment.

The black market flourishes. Russia is the only country in the world where they shoot you for supplying to people the things they want which the state is too inefficient to provide. What Prohibition did for organized crime, fixed prices in Russia (and Poland) have done for the resistance to all things Communist.

How then should you tackle a fixed price?

The simple way to do so is to challenge it! If you don't ask for a discount for cash, you certainly won't be offered one. (If you are offered five per cent discount ask for 7.5 per cent.)

If you can think of a way to change the deal you might be able to change the price. For example, what does the deal include?

Delivery and installation: how much off for uplifting and/or installing it yourself?

Parts and labour warranty: how much off for foregoing your rights to these? (You can be sure they cover themselves for repairs and defects in their price.)

184

Pay now or later: if there is a delivery delay, how much off for paying cash now – you get the use of my money?

New or 'as new': if it's £1,500 for a brand-new deep freeze, how much off for a demonstration model, a window model, a slightly bashed-in or scratched model?

Price for one: how much for two – or three? This will tell you something about the margin on the price for one.

Compatible purchase: suppose I buy the desk *and* the chairs together? ('OK, I'll take the suit *if* you throw in a tie.')

Non-compatible purchase: how much off if I buy the lawn mower *and* a set of pans from the kitchen department? ('How much off the rent of the office if I use your fax?')

Related service: how much off *if* I clean up after you and dispose of the rubbish?

Gross account: how much off the price for the pipes if I agree to place all my business with you this year?

You are unlikely to get very far with the counter clerks in a store. Higher management deliberately give them absolutely no discretion over the price – though it is worth testing this assumption just in case they do have a small margin to work with.

In clothes stores, the counter clerks sometimes have discretion over small things like the price of alterations. Almost certainly, even in big stores, you can get the alterations done free if you make that a condition of purchase, particularly if you have already taken up their time looking at lots of suits.

Naturally, they will tell you that it is company policy to charge for alterations – and so it should be if you are daft enough to accept this. Hence, you must be prepared to ask to see the manager when you are approaching a 'buy' decision. If you can't do that you're sunk.

If the clerk tells you that he cannot give you a discount, ask him who can, and invariably he will tell you to see the manager.

Now, either this is a way of telling you that if you don't believe him about the company's policy on discounts you had better hear it from the boss, *or* he is telling you that only the boss can/will give you a discount. Either way, you must be prepared to test it.

Why should the boss give you a discount?

Firstly, it's likely that he has the authority to do so, and people who have authority like occasionally to exercise it, especially if they like to impress their subordinates from time to time of the distance between them.

185

Secondly, you have probably brought him away from much more important work and the amount you are haggling for is not 'worth his time' to fight over. If he gives you five per cent off a suit or a table, he still has a 40 per cent mark-up left for his profit. And if he believes you will not buy without a discount he knows he loses the entire sale.

What is the rational thing for him to do? Agree to a discount! He didn't get where he is by being silly over 'trifles'.

Thirdly, people who have 'graduated' up from the counter like to keep their hand in when it comes to individual selling. They get promoted because they are good at selling and they are good because they enjoy it.

In management they seldom get a chance to show themselves (and their subordinates) how good they are, so your request to see him could be music to his ears. You are doing them a favour!

I always go to the top person when making a purchase, though I met my match a few years back. I went into Austin Reed's clothes store in Princes Street, Edinburgh, to look at their suits. When it came to the buy decision I asked for a discount off the price tag.

The assistant couldn't give me it, so I asked to see the manager. He came along with a smile and a 'what-appears-to-be-the-trouble' look about him.

I told him I liked the suit but not the price and asked him for a ten per cent discount. He started chatting and soon had me trying on suits again, and he indicated that I could have five per cent off the grey suit I liked but said he thought I 'looked better in the brown one'.

He also offered me five per cent off the brown one *and* hinted at a bigger discount if I bought them both.

That is what eventually I agreed to.

It wasn't until I got home that I realized I had ended up spending more than twice what I intended, had two suits instead of one (I narrowly escaped from buying a winter coat too), and had been given a 7.5 per cent 'discount' off an amount I hadn't intended to pay.

And I wore the brown suit once only! That is what comes from chasing a discount and forgetting the budget.

However, I still challenge those fixed prices. You should too. It could save you hundreds of pounds a month.

The fact that most people don't bother to challenge fixed prices is no comfort. Sure, there is a time penalty for haggling and for much of the time we simply do not have any to spare.

Twenty-five ways to take on a fixed price

1 Throw in the accessories and I'll take it.
2 At that price I must get the display unit free.
3 What discount is there for a standing order?
4 I'm a new/old customer and should get an introductory/ loyalty discount.
5 What is the discount for cash payment? (At 18 per cent per year it costs them 1.5 per cent a month for credit.)
6 If you give me 90 days to pay I'll buy now. (At 18 per cent per year, that's worth 4.5 per cent to you.)
7 What will you take off for a demonstration model?
8 If you give me a special price, I'll order right now.
9 I want a year's free maintenance, which will cost you nothing if your product is as good as you claim.
10 I want to test it for 30 days free of charge.
11 How much off if you use non-returnable/returnable crates?
12 How much off if I take the bin ends?
13 I'll take last year's stock if you take off 15 per cent.
14 I'll try it if you guarantee my money back if I am dissatisfied. ('How much off for a no-come-back deal?')
15 How much off if I recommend it to my friends/colleagues?
16 What's the discount for a repeat order?
17 What's the discount for an exclusive supply agreement?
18 How much off training if your people come to our place?
19 How much off if we collect?
20 How much off if we order but you deliver when we need it?
21 How long will you hold your prices if we order today?
22 As we are the first/fiftieth/last purchasers, we should get a 20 per cent discount.
23 As you can quote me as a reference, I'll require a discount.
24 As this is a risky/new product, I'll need ten per cent off.
25 If you have the power to give me a special price, I'll order now.

But one consequence of *never* challenging fixed prices is that we do not know how to when we want or need to. It's no good waiting until we are about to make a large-value purchase before we get experience in taking on a fixed price.

In Texas they say that business is about people with money meeting people with experience; the people with experience get the money and the people with the money get the experience.

But as Hang Ha Dong puts it: he didn't go all the way to Texas just for the experience!

Answers to self-assessment test 15

1 *(a)* A good move because it enables you to push for an extra discount for a third troll.

(b) Not so good because you have used up your leverage for a quantity discount in one go.

(c) Correct. There might be other special offers – package and posting to your home abroad free, a ten per cent sale discount off the price tag just for one, etc. – which you should know about before you then press for a quantity discount.

2 *(a)* Only if you think you can get a discount for a mint copy, otherwise you'll pay the tag price.

(b) This gives you a case for a discount to take the book off the store's hands (as long as it's readable).

(e) Yes. A strong move as evidence is a powerful supporter of an assault on a fixed price. If they still say no, leave both copies at the desk and go to a more sensible book store.

3 *(a)* Yes. If you can't face this step then you surely have not got the credibility to get a discount.

(b) You are obviously easily persuaded and lack grit.

(c) If you have ducked out of *(a)* I doubt if you will get very far with this approach.

4 *(a)* Unlikely!

(b) Right! You can see how much we are brainwashed.

(c) Not on this planet!

(d) Getting warmer.

(e) Are you serious?

Self-assessment test 16

1   You are on a sales tour of South Africa arranging dealerships for your range of industrial pumps. In Johannesburg you are told that your pumps are 'too expensive', in Durban, your prices are 'unrealistic' and in Cape Town 'the dealer's margins are too low'. Do you:
    (a) Fax head office to say the marketing people have got the price structure wrong?
    (b) Carry on your tour as normal?
    (c) Request discretion on the margins?
    (d) Give discounts off the list price in exchange for the order?

2   You are negotiating the supply of heavy pumps to a power station project and the contractor tells you that your prices are about 15 per cent above the quotes he has from a competing German firm and 35 per cent above the prices he is being offered for a totally reconditioned set of pumps. Do you:
    (a) Assure him that your pumps are the best in the world and known to be such by everybody in the business?
    (b) Tell him that the price is negotiable *if* you get the order?
    (c) Remind him that your pumps are regularly serviced and have a 24-hour emergency repair service behind them?

3   You are faxed by a construction consortium that they will accept your tender for earth-moving equipment to be shipped to Jordan if you can reduce your prices by five per cent. Do you:
    (a) Offer three per cent only?
    (b) Agree?
    (c) Suggest that it is possible only *if* the tender terms are varied?
    (d) Decline?

Chapter Sixteen

The Walls of Jericho
or how to stop conceding

Faint-hearted negotiators, faced with a challenge to their price, change their price rather than risk deadlock. They have the resolve of a wet paper bag.

Price is a predictable target in any negotiation, and you don't need to be a genius to appreciate why. Price is divisible – it's counted in pounds and pence – and many buyers (rightly) believe it pays them to try to shave prices a little.

Hypermarkets that cut a penny off per delivered bottle can share the savings with their customers, or add directly to their profits.

A wine negotiator who concedes a 'mere' penny a bottle, cuts his own company's cash flow on 50,000 cases a year by 600,000 pence, or £6,000. That is equivalent to three months of his salary. (Even a penny off per case is worth £500.)

If he concedes a penny a bottle with four of his accounts, he doubles what it costs the company to employ him!

Conversely, if he could get an extra penny a bottle from four key accounts he costs his company nothing and can spend the rest of the year earning pure profits.

A Middle East 'go-between' on a modest three per cent 'commission' (some get nine per cent) makes £900,000 on a £30 million Turnkey Project – if you can get him down 'only' a half of a per cent, you save yourself £150,000.

Is it worth trying a price challenge to save your company $150,000? Of course it is!

Is it worth his while trying to raise you half a per cent on your offer of three per cent?

Sure it is. If he gets you to agree to 3.5 per cent, his commission for acting as a 'go-between' goes up to a $1 million.

Pennies and half per cents do matter.

That is why you must expect the opposition to try some form of price challenge – they wouldn't be doing their job properly if they

Siberian gas – worst deal of the century?

Since 1984 Siberian natural gas has flowed 3,600 miles to Western Europe, thanks to a $15 billion engineering feat of Western technology – and $10 billion of European capital.

Nothing illustrates the politico-commercial skills of the Soviet Union better than the details of this deal. Their ability to get the highly-talented Europeans to put up the capital, take most of the risks, and this for only about 20 per cent of the gas (the rest being diverted into Soviet uses), is a remarkable testimony either to their negotiating prowess or to the negotiating errors of the Europeans.

How did the Soviets manage to pull off this coup? Simply by dividing the Germans, French, British, and Italians from each other. (They even managed to put one over on the Japanese, itself no mean feat.)

The Soviet negotiators went on tour from European company to European company, from German bank to French bank and then back again, each time picking up a concession here and a concession there. With their rivals making concessions, the Europeans responded with even greater concessions, to which inevitably the rivals responded too. Instead of treating the deal with a single monopolist customer as requiring a single European seller, the Western capitalist firms and their governments caved in one by one like lambs on their way to market.

The Dutch, with great credit to themselves, refused to play the Soviet game of 'Dutch auction' and tried to get collaboration across the interested parties. The Soviet response was open and brutal – they cut the Dutch out of the deal and went on to tackle the rest on a one by one basis.

didn't – and if you are not ready for them you aren't doing your job properly either.

If price challenges succeed they provide big benefits to the asker. The faint-hearted always crumble to a price challenge, and they are a cause of their company's losses – which proves that employing them as negotiators is an expensive luxury.

Of course, if you are buying you should always make a price

challenge. Never accept his first offer: test his resolve! If he crumbles, you gain – if he doesn't, you haven't lost anything.

But what of your own propensity to crumble? What can be done about it?

Quite a lot.

You can eradicate the propensity to crumble to a price challenge by learning how to fight back without provoking deadlock.

One immediate way to stiffen your resolve is to stop thinking about price in the same terms (and sometimes even in the same currency) as the other person.

He will ask you to drop your price by so much a unit, or to raise his fees by so much a day. He certainly won't talk to you about the total cost of his price change or the annual cost of his services.

Why?

Because by looking at his price challenge in the small, you forget to think about what it's going to cost you in the large.

He encourages you to think of a single bottle rather than the warehouse full of cases stacked from floor to ceiling. Are you going to think a penny doesn't matter when you multiply it by the half-million bottles of wine in your warehouse? That is the *real* cost of giving in to his price challenge.

Use a calculator if you want to see the real costs of conceding to price challenges – and let him see you using it too.

But seeing the real costs *and* avoiding them are not the same thing. The 'per unit price' ploy is aimed at making the cut more acceptable to you and is not an end in itself.

The other guy's real objective is to achieve a larger slice of the cake for himself, and therefore you need to have some weapons to hand to resist him reaching that objective entirely at your expense.

Take the case of Helmut Weber on his first overseas negotiating tour. Representing a German firm of high technical reputation, he went to South Africa to negotiate new supply and service agreements with his company's existing local distributors and some new outlets.

Helmut Weber knew something about pumps; he had graduated in engineering. However, he knew next to nothing about negotiating, and nothing at all about price challenges.

South Africans as a whole are not reputed to be handicapped in business matters. The distributors didn't know much about the technical side of pumps but they knew how to buy and sell them (and most other things) in their territories.

The square root of nothing!

The 1980–82 air freight price war in the North Atlantic routes saw extensive price slashing by air-cargo carriers.

If one carrier cut rates to get business, another would go below the cut immediately. This led a third to follow suit and a fourth to jump in with yet lower rates.

Something akin to panic set in when one cargo handler was filling space for an airline at 25 per cent off the already slashed kilo prices of the main cargo carriers.

Not surprisingly this handler's client went bust.

But the heavy pressure on rates continued.

Except for one company, British Caledonian.

To the surprise of almost everybody, they refused to join the suicidal scramble to cut prices.

'It is the easiest thing in the world to go out and fill an aeroplane with the square root of nothing,' was how a company spokesman put it.

'We have refused to dodge the issue,' he added. 'If shippers do not wish to pay our rates they do not get our services. We are not in a rate war on the North Atlantic in any shape or form.'

The result?

BCal's airfreight revenues rose 36 per cent in 1981 as it made an aggressive marketing bid for traffic at economic prices.

It was also able to expand its facilities and capacity when all around it other carriers were in severe financial difficulties.

British Airways was forced to withdraw from the cargo business altogether and other giants had to revise their rates upwards.

Obviously, BCal is not managed by price crumblers!

A classic negotiating asymmetry!

You might wonder why Helmut's company sent him on such an important mission when clearly he was less than qualified for it. That was precisely the question I put to the company president, and he said that his wife had insisted that their *son* show what he could do!

Helmut's progress across South Africa was monitored by the long trails of fax messages that accumulated on his father's desk. If they were read in sequence the trend was obvious to even the untrained eye, but his father did not need the normal German passion for order to see the pattern of his son's negotiating behaviour.

Helmut was a price crumbler.

Not that Helmut saw it that way. He was working extremely hard in what he considered the most difficult of circumstances. If asked, Helmut would have summed up the problem in one word: 'competition'.

Within two days of arriving at Jan Smuts airport in Johannesburg he was convinced that South Africa was the most price-competitive economy in the world.

Nobody denied the technical excellence of Weber pumps – though nobody praised them outright either – but everybody told him that Weber's ex-works pump prices were 'too expensive' and that the dealer margins 'were too low'. He faxed Hamburg that he had been forced to cut the ex-works price by five per cent just to hold the current order level with their largest Johannesburg distributor.

Durban was much worse: 'Weber prices are too high and your pumps will never sell at the list prices even if I take no cut myself,' was how the boss of the largest engineering parts stockist put it. Helmut faxed Hamburg: 'Our prices unrealistic. Have increased the distributor's margin by ten per cent and opened up a new dealership.'

A new distributor asked him why Weber pumps were costing more this year compared to last, which puzzled Helmut a little as he didn't know they had sold pumps to that outlet before – he would check when he got home – and as far as he knew Weber pumps had not risen in price for 15 months. He agreed however to a 15 per cent discount and faxed home that he had opened up another new dealership and an order for one of each pump type was enclosed (the dealer wanted 'to try the market' first).

Another distributor told him that he wanted to stock and sell Weber pumps but: 'The competition quotes me keener prices than yours and trade is so bad at the moment that I am not re-ordering anything'. This got the distributor a 20 per cent discount.

Helmut got different versions of the same story wherever he went, and he faxed Hamburg that he was 'compelled' to make discounts of between 15 (if he was really lucky) and 30 per cent (when he wasn't).

By the time he returned to Johannesburg he was utterly

Training staff in 'profit and loss'

The founder of a long-established family firm was puzzled by the lower than usual profits earned in the previous six months – they sold non-food products to large supermarkets. While his product ranges were under competitive pressure, sales were still healthy compared to those achieved in the recession 30 months earlier.

Investigation soon disclosed the source of the problem: the sales staff were discounting to get business. While the individual discounts they gave away (often merely because the buyer asked for one) were not large in themselves, they were huge when added together. In fact, discounts were costing this company £850,000 a year, or putting it another way, they were reducing profitability by exactly the same amount. Moreover, as his company paid the sales staff commission on their achieved sales targets, he was losing twice over!

He called in the field sales force and gave them a five-minute course in How to Avoid Bankruptcy and Keep Your Job. Briefly, he revealed to them the facts of business life. 'Every ten per cent discount you throw away,' he told them, 'halves your contribution to the company's profits'. His arithmetic was impeccable (so was his reminder that those who persistently damaged profits in this way would soon be judged to be unprofitably employed): 'If you sell £100 worth of our products to the local store,' he told them, 'we do not make £100. We have to pay out to our suppliers what it cost to buy in the goods and what it costs us to sell them (including your wages).'

'My accountant', he continued (one of his sons in fact), 'calls this the Cost of Sales. I call it £60, which taken off the £100 sales you made leaves us with £40. But before you run off with the delusion that we have made £40 profit, you should know that we still have to fork out yet more cash out of that £40 to pay for our warehouses, our offices, and our administration staff (most of whom earn a lot less than you do). These costs come to £30. They cannot be avoided according to my administration manager,' he said, mentioning another one of his sons, 'who assures me that these costs must be paid irrespective of sales and irrespective of market conditions.'

He paused while he wrote the figures on the wall: £100 less

Cost of Sales at £60 equals £40, less overheads at £30 equals £10. He underlined the final £10 and wrote beside it the word PROFIT. 'We can just manage on a profit rate of ten per cent,' he assured his listeners, some no doubt calculating how much of it they could argue for in their next performance review.

'However,' he continued, 'when you throw away a 15 per cent discount, often for no better reason than that the buyer asked for one, what happens to the company's profits?' He did not wait for an answer but returned to the numbers on the wall. This time he wrote '£85 less Cost of Sales at £60 equals £25, less overheads at £30 equals minus £5'. He drew a red circle round the £5 and wrote beside it the word LOSS.

'That, ladies and gentlemen, is what all of you are doing some of the time and what some of you are doing all of the time. It is costing the company £850,000 a year. We need that £850,000 to grow the business, to refurbish the regional warehouses, to introduce new brands, and', here he paused for effect, for he intended to appeal to their keenest sense of self-interest, 'to upgrade your company cars.'

convinced that Weber pumps would never keep a foothold in South Africa if he stuck to the company's 'ridiculous' overseas pricing policy.

He was mortified when a distributor in East London rebuked him for 'attempting monopolistic exploitation of South Africa's need for good pumps' and he reported by fax that he had conceded a 30 per cent discount because the distributor said that 'his budget for pumps does not enable me to take on your series'.

A Cape Town distributor's accusation of 'price skimming' (as Helmut wasn't even sure what this meant he asked Hamburg for an explanation!) left him depressed and the distributor with a 15 per cent discount.

When an admittedly somewhat sloshed buyer in Bloemfontein charged him with 'bare-faced profiteering', he realized what it was like to feel guilty *and* framed at the same time, so in response to the claim that 'my customers would not pay that price for a pump' he made the usual price concession.

He got to the point where he dreaded anybody referring to the high prices of Weber pumps. So much so that he got in first to discuss his prices almost as soon as he opened the negotiations and

---

The costs of competition

Getting back from a suicidal freight-rate policy to an economic one is not easy in shipping.

Customers do not like taking price increases, especially when other lines are holding their rates down below yours.

One container shipping line decided to break away from the crazy prices that operated in the business in 1982 and imposed a surcharge of $275 a TEU (Tons Equivalent Unit).

'Rates must rise today, to avoid dramatic increases tomorrow,' they announced, for rates had to reflect a reasonable return on investment.

'We re-invest our profits to increase efficiency,' they claimed, and it was from efficiency that 'you the customer benefit.'

They asked customers to think what would happen to their freight rates in a year's time if the rates war drove the line out of business.

That is what price wars are about: driving the weakest companies out of the market.

But you have a choice before the price war begins: keep out of it, and run your business without price crumblers!

---

kept referring to his prices whenever he thought the distributor was about to raise the subject himself.

He had no doubts that he had identified price as the barrier to securing a foothold in South Africa.

He reported by fax to his father that the marketing men had got this one completely wrong, that the competition was fierce, even cut-throat, and that he had been able to maintain interest in stocking Weber pumps with dealers but only at the cost of discounts off the list prices and other concessions.

He faxed home shock-horror stories galore about 'pump dumping' by the Japanese, the French, and the British. They were all at it! They were going into the dealers and selling them pumps at 'below cost' just to keep out Weber's pumps. The representatives of one Japanese firm – he was told this 'in confidence' by a Johannesburg distributor – had been instructed to 'always go below whatever price Weber quoted for their pumps'.

'How can honest men compete with such rogues?' Helmut

wanted to know when he faxed the distributor's story to his father and asked for a similar freedom so that he could get Weber pumps into that distributor's warehouse. 'If the Japanese stoop to low price tricks of that sort, we must show them what a low price looks like!'

When his father read this particular fax he held his head in his hands in despair and refused to see anybody for an hour while he recovered his composure. Then he rang his wife to tell her what an idiot of a son they had given birth to and he faxed Helmut with immediate instructions to return to Hamburg.

When Helmut got back to the office – after a few days' rest, during which his father thought carefully about what he was going to do with him – he was told to report to Fritz, the marketing manager, who gave him a thick pad of paper and a pencil and told him to write out his experiences in detail.

His reports, client by client, were read carefully and sent back to him with comments and questions in the margin. He was told to identify what each distributor had told him regarding the prices of Weber pumps ('their *exact* words please').

Long after he had wearied of this seemingly pointless task, he completed it and was ushered into Fritz's office. He realized that he was to be the object of a special grilling and naturally got apprehensive about making a fool of himself.

Fritz put such fears to rest by opening up with the statement that after what Helmut had done to the company in South Africa there was no possibility of him ever making such a fool of himself as long as he lived. Everybody had made similar mistakes (though never on such a scale, he added to himself) and they had all learned how to avoid them.

'In your opinion, what is the big problem with Weber pumps in the South African market?' he asked.

'Undoubtedly the fact that our prices are too high', replied Helmut.

'OK, let's accept that view for the moment and ask how you know they are too high.'

'Because the distributors told me they wouldn't buy pumps at our prices.'

'Did they all tell you the same story about our prices, or did they vary their stories?' asked Fritz.

'The same story.'

'Interesting,' said Fritz thoughtfully. 'How then do you explain that in your reports of each client, you mention being given not just one, but several reasons why they think our prices are too high?'

'I don't follow what you are getting at,' said a puzzled Helmut.

'OK, I'll show you.'

Fritz turned over the top sheet of a flip chart that stood in a corner and read down the page:

'Weber pumps are too expensive ex-works and therefore the distributor's margins are too low.'

'That is more than I paid for similar pumps last year.'

'The competition quotes me keener prices.'

'My budget for pumps won't stretch to your range.'

When he had finished he asked Helmut if he agreed that these were sentences from his reports. Helmut muttered: 'If you say so,' and nodded, though he couldn't remember specifically.

'Are these sentences the same?' asked Fritz.

'They are all about our prices being too high!' offered Helmut.

'That, Helmut, is where your mistake is being made. They are not the same. They are all different notes in the same song: "Get Your Prices to Tumble Down". And like Joshua at the battle of Jericho, the dealers only had to blow a note and your prices did precisely that – they came tumbling down.'

Helmut thought that a little unfair but said nothing and allowed Fritz to continue his lecture.

'Price was their vehicle for putting pressure on you to make concessions. The fact that you responded by reducing your prices does not make price *the* barrier to the deal, nor does your collapse on price automatically secure you a deal, as we can see from the number of times you offered a price concession and did not secure any business.'

'How do you mean?' asked Helmut. 'All the deals I got required me to make a price reduction. Perhaps with the others I did not go far enough down in price!'

This provoked a visible sigh from Fritz, but he continued patiently. 'Ask yourself what interest a distributor has in getting you to reduce your prices to him – leaving aside the question of whether he is telling the truth about the state of the market?'

'Well, I *suppose* it is possible that he would gain an extra margin if I reduced my price to him and he was able to maintain prices in the market, but that is not how it is in South Africa as the competition is fearsome.'

Competing ourselves out of business

Looking back on the 1980–82 North Atlantic air-cargo carriers' price war, it might be thought that they did not realize what they were doing.

That is by no means the case.

The boss of the US Flying Tigers Corporation had no doubt where it would lead.

In 1981, he warned customers and carriers alike: 'The shipper in the short term may think he has the benefits of getting low rates, in the long run he will suffer because if the free-enterprise carriers are driven from the market, he will be stuck with the government-subsidized carriers who are well able to sustain losses.

'These are the inefficient airlines and in those circumstances the price of the service will rise steeply if we are not around to discipline them.'

This situation, he added, was caused by the 'unreasonable situation where airlines are trying to protect market shares at all costs at prices which are totally uneconomic'.

'How do you know it is fearsome?'

'I could see it, of course,' replied a by-now irritated Helmut, 'and the distributors know best about the market.'

'OK, let's take the distributor's budget-for-pumps example. How do you know what his budget was limited to?'

'I remember that one. He told me he had only five per cent of his sales in pumps and showed me the racks where he kept his stocks of that Yahatsu range. They took up only three shelves out of the entire warehouse,' Helmut replied triumphantly.

Helmut thought he heard Fritz mumble something about 'Frau Hubbard.'

'And the one about the keen prices from the competition?'

'I heard that from practically everybody,' replied Helmut.

'I am sure you did, but did it not occur to you that they say the same thing to everybody? If they told you that your competitors' prices were higher than yours, would you want to raise or lower your own?'

'Raise them,' began Helmut and then realized the implication. 'I see what you mean,' he mumbled.

'Yes, I hope you do. Now consider the one about the customers not paying our price for a pump. How many pumps do we sell each year from this factory – 10,000, plus all the spares? Who buys them? Is price a barrier for those customers?'

'No, but that doesn't prove we can sell them at our prices in South Africa,' suggested Helmut.

'Maybe, maybe not, but I think the chances of South Africa being a different market to the rest of the world are pretty slim, don't you? After all, allowing for exchange rates, I should think that our pumps are more expensive in the USA at the moment and that is our second largest market. We even sell our pumps in Japan, not a million miles from Yahatsu's main plant.'

'So, I overdid the discounts a little. Next time I'll be wiser,' said Helmut.

'The discounts were only part of the problem, Helmut!', replied Fritz. 'You conceded discounts, credit terms, sale or return, free inventories, CIF shipping – the only thing you didn't give away was a promotional budget. All these concessions on top of the price concession. Have you any idea what they add up to in cost? No, don't bother guessing. I'll tell you. As of now, Weber Pumps is giving its products almost free to the richest country in the whole of Africa, meanwhile we sell at a profit to everybody else in the African continent, including the reconditioned jobs we sent to Chad. It would be cheaper to dump our pumps in the Rhine – that way we'd save on freight to South Africa!'

There was silence for a full minute. Eventually, Helmut spoke quietly: 'What should I do now?' he asked, resigned to the worst.

'How about getting a job with the competition?' whispered Fritz.

Poor Helmut. It was a heady baptism indeed. It took his company several years to get out of the mess he had got them into.

It wasn't just the price concession he had made but the way he had crumbled on price and everything else *once he believed that price was the obstacle to a successful outcome for his negotiation.*

Handling a price challenge is one of the two skills of the successful negotiator – making a price challenge is the other.

1 *(a)* Every sales negotiator believes this is true at some time or other and is invariably wrong. Anyway, marketing will not change its policies from a single fax so you are wasting your time sending one.

(b) Yes. What you are hearing is what buyers say everywhere and you must get used to it.

(c) You are weakening under pressure and could end up a price crumbler.

(d) You are a price crumbler!

2 *(a)* Every seller will say something to this effect. If it is true the contractor will know it, if it isn't you'll only annoy him.

(b) Definitely not! The first step of a price crumbler.

(c) Could be a good move because it pays to highlight benefits that separate your package from others.

3 *(a)* You are a modest crumbler!

(b) You are a rampant crumbler!

(c) Much better.

(d) Not by fax. See them first; use after *(c)*.

Self-assessment test 17

1   You are a specialist in deep-sea oil exploration and have
    been approached by a consultant engineer in Singapore to
    join his staff on a two-year assignment. In their letter offering
    you the post, they quote a salary that is within a few dollars
    of what you are earning from a company in Stavanger. Do
    you:
    (a) Tell them you want a higher salary?
    (b) Quote a figure that you would settle for?
    (c) Quote a high figure and suggest a compromise between
        that and their offer?

2   A client expresses strong objections to a price proposal you
    have submitted. He makes no suggestions as to what could
    be done about it. Do you:
    (a) Say 'no' to price cuts?
    (b) Suggest he makes a proposition?
    (c) Ask him why he is objecting to the price?
    (d) Make a proposition yourself?

3   You are negotiating an off-site sales-training seminar for an
    insurance company. They are worried about the aggregate
    cost and are pressing for a reduction. They hint that unless
    the price comes down they cannot run the course, nor the
    three follow-on courses they had planned to use you for. Do
    you:
    (a) Go over the proposal with them and see what items they
        can provide from their own resources to save you
        charging them for hiring in?
    (b) Take a firm stand on price, given your outstanding
        quality and the improvements in sales they will get from
        the high numbers they intend to put through the
        programme?
    (c) Find out what their 'best price' is and go for that if it is
        close to your own?

203

Chapter Seventeen

Don't change the price, change the package!
*or how to shape up
to better deals*

In 1801, when Lord Nelson's small fleet hove-to in sight of the Danish island forts, armed hulks and ships defending the entrance to the harbour at Copenhagen, there was more than one palpitating heart as his men gazed in awe at the menacing ferocity of what was waiting for them.

Characteristically, Nelson wrote of the Danish preparations that they 'only look formidable to those who are children at war'.

Similarly, the opposition in a negotiation is seldom as formidable as it looks and almost always looks invincible only 'to those who are children at negotiating'.

Those who feel that the competition they face is formidable ought to mind Nelson's judgment and, perhaps, emulate his grit!

Of course, it does not follow that Nelsonian grit is enough by itself for success – Nelson almost lost the Battle of Copenhagen, making it one of Britain's bloodiest naval contests – you also have to be good at what you are doing, but if you surrender, merely because of what you are up against, then they will ride all over you.

This chapter is about a key negotiating skill: handling a price challenge from a skilled and formidable opponent.

From the last chapter we know why people invariably challenge your price – it's the obvious thing to do! Helmut Weber's response was to crumble like the walls of Jericho. The people he negotiated with saw how he crumbled under pressure and, inevitably, they didn't confine their pressure only to his prices – they pushed on everything else too: credit terms, shipping and insurance, spares, returns, training, and so on.

If you concede, you open the door to an across-the-board

The kamikaze aeroplane business: I

One of the world's most highly competitive businesses must be that of aeroengines. Three or four large corporations dominate this market and the competition is murderous – almost kamikaze!

It began in 1978 when General Electric fought Pratt & Witney for the engine contracts of the Boeing 767 and the Airbus A310.

The 'giveaways' they offered the planes' users reached 40 per cent of the initial prices of the engines!

In 1980 the Saudis were 'persuaded' with offers even they could not refuse. They chose the Pratt JT9 over the Rolls Royce RB 211. Rolls accused their competitors of 'buying business'.

They claimed that Pratt offered cheap spares, training, free maintenance, tooling, free rebuilds on existing engines, free access to worldwide maintenance bases for their aircraft and even special finance.

And all this to the richest country in the world. Naturally, the Saudis took the deal – if people want to give them millions of dollars for nothing it sure beats giving them oil for it!

challenge to everything in your package (and possibly some additional issues you had not even thought were negotiable).

Once the price walls tumble down, so does almost everything else! Hence, it is important to hold to your price if you possibly can.

How do you do that?

By repeating 'no'? By doing without a deal? By having a policy of fixed prices only?

Not at all!

The idea of fixed prices implies fixed packages, and the reason why there is no such thing as a fixed price is because:

There is no such thing as a fixed package.

Everything that is negotiable has different attributes for different people. Take a chair, for instance:

I see a means to comfortable seating.
Somebody else sees an item for decoration.
A third person an antique.

A fourth person a stage prop.
A fifth person an investment.
A sixth person some firewood.
A seventh person a pile of old junk.
An eighth person a wedding present.
A ninth person a hole in his bank balance.
A tenth person part of her image.
And so on.

The attributes that people see in the same object are as endless as there are people. And as each person's perception of the object is subject to change, the possible attributes of the object for any one person increase through time; today's fashionable furniture is tomorrow's junk (and among the 'trendies' the exact reverse!) etc.

Also, a black chair may not qualify as a wedding present but might as a stage prop. Offer to sell her a white chair and the uses may reverse – and may change again when the price is quoted!

People do not purchase objects – they purchase the *services* that the objects provide for them, and these may be tangible or intangible, specific to the person, or general to everybody. Sometimes we put up with an object that meets our needs imperfectly and other times we insist on a most exacting match of our needs with the services derived from the objects on offer.

This is the foundation of all good selling and buying practice: find out the needs of the customer and fit what you have for sale to those needs and you'll get their money: find which object provides the services you need and you'll not regret your purchases.

In principle, the price of any particular object, when all else is said and done, is what somebody is prepared to pay for it: you match the service provided by the object to the price they want for it.

If they press you on your price that may be because they don't think the services they derive from the object are worth what you are asking for them. Alternatively, if they believe the services they obtain from the object are very valuable to *themselves*, they may be willing to pay a great deal more for it than they tell you.

On the other hand, there are other reasons why they may not agree to your price:

1　Most commonly, the other person may just be testing how firm you are on price.
2　He may just be mean – some people abhor spending money.
3　He may genuinely believe you are ripping him off.

4 He may not be able to afford it (the cupboard really is bare).
5 He may like to bargain for its own sake (good man!).
6 He may want to use your price concessions against your rivals – (a 'Dutch Auction').
7 He may be using price as a camouflage to back out of the deal.

Now you are not likely to know beforehand which of these is behind the particular price challenge you face in your negotiation – yet another dilemma for you as a negotiator!

The first thing to do when you hear a price challenge – as in other critical moments in negotiation – is ask: 'why?'

You don't naively need to accept his answers but they are a better start to handling the challenge than to assume that, because he tells you your price is too high (or too low for that matter), this is necessarily *the* barrier to the deal and therefore you must cut your price to get the deal.

Cutting your price because of a price challenge could be the worst thing you can do. Looking at the reasons for his challenge we can see that a simple price change is not your best move in any of them – this was Helmut's real mistake in South Africa.

If they are testing your resolve with a price challenge, it does not make a lot of sense to show them that you have none. They will only press for more, until they are convinced that you have nothing left to give – and as they still may not agree to a deal, you ought to stick where you start.

Meanness is a very difficult attitude to cope with and it flourishes in small pockets all over the world. It is not confined to any class, race, political system, religion or nation, nor is any grouping you care to name entirely free from it.

It is most often prevalent among people who know the price of things but not their value, and because reducing the price of something does not increase its value there is little point in you doing so.

As for the person who believes that you are ripping him off there is no surer way to confirm his suspicions than to reduce your prices! The person who cannot afford the deal you are offering may be open to another deal and it is up to you to find it (of which more in a moment) and the person who likes to bargain for its own sake is not really a big problem – indeed in a sense he is the easiest of the lot to deal with.

When you suspect that the other person is using you as fodder for a

The kamikaze aeroplane business: II

Aeroplane manufacturers have also got in on the kamikaze competition act.

Boeing snatched the Trans World Airlines contract from Airbus Industrie by making a fuel-economy commitment which they are unlikely to meet and, if they do, TWA still gain.

They promised TWA that for every percentage point which their 767s' fuel consumption exceeds their design claims, they will pay to TWA $20,000 a year for each of the ten 767s they will be flying.

If they fail to meet their fuel targets even by three per cent it will cost Boeing $15 million over 20 years. Thus, effectively, TWA would be getting the ten planes at a discount of $1.5 million each.

Also, Boeing effectively waived the progress payments that TWA would normally have been expected to contribute up to the delivery of the first aircraft in 1985 — Boeing is 'lending' TWA money which they hand back as progress payments!

Who says you can't put a deal together?

'Dutch auction' with the competition, you will not frustrate this tactic by cutting your prices – as that is exactly what he wants you to do it must be self-defeating – so don't.

The same is true of the person who is using a price challenge in order to get out of the deal. Nothing you do on price – except in a totally humiliating fashion – will keep someone in a deal who doesn't want to be there.

It's more likely to give him yet another excuse for not agreeing – 'If your boat is now reduced by 20 per cent in price, you were obviously ripping me off in the first place.'

How then do we handle a price challenge?

Few deals are decided solely on price. There is almost always more than one variable in any deal and where there is a variable there is a possibility of a negotiation. Therefore a price challenge is a challenge to only one of the, possibly numerous, variables available for negotiation.

We know already that to give way to a price challenge is to invite a challenge to the other variables. So consider the consequence of using the other variables to protect your price. If they want to change the price variable in the package, it is legitimate for you to adjust the other variables. Indeed, make it a condition for the change in one variable, that some others must be changed in compensation.

You can sum up this strategy by:

For this package there is one price, for another price there is another package.

I can illustrate this strategy with the subsequent career of Helmut Weber. After his debacle in South Africa, he decided to resign and start again, not with the competition, as the marketing manager had sarcastically suggested, but in an entirely different line altogether.

The spur to Helmut's redemption was the German passion for chocolate. The Germans are very competitive with the Austrians and the Swiss in the production of chocolate delicacies, for chocolate is to the Germans what cheese is to the French – there are hundreds of different types, many eaten only in the locality where they are made.

Chocolate is made from cocoa and cocoa comes from West Africa. The cocoa beans grow in Ghana, Nigeria, Togo, Ivory Coast, and Cameroun, and are shipped in 130 lb sacks to Europe. There they are processed and sold to chocolate manufacturers who add their own ingredients (mainly milk and sugar, but also nuts, raisins, cream and jam) from their own recipes.

Some of the chocolate is made into popular products for the supermarkets and some into local varieties. The packaging and marketing of these brands is a highly diversified business, with some large companies and lots of smaller ones.

It was into this business, as a cocoa broker, that Helmut threw himself, originally in a quest for his father's approval but latterly because he enjoyed it. This was how he discovered packaging. Not the stuff they wrap the chocolate in, but the way that negotiators go about getting a deal.

Chocolate, like pumps and most other products, is no stranger to prices.

In a market economy, price is a great storer of information; it is an efficient indicator of a product's standing in relation to supply and demand.

But man does not buy chocolate only on price, any more than he lives by bread alone. The cocoa processors who buy tons of beans a month are not just concerned with price. If they were they might very well end up producing an inferior product, and if they won a reputation for inferior – or even variable – quality, their sales would plummet.

Thus, the quality of the beans, and the consistency of that quality, is an important variable in the deals they negotiate with the shippers of beans from West Africa.

Quality is a variable in a technical sense, for not all variations in quality are critical to the production of highly consistent output in each type of chocolate. It depends on the type of chocolate a particular batch of processed cocoa is to be used for.

Helmut had to learn in buying processed cocoa to get the right trade-off between price and the minimum quality required in each process. For instance, cooking chocolate can take a lower-quality cocoa than confectionery chocolate. Top-class table chocolate – the kind you would give your loved one – requires top-class cocoa.

With some processors the quality control is so reliable that you need fewer sample inspections and risk fewer rejects than with those others whose quality is a bit of a lottery and whose output generates substantial wastage during the making of choclate.

The quality variable throws up several other related variables: inspection criteria, rejection policy, credit or replacement for rejected batches, payment on delivery or after processing to take account of acceptance levels and so on.

These variables had to be considered when prices were negotiated. If the processor pushed up his prices, Helmut learned to adjust the package he proposed to take account of the risks his company ran and the appropriate compensatory measures it required either before or after delivery and payment.

It could be that for a particular reason he would agree to a higher price per ton of cocoa if the supplier agreed to accept later payment and a higher inspection standard, and sometimes he did the reverse.

He certainly did not just change his price upwards or downwards because the processor told him how 'fearsome' the competition was or how lousy his prices were.

This does not mean to say that Helmut was not interested in the competition. On the country, he made it his first objective to learn about the business he was in and how the industry was organized. He knew about the real competition and how it was faring because he studied it and consequently he was never hustled by processors or manufacturers and their fairy stories.

In this respect, he lost count of the times buyers told him ('in confidence', of course) about a Dutch, Danish, or Swiss company – the nationality varied each time (he even heard it once about a Japanese supplier) – that 'was given instructions to beat whatever price Weber's company offered'!

Helmut took an interest in processors out of a healthy concern for ensuring continuity of supply for his customers, the chocolate manufacturers. If a processor was totally dependent on cocoa supplies from a single West African country, then this was of significance to Helmut, particulary if political conditions in that country were unstable.

The prospect (highly probable) or actual occurrence (frequent) of a military coup influenced the way he approached a supply contract both as a buyer and as a seller. With those processors who were not dependent on a single source for their cocoa but had several sources, he had to face the question of the compatibility of their cocoa from the different countries that they got it from.

Blending compatibilities could be reflected in the price he was prepared to pay per ton or the credit terms he sought and the prices he could get from the manufacturers – who insisted, like art dealers, on knowing the provenance of the processed cocoa he supplied to them.

Sometimes, in periods of tension or calamity among the West African growers, the payment terms switched one way or another between Helmut and his suppliers. If supplies were unsettled the trade-off could be to shorten the payment period; if they were fine, the payment period might lengthen, or it might stay the same and the price per ton change.

There was always the possibility of longer-term contracts for at least some amount of the output of certain suppliers. Helmut had to make a judgment about whether to get locked in at too high a price or risk being locked out if he didn't offer enough.

For each negotiation there was a different set of tradables to consider and the skill that Helmut developed was that of packaging the best deal he could out of the deals that were available.

The supplies that were earmarked for Helmut's company – and they could be counted in anything from thousands to tens of tons – could be stored with the processor (at whose expense?) or with Helmut (at whose risk?). It could be delivered in large silos (who paid for them?) or in containers (who owned the containers?).

The negotiators had to decide who was responsible for the

processed cocoa when it was in their stores and what access to what minimum amounts was possible if supplies were needed urgently. These are only some of the many tradables that Helmut learned about in his new job as a negotiator with the cocoa processors, and this represents only *half* of his job.

He only bought processed cocoa in order to sell it to chocolate manufacturers, and while dealing with one side of a transaction – buying in – he could very well be dealing simultaneously with the other side – selling out. On occasion, Helmut also dealt direct with the retail outlets, though on a small scale (he has ambitions to produce his own chocolate brand – Weber's 'African Delight').

In selling, the same tradables emerge. Manufacturers require consistency and continuity of supply. They may want to vary the supply over a production cycle – they need more chocolate for Christmas than they do for the height of the summer, for instance.

The issues that have to be negotiated as part of a package include: who holds the stocks surplus to current requirements and who pays what for the cocoa, and when, between contract and delivery?

To what extent can a price variation be traded-off in the returns of inferior or damaged supplies? How much of a promotional budget would a manufacturer contribute for its branded products and what effect does this have on the order levels of the hypermarket chains?

And so it could go on. The tradables that emerge from a simple product like chocolate are clearly very numerous.

In the real world, whatever it is that you sell or buy, there may be many tradables that you have not considered recently, or at all. It's time you did, because it is in the tradables that you will find the defence of your prices.

At my Negotiating Clinics we require participants to identify all the negotiable tradables in their business. The results sometimes surprise even the old hands.

Routine approaches to their business can exclude glaringly obvious tradables from consideration which must diminish their negotiating ability to package and repackage deals. Constant reviewing of the negotiable tradables is a necessity for successful negotiating.

In one seminar, for a multinational company, the various national divisions produced from their syndicate sessions lists of tradables that directly contradicted each other!

It was an illuminating experience to watch the syndicates explain why they had grouped some tradables as 'non-negotiable' while

Tradables and constants

What are the *negotiable tradables* in your business?

It is well worth spending some time writing down a list of the tradables you negotiate in your particular line of work. Then add to the list all the things you could negotiate over at present, but, for one reason or another, you don't.

The list should be a long one. If it isn't it may be you are missing opportunities for negotiating better deals. If you get stuck with a small list, start from the other end and write down all the *non-negotiable constants* in your business – the things you do not negotiate over.

Ask yourself why you don't negotiate over each constant?

Who said you shouldn't? What good reason is stopping you? Is it a matter of habit, tradition, custom? Is it an ethical matter?

As you ask these questions you will gradually find reasons to move those constants into the variables column.

The boss of one of Britain's largest life assurance societies said in 1981: 'You need a big crunch every now and again. Out of that you get a lot of ideas. In a big organization it is amazing how many sacred cows are created – and it is hard to slaughter them.' (*Financial Times*, 6 October 1981.)

How many sacred constants have you got around your organization and its activities in the competitive markets you deal in?

their overseas colleagues considered them 'negotiable'. This was all the more interesting when the Canadians disclosed they were negotiating on some issues that the English traditionally held out on. The English were not slow to wake up to the real explanation as to why they had lost business over the years in the United States and Mexico – their clients had switched to the Canadian branch of the company instead!

Once we stop seeing price as *the* issue in a negotiation we can really put some good deals together; deals that are good for us and good for them. All the tradables in and around the deal can be used to improve the deal and protect our interests.

How?

By concentrating our attention not on the huffing and puffing about price but on the total *shape* of what is proposed.

Consider some illustrative tradables that are present in most deals. They were present for Helmut Weber in South Africa but he didn't see them, and they are present for you in your negotiations if you look for them. Take *money* as a tradable. Can we adjust:

The way we pay?
What currency we pay in?
The credit terms – 30, 90, 120 days?
The discount for early payment?
In advance or in arrears?
The intervals between progress payments?
With revocable or irrevocable lines of credit?
To a third (neutral) party?
Cash on delivery or after acceptance? (Whose inspection?)
Consequences of default?

Or consider *delivery* as a tradable.

In what quantities can it be delivered?
Any advantages for smaller packs/larger loads?
Who pays for delivery and insurance?
If in a container, who pays for damage?
What packaging is used? Possibility of own branding?
How wind-, water- or rodent-proof the storage materials?
Who stores surplus requirements?
Who pays for storage?
What minimum loads can be got quickly?
What and whose inspection of deliveries is acceptable?

What about the *specifications* as tradables?

What are the critical specifications?
Can they be varied without risking quality?
Do we need 95 per cent reliability?
Is a doubled working life worth a trebled price?
How much do we save by marginally reducing a spec?
Should the extras be standard or some standards extras?
Which features are attractive and which actually used?

What about the *relationship* as a tradable?

Is it worth anything to be a sole supplier?
Is it better to spread the business among several suppliers?

How long should a sole-supplier contract run for?
How long should any contract run for and what is duration worth off the basic price?
If we deal with them solely how much advertising and promotion will we get them to pay for?
What about joint promotion?

Is there anything tradable in the *risks*?

Who pays for insurance?
How much insurance should we go for?
Who pays for replacements and how are they credited?
Who defines *force majeure*?
What is a warranty worth?
Who guarantees quality and inspection?
What about performance measures and third-party liability?
Share of insurance payouts? What expenses are covered?
Whose liability for patent breaches, copyrights, etc.?
Whose liability for local taxes, sundry debts?

Is *time* tradable?

When is delivery to commence?
Over what period is the contract to run?
How late is late delivery?
When do we get access to the product?
When will proportions of the project be released?
In what order will things happen?
The timing of progress reports?
The closing dates for inspection?
How flexible is the completion date?

If you handle price challenges this way, the people across the table will learn from your behaviour that if they want to change the price, they will have to face the inescapable consequence that you will vary the package.

For you, everything must be negotiable!

There are no circumstances in which you agree to back off a price unilaterally. This is negotiation, not a Dutch auction in which you keep shouting out lower and lower prices until somebody agrees to take the deal.

If the person does not like your price for the package you propose, then you are happy to quote him another price for another

215

How to win price wars

Faced with stiff competition many negotiators turn first to price cuts as the road to salvation – it is in fact the road to ruin.

Every negotiator must eradicate the view that price cuts win business; they are often the first resort when they should be the last.

If the competition is tough it is the time to wage a relentless war on COSTS. All costs must be pruned to the bone. Inefficient plants should be closed or re-organized; all deadwood eliminated; sentimental symbols scrapped; workforces slimmed down and all expenditure that is not connected with the productivity of the assets postponed (in some cases for good).

As costs come down, profitability goes up. With higher profits the beleaguered firm has an alternative to a kamikaze price war.

The beer business is extremely competitive and it is getting tougher as younger people turn to other beverages.

In some cases, beer companies, having rammed down their prices to grab market share, seize a temporary advantage and provoke price crumblers to panic.

The firms that will survive resist joining in a price war. They go first for profits and use them to increase their marketing impact.

Distributors and retail outlets are trained in grass-roots financial management so that they can see for themselves the margins on each of their lines, the turnover per asset they use, the sale per customer, and even the profit per use of shelf space in their operations.

Everybody becomes cost- not price-conscious. Marketing support is demanded by the people selling the beer to the drinkers because they want to sell more of the most profitable beer brands. Their attitude changes from demoralized people looking for price cuts to people 'struggling to be humble' because they are proud of their profitable products.

package. It may be that the new package you propose meets his needs closer than the original one. In moving to alter the *shape* of one or more of the components of the deal, you could be moving closer to what he really wants.

His price challenge is a signal that there is something wrong with the proposed package. That is how you must interpret it. If the other person insists that he is flying a different signal, then, like Nelson at the Battle of Copenhagen, put the telescope to your blind eye and tell him you 'really don't see the signal'!

The rule that Helmut Weber had to learn ought now to be abundantly clear:

> *Don't change the price,*
> *change the package!*

Answers to self-assessment test 17

1　*(a)* A strong move if you are confident they need you badly enough to make an offer and you are not too fussy whether you get the job or not, but as you don't tell them what would be acceptable they don't know how far to pitch it. You would need to explain why you accept their rate from your present employers but reject it from them.

(b) A definite move but vulnerable to a 'split the difference' response.

(c) No! This indicates weakness in your position and will likely get a negative response. Better that they reply to *(b)* with a compromise than you offer one yourself.

2　*(a)* A negative move. Does not give them anywhere to go but to back off their price expectations or deadlock.

(b) Implies that a price cut is possible. He should go in tough on you and get a compromise.

(c) Good. You need more information about his reasons for objecting to the price.

(d) Weak. Don't offer price cuts just because they ask for them!

3　*(a)* One way to break a deadlock at no real cost to you unless your charges for these items are padded.

(b) A strong defence of your prices is essential if you are to have credibility in the negotiations. A good lead into *(a)*.

(c) That only teaches them to make price objections.

Self-assessment test 18

1 You are in the market to buy an executive jet for a small
   courier air service you intend to set up out of your hard-
   earned savings and small borrowings from a local bank. The
   company selling new and used aircraft of the type you want
   is located on the 72nd floor of the World Trade Center in
   Manhattan. The President's office is as big as an aircraft
   hanger and the carpet pile is up to your ankles. The
   elegantly dressed man behind the 20-foot mahogany desk
   sits in front of a Picasso original. There is a Henry Moore
   sculpture in one corner of the room and a fountain spraying
   quietly in the other. Do you:
   (a) Think you will get a bargain price?
   (b) Wait and see?
   (c) Believe you are likely to be pushed to the top price?

2 The man who has come to see you wears a beautifully cut
   Saville Row suit, a gold Rolex watch and Gucci shoes. If
   asked to rate his status, would you rate him:
   (a) Low?
   (b) High?
   (c) Indeterminate?

3 When he leaves, how would you rate him (high or low) if
   he:
   (a) Waited at the curbside for a cab?
   (b) Had your secretary call him one?
   (c) Got into a compact car he had parked round the corner?
   (d) Got into a chauffer-driven Rolls Royce?

Chapter Eighteen

All that glitters isn't gold
or how to resist intimidation

Have you wondered why some corporations go in for highly expensive waste space?

They locate themselves in glass palaces, downtown in the most exclusive real estate they can find, or out in the wide open spaces of the far-flung suburbs, surrounded by acres of pretty flowers and healthy trees.

The entrance to the glass palace is like a scene out of Cleopatra: vast columns rise towards the heavens, marbled staircases wind majestically upwards, fountains and waterfalls abound everywhere and there is solid dark wooden furniture dotted about like little fortresses on a plain. The only thing missing is a trumpet voluntary announcing arrivals.

Batches of people cluster at the mouths of high-speed lifts and the doors swish open and shut disgorging and swallowing their fare effortlessly.

Behind the front desks sit immaculately groomed receptionists chosen presumably for their perfect smiles and expensive teeth, and an ability to suffer boredom gladly.

Nearby, the security guards hover, looking busy but doing nothing much. Each is turned out like a Marine drill sergeant who has had nothing else to do since his last war. When a phone rings, it does so quietly and is answered with manic precision before the second bell.

When you arrive for an appointment you are treated as if you are in danger of becoming a lost parcel. And just in case you have an identity crisis while on the premises they give you a pass to tell you, and anybody else who asks, who you are.

If they are really pulling out the stops, they take a quick photograph, seal it with plastic and pin it on your chest so that you look (and feel) like an immigrant at Ellis Island in the 1920s. When you go anywhere you are escorted politely by a junior clerk (or a spare gorilla out of security).

Lifts, corridors and waiting rooms are furnished to give you the impression that you are passing by Big Events that are taking place behind the closed doors that hum with purposeful activity. The way the staff move about is proof that *something* is happening.

When you get to the person you have come to see you enter an office that is as large as an aircraft hangar and has carpet pile up to your ankles. It also has the odd Picasso or Van Gogh on the wall and some tasteful sculpture in the corner.

This is the moment when you make your most important mistake.

You foolishly believe that all the trappings of corporate wealth you have seen are for the benefit of the people working for the outfit and are their reward for loyal service to the corporation and an exhibition of their successful endeavours.

Nothing could be further from the truth!

It has nothing to do with the comfort of, or praise for, the employees, loyal or otherwise. If they benefit from working in such munificent surroundings, that is an unavoidable and minor consequence of the main objective of all the splendour.

Everything you have seen has been put there specially for *you*.

It is your perceptions that they are working on.

Everything you see from the moment you step through the front door is pure theatre. You are being got at by props, all carefully designed to create the right impression in the minds of visitors.

The purpose of the design?

Simply to *intimidate* you!

And unless you are very strong-minded, or prepared, you don't stand a chance.

Why?

Because intimidation of this kind works.

The building oozes success. Power creeps out of its every pore. You are seduced into asking yourself: 'If they can spend that kind of money on this kind of foyer, what must they be making out there in the harsh competitive world that I am struggling in?' leading to: 'Boy, do I want to do business with this company!'

One thing you feel for sure. They are making a lot more money than you are. How do you know that? Because you are on your way to see them; they are not on their way to see you. And if they did visit you, how would your entrance and foyer compare?

A wee orange box of an office, an old desk and chair and last month's rent overdue? You either have a bigger glass palace than they have – in which case you wouldn't even notice the splendours of theirs – or you haven't – in which case you do.

Big and little cons

Practically every known con starts with the use of props. That is why the use of props in business runs a thin line between probity and fraud.

Just because a person is living in a penthouse suite it does not mean that he is productively using the funds he collects each week from gullible investors.

He may just be using each week's 'contributions' to pay the bills for his exotic lifestyle so that he can con new contributors to pay his bills next week.

More than one real-life bankrupt flies the Atlantic by Concorde – it makes creditors less anxious about their money if they associate the person with the trappings of wealth and power. If the bankrupt switched to economy stand-by tickets to save cash, the creditors would begin to worry about their money.

There is a constant stream of programmes on TV about dubious business dealers who drive Rolls Royces and Mercedes and live in small palaces. Hence, *caveat emptor*.

Also, there are several religious cons that involve substantial transfers of wealth to high-living 'saints' – the more material wealth they display the more their followers are convinced that they are divine.

The source of the problem is a logical distortion: the successful have high living standards and conspicuous evidence of wealth (yachts, helicopters, country houses, etc.) hence – so the 'logic' runs – people with high living standards are successful. Almost all cons rely on that sort of 'logic' in the minds of the marks (victim).

If you are intimidated by the other (honest) person's props you are a victim of a mild con. If this results in you settling for less you might as well be in a bunco booth!

If you notice it, you're half way to being conned.

It'll get to you and when it does it will influence your attitude to the way you go about doing business with them.

You'd better believe that it will.

It's your impression of their strength that they're working on.

Why?

Because through intimidation they subtly get you to undersell yourself. In its extreme form this kind of intimidation can turn you into a cowering cheapie.

Once you've been through the intimidating treatment and are in the presence of the Very Important Person who has granted you some of his precious time, there is no doubt that you are likely to be grateful for whatever he feels you are worthy of.

And that is before he has even begun his 'pitch' (it doesn't matter whether he is buying or selling). Covert intimidation is the least-talked-about aspect of the negotiating relationship.

Screeds have been written on overt and actual intimidation through the use of threats and so on. Yet covert intimidation is probably more prevalent and is certainly more efficient in that the person who is intimidated in this way is less likely to realize it and, not realizing it, is less likely to resent it.

If someone bullies you to take a lower price, you resent their exploitative behaviour – especially if you might have to take the deal as well. But if they psych your perceptions through covert intimidation you cannot resent them for what you do to yourself, can you?

Some sales training programmes prepare the participants for some forms of intimidation by buyers, but not for others. They cover those aspects of buyer behaviour that are designed to intimidate the luckless seller who is unprepared for them.

The tactics used by such unscrupulous buyers are now well-known in the folklore of the downtrodden salesman. Ask anybody who has been out selling in the real world for his atrocity stories of how buyers can behave, and he or she is bound to include one or more of the following:

You will be kept waiting outside his office, or the appointment will be postponed, rescheduled or clash with another he has with a far-more-important person than you.

When you do get in to see him he directs you to a seat that is smaller than his.

It's also lower down – and probably wobbly as well.

Also you are facing a brightly lit lamp or the sunny window.

On being hustled

A young manager decided to invest his savings in land which he saw advertised in a New York paper. He visited the site where the broker assured him of the stiff competition for the lots, recently zoned by the State for housing development. He was not persuaded by this but was marginally interested in the proposition.

However, as he was talking over the deal another man entered the room and interrupted their conversation, asking to buy some of the lots (including the ones that he was interested in) for a house-building programme. The broker told the man, who apparently was a local builder, that he would have to wait a moment.

The builder replied that he was ready to place an order for the unsold lots there and then and he ought not to be kept waiting as he had the bank behind the finance.

The young manager hearing this realized that if building commenced on the site, any lots he owned would realize an early profit to him on his investment (and therefore he could afford to buy more than he had originally intended).

He told the builder that he had first option on the lots in question and that he was about to write a cheque for a signed title agreement. This he did.

The builder was not too happy about this and demanded to have the right to purchase the surrounding lots. The young investor left the two men in the office deep in argument about the remaining lots and their price.

He felt very pleased with himself, and this feeling persisted for about a year until it became obvious that no houses were being built in the area he had purchased. Had the builder changed his mind? Or was he the victim of a set-up by the broker and a so-called 'builder' to hustle him into believing there was competition for the unsold lots? (What do you think? No prizes for my guess!)

It took him five years to get out from under with a capital loss of three-fifths of his savings.

The door will be left open and you can hear people moving about outside and the secretaries might walk in and out looking for papers.

The room is too cold, too hot, too stuffy, too open or too draughty (and guess who is sitting in one?).

The phone rings incessantly as you make your pitch.

There are other interruptions, such as staff knocking loudly on the door and entering to discuss business or social affairs with the buyer.

The buyer tells the secterary to hold his calls for a couple of *minutes* – indicating your time is nearly up – and he'll keep looking at his watch.

Other times he meets you in the foyer or waiting room with other people milling about and proceeds to conduct a conversation.

He gets your name wrong and that of your company (repeatedly).

He looks bored – painfully bored – and stares as if he is not listening.

If you hand him some literature he throws it casually to one side or doesn't study it at all (though he will certainly spot a blemish on it if it is torn, stained or written on).

He will avoid touching any samples of your product and only give them a cursory glance – he certainly will not show any interest in seeing them operate.

He will make disparaging remarks about you, your appearance, your weight, your hair loss, your teeth ('do you smoke a lot?'), your accent, your ethnic origins, your background.

He'll do the same about your product, your company, your deliveries, your quality control, your invoicing, your previous promises, your superiors, your employees, your track record and your chances this time.

He'll do the opposite about the competition, using their first names and personal details of their background ('did you know that Henry, their marketing boss, won a gold in the Olympics? Of course, he's a fit, good-looking man for his age, and never lets me down.').

He'll also praise their products, their efficiency, their accounts, their integrity and their prices.

He'll ask you questions aimed at identifyng your social inferiority – which clubs you belong to, what car you drive, have you been to the Seychelles, do you know the president of the steel company in your home town, what do you think of the Hotel Al Khozama in Riyadh, how are your stocks going and which way will Dow Jones go, what do you think of the Archbishop of Canterbury's library, have you seen the price of gold this morning, who is your broker, your banker, your tailor? And so on.

He'll stall over decisions, announce that he doesn't make them and the person who does is not available.

Next time you go there you have to begin with somebody else; if he has higher status than the first person, you are in for a tough fight over the deadlocked issues and if he is of lower status it's going to be even tougher!

He'll require everything in writing and all your prices have to be your 'best prices'.

The purpose of these tactics is to intimidate you into a submissive attitude and every seller has to learn how to cope with buyers who use these methods.

Fortunately, some sales training programmes show you how (and buyers' programmes teach them the counters!) and you'll pick up some ideas from Thank God it's Friday seminars with your colleagues.

But these well-known stress tactics of buyers are small beer compared to the self-induced intimidation that comes from downgrading yourself because of the way the other person's corporation spends its money on props.

These latter tactics are far more intimidating because they operate in your mind as 'own goals'. You see, deep down you really want to acquire the trappings displayed in the corporate headquarters yourself and when you see them around somebody else you assume that the other person has got them already because he is better than you, or has more power than you, or knows better what he is about.

I was given a very clear example of the power of subtle intimidation through the use of apparently expensive props when I was involved in negotiating the sale of a hotel in the Highlands of Scotland – just across the water from the Isle of Skye – in 1976.

The owner had offered me a commission if I could close a sale with the third set of buyers he had tried to negotiate with, the other two falling out after meeting him.

I had driven up overnight from Edinburgh to be ready for the arrival of the prospective buyers the next morning, and five minutes before the meeting was due to begin the owner began to get anxious as the other side had not yet arrived.

We could see about four miles down the road towards Fort William and no cars were coming our way. Was it a no-show? I too was a trifle anxious as I was to get my commission for arranging a sale and without the other party there would be no negotiation.

At one minute to twelve, we heard a loud noise approaching and sure enough in swooped a helicopter right into the hotel's car park and set itself down a few yards from my Mercedes – which the owner had been impressed with on my (quieter) arrival the night before.

There is no doubt that it was a magnificent entrance for the buyers to make. They totally upstaged me in the eyes of my client and in doing so weakened his resolve (but not mine!) on price.

I am certain that this knocked about £10,000 off his aspirations for what he though he could get for his hotel. He literally fell over the buyers for the two hours or so they were there and clearly no longer regarded them as the 'mugs' he thought they were going to be in our conversation over dinner the previous night.

The helicopter had intimidated him.

He believed he was dealing with *real* money when he talked to those guys and was more than grateful when they treated him and his business with some respect. This made him feel, almost, like the kind of guy who one day would ride around in a helicopter!

If he had thought about it (as I did on my way home by car) the cost of hiring a helicopter for a round trip from Glasgow via Fort William was about £800. If that knocked £10,000 off the top price the owner was looking for for the hotel, it had to be a good investment.

And it was. The buyers got extended credit on part of the sale price, a generous assessment of stock at valuation and were required to pay a very low deposit on contract.

Also, I had difficulty in getting my full fee out of him!

I had pressed hard in the negotiations for a price about £3,000 more than the owner finally settled at and also for stiffer terms. He instructed me to accept the lower price and the softer terms and even suggested *publicly* that I was threatening *his* deal!

When the agreement was signed and it came to my turn to get paid, he had the impudence to suggest I should take a smaller fee as I had not got as much for the hotel as he had anticipated.

Fortunately, I had a signed letter from him confirming my fee and I waved it at him. Also, in view of his attitude, I insisted on cash or kind and told him I was quite prepared to load the Mercedes with Scotch if he didn't have the 'readies' to hand.

We settled on a bit of each, with the whisky valued on the same terms he had given to the new owners.

Intimidation through props is not easy to combat.

In business you make status judgments all the time. Practically everybody – with the possible exception of bankers who know what real money is, who has it and what it should or should not be doing –equates the trappings of status with the possession of power.

That is why there are so many burned fingers in the negotiating business and why so many people are conned every day by acting upon what they think they are seeing.

Every hustler knows about intimidation. They know that you judge the quality of someone by the possessions they have around them. If you notice and are impressed by ostentatiously visible possessions, you are almost hooked and the rest is easier than it would be if you weren't.

What will intimidate the average negotiator? Any or all of the following:

A prestige headquarters exquisitely furnished.

A list of international offices.

An executive jet, or better still, two, or a helicopter.

A yacht cruising in the Mediterranean or Caribbean.

Rolls Royces and other big gas guzzlers.

Minions running around at the whim and behest of the boss.

Expensive clothes, accessories and gizmo gadgets.

An obvious ability to get other people to fawn.

A facility to talk in large numbers and work out percentages of awkward sums fast.

Association with 'important names' in society.

Evidence of cash resources, credit cards, and lines of credit.

The appearance of being unrushed, and unworried.

Evidence of constant international travel.

A much larger business than the negotiator's.

Some evidence of 'kindness' and 'respect' from the 'big guy' with a reputation of ruthlessness towards others.

All of these are pure intimidation. They are the business versions of see-through blouses and tight jeans (indeed, it is not unknown for ostensibly non-business intimidation to be used to facilitate a negotiated outcome).

The antidotes?

Recognize the signs of intimidation for what they are – don't psyche yourself into becoming a victim of your own fantasies. All that glitters is not gold and the apparent access to props is no proof of the actual power relationship between you and the big guy in the corporate suite.

If you are not intimidated you have nothing to worry about, no matter who you are dealing with. In a practical sense you can steel yourself against their intimidation by avoiding any overt references to their props. You give the game away if you make it obvious how impressed you are with the props for this automatically acts to strengthen the other person if he basks in your approval and you gratify his self-esteem.

Hence, do not exclaim how wonderful their building is or even make a remark about the view from his office (no matter how magnificent it is – that's why they pay for it).

If you are there to see a head guy, and you are kept waiting, always ask the receptionist to use the telephone to ring home, the office or your next appointment. That will change her attitude towards you (remember she is part of his team not yours) and when the boss hears what is delaying your admission it undercuts his tactics of keeping you waiting.

If the wait is likely to be a long one (he is delayed at an 'important' meeting, i.e. his lunch, a round of golf, or coffee and doughnuts with his girlfriend) make some more phone calls – think of the money it's saving you – and, if you really want to fight back, make a long-distance call by direct dial. Or better still ask to be connected to the fax room!

Whatever else you do, do not read the magazines they leave out for visitors in your predicament because that is your first step in the dance to their tune. I always bring a book to read in these circumstances and when he looks out of his door he sees me immersed in something from the Top Ten list (hardcover not paperback), but certainly not *House and Garden, Vogue,* or his company's *Annual Report*.

It doesn't always pay to be an MBA

A multinational shipping consortium faced a severe drop in earnings caused by a world trade recession. It decided to rationalize its operations and called on the various national components to submit survival plans.

The US end of the operation took the problem on board much in the manner of a Harvard Business School case study, i.e. a problem to be solved rather than a fight for national interests.

They set up a ten-man survival team, seven of them with MBAs, and produced a detailed survival report for the meeting. In presentation terms it was a well-produced document – stitch binding even! – and was supported by a slide projection programme.

The other members of the consortium were less than impressed with the hundreds of man-hours that had been used in producing the report and its obvious professionalism. They recommended that the US office be demanned by 15 per cent as they obviously had too little to do if they could produce such magnificent reports with their available staff.

One man I know fights back by going to sleep, he says it gets him into the right unintimidated mood. Another only talks business with clients, never anything personal. That way he can't be intimidated by the (often entirely phoney) international jet-set image his clients like to create for the impressionable. He finds no need to explain himself as a person or to account for his wordly adventures. He just sticks to the deal, the whole deal and nothing but the deal.

So should you.

Beware, however, of trying to out-intimidate the other person with your own props and phoney lines. Stick to the use of your skill in negotiating and leave the manipulative moves to others, because it is sufficient for you *not* to be intimidated by what they do. It is not necessary for you to work out how to intimidate them by what you do.

If you're good at your job, that is all the intimidation you require, for there is nothing so awe-inspiring as a richly-deserved reputation for being good at your business.

1 *(a)* You have not been intimidated by the props of power. You live in hope.

(b) The right approach to a deal. His props may hide an imminent financial disaster unless he can off-load some planes quickly.

(c) You've been intimidated and deserve to pay more.

2 *(a)* Surely a trifle perverse!

(b) You've been intimidated.

(c) Good. You do not judge status by props.

3 *(a)* Low (he should have ordered one).

(b) Low (a power prop is not status).

(c) High (absence of a prop means nothing).

(d) Low (intimidation!).

Self-assessment test 19

1 You manage a small engineering plant and one of your large customers owes you for three deliveries. You feel you are getting the 'run around' from his accounts department and another delivery of parts is due next week. Do you:
   (a) Tell his accounts department that you will hold back the next delivery unless they pay up?
   (b) Continue to demand payment for the overdue accounts?
   (c) Tell the user department that you will hold back delivery until the overdue amounts are paid?

2 A small supplier of valves has delivered a batch which failed your quality-control tests and you put them into your own workshop for corrective machining. Do you:
   (a) Demand a reduction in the invoice for your machining costs and warn them about future quality?
   (b) Deduct your costs from the invoice and pay the balance?
   (c) Pay the invoice but demand a guarantee on future quality?
   (d) Wait until you hear from them about their unpaid invoice?

3 The supplier demands payment in full. He argues that your machining costs are excessive and that allegedly rejected work should be returned for their inspection and replacement. Do you:
   (a) Reject his invoice again and insist on your reasonable costs being met?
   (b) Tell him that if he insists on full payment you will cease to do business with him in future?
   (c) Pay the invoice but demand a guarantee of future quality?

Chapter Nineteen

On being Russian-Fronted
or how to cope with threats

Consider young Lieutenant Wolfgang Mueller's predicament in Paris in 1943. He was dining with his girlfriend in a bistro just off the Boulevard St Germain, in the Rue De Bac, when his Colonel walked in and took a fancy to his companion.

He called Wolfgang over and ordered him to go for a walk, to which order Wolfgang protested. The Colonel told him: 'Either you do as I say, or I will have you sent to the Russian Front *tonight*.'

'Mein Gott,' said Wolfgang. 'The Russian Front! Anything but the Russian Front!'

And he went for a (long) walk.

Why?

Because Wolfgang believed that the Colonel fully intended to get his way or send him to the Russian Front, which, Wolfgang also believed, would be absolutely disastrous to his interests.

If you believe that the threatener fully intends to carry out his threat and has the capability to do so in such a way that you are damaged by the consequences, it is bound to influence your judgment about the appropriate courses of action for you to follow.

If this causes you to alter your previous intentions in any way, you have been 'Russian-Fronted'!

When was the last time you were Russian-Fronted?

You may remember your feelings of resentment at being forced by circumstances to accede to a threat. True, you get a choice, but the choice is between something so unpleasant that the alternative, unpleasant as it may be, is less unpleasant than the Russian Front.

What is the role of a threat in negotiation?

The evidence is overwhelming that threats, sanctions and their counters are familiar features of negotiating practice. They are used frequently in many negotiations – industrial relations, international conferences, commercial disputes, domestic altercations, and so on. Sometimes they are used as pressure tactics in the aftermath of a deadlock and other times they are a part of the negotiation itself.

Threats and sanctions can be used as a substitute for negotiation, such as in hijacking and kidnapping, though the more you can get the hijacker or kidnapper into a negotiating relationship, the more likely you are to resolve the issue without giving in.

To see the tactical use of threats, consider the case of a small components firm that had not received payment for the last three deliveries it had made to a large Brazilian engineering corporation. All three deliveries were on time and all of them were accepted by the customer's quality-control people.

Naturally, it had chased the various departments concerned for its money and had been fobbed off by various managers, including the accounts department, each time.

The managers of the small firm were of the opinion that they were getting the proverbial 'run around' from the corporation's employees who gave no explanation for why payment was delayed – only references to 'it's in the system'. The failure to pay was causing a serious cash-flow problem and they did not have the resources to sustain themselves beyond a few weeks.

The next delivery of components was due in two weeks' time and a letter was sent to the head of the particular division that used the components, informing him that until the previous accounts were paid delivery would not take place.

The day before the delivery was due, a cheque for the outstanding amount arrived without explanation or apology.

The small firm had successfully *threatened* the larger firm.

However, threats can sour a good relationship, and make a bad relationship worse, by leading to outright warfare and mutually damaging behaviour.

Nobody likes to be threatened.

In fact the chances are very strong that a person who is threatened will resent it so much that they will make a counter-threat, *even if the implementation of that threat will lead to large mutual losses for both parties*. For once a threat/counter-threat cycle gets underway it is very difficult to reverse it into a reward/counter-reward cycle.

Threats beget threats, probably more often than they produce compliance.

A North American aircraft corporation, for instance, received a batch of valves from a supplier which failed to pass its quality-control sampling test. Following procedure, every item in the batch was individually inspected and the failure rate reached 24 per cent.

The rejected valves were re-machined on site and the supplier

When arbitration is worse than robbery

The British warship builders, Yarrows, were nationalized in 1977 and for several years fought hard for what they considered to be a just compensation.

Yarrows valued their shipbuilding assets at £16 million and the British Government valued them at £6 million (at least that was the total compensation they offered).

Two other formerly independent companies contested the amounts of compensation they were awarded. However, one of the former yards settled with the Government – under protest – and a week later Yarrows followed suit.

They had been disappointed that the Conservative Government did not endorse their fight against the previous Labour Government's nationalization formula.

They were also advised that the only recourse open to them was to go to arbitration. If they did so, they were told there was no assurance that any award made would be any better than they had already, and there was also the risk that it might be worse.

Faced with that as an alternative, Yarrows decided to settle for what they could get.

They had been Russian-Fronted.

was notified that its charges had to be adjusted downwards to take account of the (itemized) additional cost of labour and machine time to the aircraft company. They were also issued with a warning on quality standards.

The supplier refused to accept a reduction in their invoice and insisted on full payment. Allegedly defective materials should be returned to them for re-machining or replacement, they argued, and they did not accept the customer's machining costs which they considered were 'overpriced' compared to the costs they would incur in their own plant for the same work (this also told them something about the cost margins between their work and their client's and suggested that they were quoting for work too cheaply).

The aircraft corporation threatened the supplier that unless they agreed to cut their invoice by the stated amount and guaranteed quality for the future, their contract would be terminated forthwith and they would 'never earn another dollar from them again'.

After a delay of some weeks, the aircraft corporation received an invoice for the same amount by certified post and a demand for full payment within 30 days otherwise the supplier intended to go to court over the issue.

A week later, the supplier received a cheque and formal notice of their removal from the list of approved sub-contractors.

Neither side have done business with each other since.

The corporation *threatened* the supplier and the supplier *counter-threatened* the corporation. The corporation *implemented* its threat (not to do business with the supplier); the supplier didn't have to implement its threat (to take the corporation to court).

But who, if anybody, won?

The capacity for people to act 'irrationally', i.e. against what a disinterested onlooker would judge to be in their best interests, is not related to the level of intelligence of the parties.

Geniuses can engage in mutually destructive behaviour when they are in contest over something – who 'discovered' something first, for instance – so it is not surprising that 'mad' behaviour is commonplace among the rest of us.

When threats appear in a negotiation there is a higher chance of deadlock than when they don't.

There is a lesson here: avoid making threats in a negotiation. They are often unproductive for being made explicit.

As a professional negotiator I almost always raise at least one eyebrow (two if the timing of the threat is utterly ridiculous!) when a threat is clumsily articulated by the other person.

Why?

Because I regard it as a sign of impatience, of amateurism, even, that the other person thinks I need to be reminded of the power balance between us. Threats are put-me-downs, like drawing attention to my accent or my clothes.

If he thinks I need reminding of the power balance he is trying to intimidate me, or he has no respect for me as a negotiator. On the other hand, when a negotiation is in deadlock – or stalled due to a party's tactics of prevarication – it may be that only threats will get things moving satisfactorily. In this circumstance the threatener regards the risk of upsetting the overall relationship as less damaging than letting things slide indefinitely.

It all depends on context.

Some types of negotiation involve the frequent use of threats and counter-threats by both parties. International disputes between

Rum deals in the pool

A vice-president of a UK beer company was on a business tour of South America and was telexed by his head office to go to Jamaica on his way back and meet with the management team of one of the local rum exporters. His problem was that he did not have the work permit required for a business visit to Jamaica, nor on his tight schedule did he have time to acquire one.

Hence, he went into Norman Manley airport, Kingston, as a tourist. His problems began at immigration, because it was obvious from his previous itinerary and correspondence in his briefcase that he had been on a business trip. He claimed to the officials that he was in Jamaica for a few days' recreation before returning to London.

He booked into his hotel and phoned the rum exporter he wanted to meet. Later at the hotel he was interviewed by an immigration official who accused him of being in Jamaica for business purposes without a proper work permit. The official told him that he was being watched and that if he did any business at all he would be arrested, fined heavily and deported.

For two days a policeman shadowed him everywhere and forced him to spend the days and evenings like a tourist. The visit was clearly going to be a waste of time and money.

Before leaving, however, he met with the rum exporter and they did a deal right under the nose of the police.

The hotel has a patio bar, one side of which is built into the pool for swimmers to sit beside while in the water. While a policeman sat keeping a sleepy eye on him, he sat at the bar in the pool talking to the barman and a young woman who joined them.

The policeman assumed that he was merely idling his time talking to a barman and flirting with a guest. In fact he was negotiating with the head of the rum company who was behind the bar dressed as a barman. His secretary was the 'guest' undressed in a bikini in the pool.

Moral: initiative can beat any bureaucratic nonsense aimed at stopping people doing business.

countries and labour disputes with managements are two familiar contexts in which threats and sanctions (or implemented threats) are regular features of dialogue.

In business negotiations threats are also common – much more than is admitted – though they are often disguised or buried in subtle hints and the parties can miss them when they are made.

Anyway, properly prepared negotiators are aware of their vulnerability in a deal without the heavy-handed needing to remind them. The purpose of every threat is intimidation and there are two ways to intimidate people by using threats:

> You want the kids to cut the grass, so you threaten them with no television for a week.

This threat is a *compliance* threat that compels the kids to do it or else.

> Your spouse wants you to stay home and sober, so you are warned if you go out to expect the house to be deserted when you return.

This threat is a *deterrence* threat that deters you from doing it or else – you may do almost anything else instead.

To illustrate the difference between these types of threats more clearly consider the unhappy (for the hostages) experience of hijacking or politcal kidnapping.

An aircraft hijacker's demand for the release of terrorist prisoners (or similar) is a compliance threat; the passing of a law that requires a mandatory life sentence for hijacking is a deterrence threat.

How should we respond to threats? This is a very difficult question to generalize about. The question that must be uppermost in a negotiator's mind when contemplating making a threat is:

> What is the likelihood of the threat succeeding as an intimidator?

That depends, as with much else in negotiating, on the context of the threat. Specifically, it depends on two interrelated but nevertheless distinct factors:

1   The credibility of our intention to carry out the threat.
2   The capability of the implemented threat to damage the other party.

These have both objective and subjective aspects.

If the threat has high credibility and its capability to damage us is extensive, we are likely to accede to the Russian-Front tactic. There is no point mincing words about this: if they have you by the 'short and curlies' the prospect of resistance to their demands is purely academic.

But if they have you that way cold, why are they negotiating with you?

On the surface there is no reason, but if you examine it more carefully you will see that your position is not as weak as it looks.

In the unhappy circumstance of a hijacking or kidnapping, your only chance of getting out from under *without giving in* is to find something to negotiate about.

The hijacker holding a plane-load of people hostage needs material things from those he is threatening. He needs fuel to get away, he needs food, water and, perhaps, medicines, while arrangements to meet his demands are made (you can spin that out to increase his dependence on your goodwill which has the effect of lowering the pressure on you too), and he needs good communications otherwise his threats slacken by an inability to reinforce them.

Experience suggests that long negotiations between the authorities and the hijackers weakens the pressure from the latter and produces a stalemate, and the longer the stalemate the more the hijackers will reduce their demands (down to a final one – escape).

The hijackers can increase the pressure by carrying out their threats, or they can avoid the pressure of a stalemate by changing location. The first may provoke a violent ending to the hijack and the second weakens the pressure on the original target.

The delay in gaining their ends also increases the chances that they can be disarmed successfully by special anti-terrorist units. The hijackers get tired, jaded and mentally stressed as each hour passes. The assault troops are well-trained, rested and fresh and need only be brought into contact minutes before the assault.

In the case of a kidnapping, we are in an entirely different environment. You know where the hijacker and his hostages are – sitting out there on the tarmac with the world's TV filming every move – but you don't know where the kidnapper's lair is.

The kidnapper issues demands from a secret hideout, shuns physical or visual two-way contact with his target, relies on his own resources of food and water, and is able to cut out if things go wrong.

But the kidnapper's Achilles heel is the line of communication between him and the target for whatever it is that he is demanding. If it's money he wants, he has to get it delivered somewhere without being arrested in the process of collecting it. Negotiations on the means of delivery, the denominations of the currency, the dropping zone and the involvement of the authorities all take time.

The longer the time these negotiations take, the greater the chance of the kidnapper releasing his hostages.

The more difficult problem occurs when it is something political that the kidnapper is after – release of colleagues in prison, dismissal of a government official, distribution of relief to the poor, publication of a message by the media, ending of some programme that helps a racial or religious minority and so on.

For reasons of state, many governments refuse point blank to negotiate under the duress of a kidnapping for political demands on the grounds that this will lead to repetition by other ruthless and determined groups.

For tactical reasons the authorities might pretend to be negotiating with the kidnappers when in reality they are using whatever information they can glean in the negotiations to catch them. Or, they could be negotiating in earnest but a slip by the kidnappers could give the authorities another option.

So, in general, if threats are used against you in a negotiation it does not follow necessarily that you are trapped cold. If you have some room for manoeuvre you have a choice, *however limited*. Identifying that room, and expanding on it, is a task you have to face if you prefer not to comply with their demands.

Otherwise you are stuck with the 'lesser evil' they offer you as an alternative to their Russian Front.

In negotiating, each party has a veto – you don't have to agree to whatever is on offer – though this may have consequences for you. The plant could go on strike, they may try to get their way by force, you might have to do without supplies or you might be taken to court and so on.

It is legitimate in a negotiation to draw the attention of the other person to the consequences of his persistence with a deadlocked position, though there are ways in which this can be stated without provoking the charge that you are threatening them. Timing is the essence of making clear the consequences of deadlock without necessarily creating resentment.

In commerce you have the option to take your business elsewhere. The implicit 'threat' to do so is present in every negotiation and is widely accepted as being legitimate. By legitimate I mean that it is regarded as being within the norms of everyday negotiating.

The acceptability of the implicit sanction of not doing business if you fail to agree is a matter of degree.

The buyer (or seller) uttering the 'killer' sentence, 'you'll have to do better than that', implies that if you don't (can't) you won't get his business. That *might* be acceptable as a negotiating tactic if it is confined only to a relatively small transaction out of your annual turnover with him.

If you say that not only will he not get your business in the case in dispute, but he will not get *any* business from you at all, the sanction threat begins to move towards being unacceptable and you run the risk that your threat may dig him deeper into his position precisely because he resents your blackmail and cannot be seen to give in to those tactics.

If you use the threat of possibly large-scale damage to his business in pursuit of a relatively minor matter, he is likely to perceive your intentions as being hostile to him and his interests and his reaction could produce an equally negative response.

His quandary is (and ought to be) that if he appears to give in to a large-scale threat over a relatively small matter, how does he protect himself in future?

If you threaten that you will stop him doing business with everybody else in town, the territory, the country, the continent, even the world, your threat is pure blackmail, assuming that it is credible. And if it isn't credible you cannot possibly retain his respect.

As large-scale threats are less credible in pursuit of small objectives than they are when in pursuit of large-scale objectives, there is a natural limitation on using them in this way, without provoking legal intervention, public hostility or outright disbelief that you intend to do what you threaten.

If a man in a bar says 'pass me the ashtray or I'll kill you' it is unlikely that you would take him seriously (you would certainly doubt his sanity or sobriety or both!). Most people would pass the ashtray without such a heavy threat, but a lot of people wouldn't if they were treated that way. (In some bars that could be fatal.)

The United States – or for that matter the Soviet Union – doesn't use (hasn't so far, anyway) the threat of nuclear *attack* when in dispute with a smaller non-nuclear power. They reserve the nuclear option for retaliation if they are attacked by the other.

If you compared in 1973 the absolute capacities of the United States and North Vietnamese militaries to inflict damage on each other, there is no doubt that the US arsenal of nuclear weapons made it by far the most formidable of the two.

However, using nuclear weapons is not the same as having them. The North Vietnamese could, therefore, safely disregard the US nuclear arsenal in their calculations of the balance of forces.

The magnitude of the threat ought then to be relative to the issue at stake. This is the more so, the earlier in the negotiation that the threat is made: when a threat is a *last* resort, it has more legitimacy, i.e. it is more acceptable as a negotiating norm, than when it is the *first* resort.

To open up earlier in the negotiation with a threat is likely to raise the other party's eyebrows if not their hackles! It provokes more resistance than it overcomes.

Actually implementing a threat may also impose costs on the party doing the threatening – for a start you would have to do without their services, and they yours, at least in the short run. This is also your opportunity because it is rare to find the dependence only running one way.

Most of the time, just as we are vulnerable to a threatened action from the other person, he is vulnerable to some form of threatened counter-action from us. No wonder then that most threats do not provoke immediate compliance – they provoke retaliatory counter-threats instead.

One of the most devastating counters to a threat is to imply that it does not concern you all that much if the threat is implemented. The other person has to contemplate whether you are bluffing and what the cost is going to be to himself of implementing the threat.

If, however, you are the only supplier of a particular product which the other party must have (say, a drug company negotiating with a hospital), there is a strong moral pressure present (often backed up by a legal deterrence) for you not to exploit that position and make 'unreasonable' demands.

Market economies normally have legislation to limit monopoly powers, though the limitations vary for different types of monopolies and may be applied with more or less vigour. For instance, labour monopolies tend to be less regulated than corporate monopolies.

A threat raises the costs of disagreement – assuming that the threat will be implemented if we disagree and that it is not just a

A discount, or else!

A hotel chain selling a branded vodka in its bars decided to widen its profit margin on sales by increasing the discount it got from the supplier.

The negotiators deadlocked when the vodka people insisted that the chain was already on a top discount and anything more 'would make it unprofitable to supply them at all'.

The hotel chain was adamant in its demands as it had been offered by another company a 'hotel brand' vodka at a higher discount.

The last statement of the vodka people was taken as a threat to withhold supplies. In fact, the so-called 'threat' became the main issue at the next meeting, but the other side heatedly denied they had threatened anything at all – they were 'just drawing the attention of the hotel chain to the financial realities'.

The hotel negotiators insisted on a larger discount and added that if they did not get one they 'would stop buying the branded vodka altogether'.

The vodka people took this as a threat – 'blackmail' they called it – and the negotiatons broke down.

The hotel chain changed its vodka suppliers and customers were offered the in-house brand when they asked for the other company's (well advertised) vodka. This did not always go down well with those customers who asked for the vodka by name.

It might have been possible for the hotel people to get a better financial deal if they had simply switched from a demand for a discount to a demand for extended credit. This (minority) view was expressed at the time but was overruled once the hotel chiefs got their tails up at the alleged threat not to supply them with vodka.

Casual remarks can be taken as threats, and can be thrown back as a challenge. If the negotiations break down the threat may have to be implemented.

bluff. If you are dependent upon the other person, you are vulnerable to a threat from him.

Wolfgang's problems was his dependence on his colonel who had the power to decide where Wolfgang fought in Hitler's War.

Being dependent upon the other party increases the possibility of being Russian-Fronted. It follows that lessening your dependence improves your chances of being able to defy threats, ill-timed or otherwise.

Chain stores that place their orders with small suppliers can get a lot of negotiating leverage into their hands if they can come to represent the bulk of a small supplier's sales. They can do this by placing large orders – which the small firm may at first be grateful for – or offering credit to buy machinery and such like.

They can (and often do) squeeze down the price of the goods they buy from totally dependent sources by threatening to cut them out as a supply source. They also take longer credit and insist on higher quality. At the very least they can determine the supplier's policies in areas where normally you would not expect to find them operating, e.g. hiring standards, trade union membership, even ethnic balance.

They also tighten the squeeze on dependent suppliers by locking them into exclusive purchase agreements, thus preventing them expanding out from under their dependence by acquiring other customers.

The threat to cut them out need not be made incessantly, because every time the smaller company looks at its markets (or lack of them) it gets the message. So the latent threat to cut them out – through, perhaps, the occasional demonstration of the disciplining of a 'troublemaker' – is enough to get the desired result. Many a large business has grown by swallowing up smaller suppliers that either needed cash for expansion or got into debt to their 'customer'.

Breweries often pick up hotels and bars because their owners fall into debt to them; retail stores acquire clothing manufacturers because they become so dependent on their customer that they cannot survive at the prices imposed on them for their clothes; petroleum companies take over garage outlets, and franchise operations acquire faltering businesses or the real estate left after debts are paid off.

You can save yourself a lot of grief at the negotiating table if you refrain from getting too dependent on one source and thus increasing the costs to you of disagreement with the other person on what he regards as being a substantial matter.

All threats boil down to some version of the Russian Front, forcing you to choose between unpleasant alternatives. If you believe they have the power to damage you and that they will do so if you don't comply or are not deterred, you will be Russian-Fronted.

However, unlike Wolfgang, you might have a choice.

Answers to self-assessment test 19

1 *(a)* If you can wait it might be better to do so, *up to a point*, because fighting for the money has risks.

(b) The wrong people to pressure. Accountants are unlikely to worry about missed deliveries – it gives them an excuse for delaying payment further!

(c) Yes – put the pressure on the people who feel it sharpest – they will put pressure on accounts for you.

2 *(a)* The course most likely to lead to a negotiation.

(b) Might work if they decide not to fight. Otherwise, it reduces the pressure on them if they do fight.

(c) The weakest move, unless the sum is trivial.

(d) Changes a grievance into a mere late payment.

3 *(a)* The course most likely to lead to negotiation.

(b) The move with the highest risks of total breakdown. Unlikely to succeed.

(c) The weakest move, unless the sum is trivial.

Self-assessment test 20

1   You are in dispute with a shipper who has managed to lose a 20-foot container between your factory and Benghazi. This is the second shipment that has gone missing – the first turned up weeks behind schedule – and the Libyan client is threatening to cancel the contract unless you deliver on time. In a meeting with the transport agents that is long on verbosity and short on details, do you:
    (a) Insist that they admit liability?
    (b) Ask them why they let you down on this occasion?
    (c) Ask them how they can claim to be efficient when it is the second container to go missing?
    (d) Tell them their schedules are hopeless?

2   You are a contractor in East Africa and the project is running behind schedule. The Minister in charge constantly interferes with the project, changes his mind on details, holds up papers needed to clear supplies through customs, and makes untrue and slanderous public statements about your company's efforts. As a last straw, he issues a public warning that he will cancel the contract and arrest your staff for 'malingering', 'corruption', and most ludicrous of all, 'spying'! The local TV station asks you for a comment. Do you:
    (a) Tell them what you think of the Minister's mental age?
    (b) Deny the charges and give your side of the story?
    (c) Say 'no comment'?

3   You have been negotiating the rental of your office with the landlord for some months. He has made tough demands and you cannot budge him. The negotiations are taking up a lot of your time and you are fed up with the arguments: Do you:
    (a) Accept the rent because it is close to your top price?
    (b) Decide to fight him in any way you can?
    (c) Look for another office?
    (d) Have another go at finding a negotiated solution?

Chapter Twenty

The Lazarus Shuffle
or how to cope with deadlock

Deadlocks are a familiar experience for negotiators.

They occur frequently in negotiating and in extreme cases they can occur over every single point at issue.

Sometimes both parties are unprepared to compromise, or they have not discovered anything suitable to trade off. This provokes the kind of deadlock that endures and no amount of time spent trying to unlock it seems to work. The parties get entrenched where they are and the negotiation grinds to a halt.

In some circumstances, the relationship of the parties degenerates into outright hostilities that kill the prospects of a deal. And there is nothing deader than a dead deal (except perhaps the parties if they end up killing each other).

In business, it is not uncommon to find that some former clients will have nothing to do with each other, even though they were once trading frequently, because of some unbridgeable gulf that opened up between them during the course of their dealings.

It doesn't always take much to do this – you missed a due payment by careless oversight; you pressed just too hard for a rebate; you let the other side down in special or commercially embarrassing circumstances; or your interests clashed diametrically on an issue.

On other occasions the differences are long in germinating – constant let-downs, frequent bickerings, startling revelations and accusations and such like, gradually erode the trust between you and when that is gone the entire relationship collapses.

Also, it is not unusual for negotiating relationships to exist in an atmosphere of suspicion and hostility. The parties bring with them to the negotiations their reputations, or the history of their 'atrocities' on friends or predecessors of the other party.

Cease-fire negotiations, for example, are never easy and they are made even less easy by the images of the two parties in each other's perceptions. The Arab-Israeli conflict is an obvious case in point;

Private communication might prevent public blasting

Landing charges were raised recently on aircraft using Heathrow Airport, London. The 18 international carriers who use Heathrow protested in the strongest terms both privately and publicly.

The issue became very heated between the carriers and the airport and much abuse flowed across the media about the motives of the company that raised the charges.

The carriers decided to sue the airport owners for imposing 'illegal and excessive' charges.

The owners issued a statement, saying that 'differences between partners should be settled by negotiation, not by public and expensive squabbles'.

The spokesman for the carriers replied: 'We would not have recourse to litigation if there had been any prospect that you would have been willing to settle the differences between us by negotiation but in view of your statement we are prepared even now to enter into negotiations upon any sensible and realistic basis to reduce charges.'

If the option of negotiation was present there was no need for media blasting or litigation.

But whose responsibility was it that the issue blew up? The airport owners who unilaterally hiked the landing charges or the carriers who got cross about it?

---

the splintering of Lebanon is another; as are the differing traditions of Ireland and the histories of India and Pakistan.

Intractability is not monopolized by political conflicts, the scope for intractability in everyday business is limitless.

The issues may be less serious – in life-or-death terms – but the fact remains that soured relationships stay sour.

The question asked in this chapter is: can we get a 'yes' or 'maybe' instead of a 'no' or 'never'?

This amounts to asking whether there is anything we can do in our negotiating to get back from the dead.

There is.

We can try the Lazarus Shuffle!

How does this work?

Basically, it is an attitude rather than a prescription. It aims to separate the negotiators from the emotional tensions and commitments of the issues in dispute and shuffle them slowly towards a settlement.

Why?

Because people are the biggest problem in negotiating!

They bring to the negotiations their hopes, fears, prejudices and offensive behaviours – if they came without these there might be fewer deadlocks but then the people would hardly be normal.

How do we achieve this remarkable result?

Let us work our way through the Lazarus Shuffle and see what pointers it has for our negotiating behaviour.

Having chose to negotiate a settlement we have by implication abandoned the alternatives which include legal remedies, violent confrontation, outright warfare, guerrilla action, sabotage, blockade, boycott, bribery, demonstration, hunger strike, legislation, or just some good old publicity.

If for good reason we reject the alternatives as being inappropriate, excessive or too risky (or we have already tried them and failed!) and we commit ourselves to a negotiation, this must be our *only* means. In other words we must approach the negotiations in good faith and with an open mind.

If the real estate company wants to increase your rent or shorten your lease, you have the alternative of fighting them. You can refuse to pay up or to leave – even barricade yourselves in – or you can threaten to go to court and seek a legal injunction to prevent them repossessing the property.

They too can engage in similar behaviour. They can send in their 'heavy squad' to intimidate you, cut off your utility supplies, or get a repossession order from a court.

The publicity value of your predicament ('rogue landlords terrorise defenceless families') is contrasted with theirs ('skiving tenants snub the law').

The grievance cycle is going to escalate rapidly if this behaviour is the sum of the relationship. Each side takes a public position and seeks to strengthen it relative to the other. The consequence of this is to weaken the possibility of negotiating a compromise, because any compromise by either party is a 'defeat', a 'loss of face', a 'climbdown', etc.

Fighting them may not be your first best alternative. It might not be your second or third best alternative either.

It certainly helps your prospects of negotiating a settlement if you have not done anything (or at least haven't done enough) to set the relationship on such a collision course that you are both straining on the leash to get at the other's jugular.

Your behaviour, therefore, does influence the prospects of a settlement. Provocative behaviour does just that: provokes! And what is regarded as provocative is not within your control – it is the other party's perception of your actions that counts.

Who can provide you with the best description of how they perceive your actions? The other person, of course! So ask him questions – incessantly – about how he sees the situation and don't argue the toss over anything he says. He may get repetitive, but you'll soon know what you are up against.

When I say 'find out how he sees it', I do not mean that as a prelude to surrender. You need to know what he is on about if you are going to find the bridges between your side and his.

You, quite rightly, see a rent increase as a reduction in your standard of living (and an increase in the landlord's – who by your definition is richer than you are as he owns what you are renting).

He, quite rightly too, sees the rent increase as a means to preserving the integrity of the property by funding the necessary repairs – his ownership of the property gives him responsibilities which he can meet only if there is an adequate income from the rents and to expect repairs in any other circumstance is to reduce *his* living standards (and increase yours).

A bridge to think about is present: both of you want to maintain your living standards, and an adequately maintained and repaired building is common to the living standards of both of you.

Attacking the other person is not conducive to making him help your interests when his own are at stake. It never ceases to amaze me to listen to negotiators attack the other person – oft times ferociously – when their strategy requires the same person to compromise his interests in some way. Why they think that abusing him makes him warmer towards them, I do not know.

If you attack someone, they will defend themselves. That ought to be self-evident. 'It's your fault', 'No, it bloody well isn't!' 'Oh, yes it is!' and so on, are fairly familiar attack-defend cycles. So is the (bad) habit of point scoring:

Before I respond to what passes for a proposal from you, I cannot

How not to tackle a suspected rip-off

I was minding my own business at Gothenburg airport when I was approached by a businessman who asked if I was travelling Business Class and if I was would I join him for a drink (I said yes to both questions). He wanted to talk about something that was exciting him greatly and when he heard I was a consultant negotiator his tale poured forth.

Briefly, his story was that he had been selling children's clothes to a Swedish chain store for three years. On this visit he had arrived early and had taken time out to casually wander through one of the branches of this chain, and, naturally, he had gravitated to the children's department and looked out for his company's products.

What do you think he found? Yes! His clothes were there and were prominently displayed. This pleased him immensely and in his pride he informed the staff that he owned the firm that made what they were selling. They were most impressed and told him that there was a steady demand for his clothes, given their excellent quality.

He was in turn very pleased at this news and after a while he left. One thing, however, stuck in his mind and that was the price tag on one of his lines. It wasn't until he left that he realized that the Swedish Kroner price represented in sterling a mark-up of several hundred per cent on his selling price to the store.

Such was his concern that he went back to the shop and noted down all the prices of every one of his products. He worked out the mark-up and found it was consistent throughout – the chain store, whch had always pleaded poverty and tight competition as reasons for squeezing his prices, was, he said, 'ripping me off'.

He was upset about this, even though the price he had got for his product was profitable to his business. He raised this immediately with them in the negotiations later that morning and told them he felt they had been cheating him. They were obviously offended at this charge but after much discussion they agreed to raise their purchase prices. They claimed this would squeeze their profits because of their very high labour costs and taxes on their stores.

He was now even more worried because he felt he had overreacted and gone in too strong and perhaps damaged their good relationship. I suggested it would have been better if he had raised the question of their retail pricing policy quite neutrally and let the implications of that lead them to either a credible defence of their mark-up or to a revision of their purchase price. By charging in he had risked causing offence when none was necessary and whatever he had gained in the immediate trip might be followed by a falling off in orders as they eased out an obviously disgruntled supplier. By paying him more they partly confirmed his feeling of being cheated, whether this was the case or not.

let you get away with the snide and ridiculous remarks you made a moment ago.

The result? Certainly not peace!

The taking of firm stances is a form of attack. If you declare a firm, unalterable, position, it is more than likely that they will, and there you will sit glaring at each other across the battlements.

It is a negotiating tactic (discussed with the others in the next chapter) to make a public commitment to a position and use that as leverage on the other party who is supposed to appreciate that, as you are unlikely to move off your declared position without considerable loss of face, he had better accept your position.

Playing 'chicken' with a dedicated ('irrational') opponent in fast cars on a highway is also a fast way to die. In negotiating, a mutual chicken game is known as deadlock.

'I will *never* pay an increased rent!' is one way to provoke the response: 'I'll see you in hell if you don't!'

Firm declarations of commitment are to be avoided in moves to unlock deadlock. A moratorium on public statements would greatly assist the negotiations (Sadat and Begin meeting in total privacy at Camp David for instance). No interviews with the media during delicate labour or commercial negotiations is always a good policy.

How can we state our perceptions if we do not let them know of our feelings?

Feelings tend to be resented if they are made in the form of an attack but there is a world of difference between saying that you feel let down and accusing them of screwing up your business.

You can always translate statements from accusatory attacks into more acceptable feelings:

> You've ruined my delivery schedules!
> You let me down on this occasion.

The very translation of attack language into neutral statements of our feelings highlights the perceptions we have of the problem and suggests ways in which it can be tackled.

It is the problem that requires solution not the attacks that need responses. Highlighting what the problems are suggests ways in which the bridge can be made.

For the problems to produce solutions it is necessary for you to be clear what it is that the other person is interested in. This may require some very careful questioning on your part:

> Let me be clear what it is that you need.

Or:

> Are you suggesting that we arrange dual inspection on site at weekends?', followed, if the answer is affirmative, by 'What do you mean exactly by *dual* inspection?'

Once you are both discussing *how* something should be done, as against *why* it wasn't in the past, or *why* they don't trust you to do it, you can move on to discuss what sort of packages would be possible that could incorporate the safeguards both of you are legitimately seeking. (You can see that this is really a chapter for those who have graduated from merely stating grievances to proposing remedies!)

However, the road to melting the deadlock cannot be traversed without first defusing the causes of deadlock, and the most productive way to do this is to ask questions. Now questions can be either helpful or irritating, they can soften up a deadlock or ice it over. It's a matter of content, tone and timing.

Much has been written by psychologists on the role of questions and my summary here is more in the form of a whistle-stop tour than a comprehensive treatise.

Let's look at some no-no's.

If you want to start or continue a fight, ask provocative questions, show them you don't believe their answers, ask sarcastic supplementaries, challenge their veracity, contradict their answers, interrupt them before they have finished, and dismiss their answers with one-liners (examples include: 'rubbish', 'crap', 'balls', 'lies', 'oh my God', 'you must be joking', 'you don't really believe that', 'remember you are under oath', 'tell the truth now', 'be honest', and 'if you think I'll fall for that one, you must be out of your tiny mind!').

Any attempt to use questions as battering rams against the other person's position is bound to be self-defeating in the retaliation that it provokes. Before long you will be up to your necks again in accusations.

The same applies to questions that are directed in an antagonistic way, such as:

1 *Loaded questions*: 'Do you believe you are always right?'
2 *Impertinent questions*: 'How long are you going to continue waffling on about nothing?'
3 *Perry Mason questions*: 'How can you claim to be innocent when you have just admitted to five cases of missed deliveries?'
4 *Boomerang questions*: 'Don't you agree with me that you lot made a monumental cock-up of the scheduling?'
5 *Gotcha questions*: 'Wouldn't you do *anything* to save your country's reputation?' – if you say 'yes' or 'no' they've gotcha!

To see why the content, tone and timing of questions is so important, we must consider the purpose of questions in the Lazarus Shuffle. A question can imply that:

You want to receive information.
You want the other person to think about the implication of something by his answers.
You want to give information.
You want to defuse tension.
You want to facilitate communication.
You want to make a decision.

The same is true, hopefully, for the other person.

Moving the discussion into a question format has a number of advantages, not the least that it releases the tensions associated with deadlock.

Hence, as your questions are aimed at ending a deadlock it follows that you will make most progress if your questioning style facilitates your aims rather than undermines them.

It is best to start with questions that *open* up the discourse rather than track it into a monosyllabic exchange. Closed questions can be answered with a single word: 'yes', 'no', 'maybe', or 'never'. They must be avoided, especially in the early high-tension part of the negotiation.

Open questions are preferable because they require more than one-word answers and invite the other person to expound his views at length – the length of the answers increasing as the hostility level drops.

Once you both get talking the tension will begin to drain, if only slightly at first, until it is at a manageable level. You might remember how to ask open questions by prefacing your questions with the key words in Kipling's little ditty:

> *I keep six honest serving men*
> *They taught me all I knew*
> *Their names are* What? *and* Why? *and* When?,
> *And* How? *and* Where? *and* Who?

The purpose of the dialogue is to lead yourselves to a break in the deadlock. This suggests that the next step is to get agreement on the next step! You can do this by summarizing the benefits of an agenda, a timetable, an exchange of views in a 'safe' environment, a procedure for adjudicating issues, a forum for discussing informally at high level, the main headings of an agreement, etc.

The question that is posed after such a summary is of the form: 'Is it possible to agree to proceed in such a way?'. The answer *leads* the negotiation to the next stage because the question is a *leading* question.

Such questions have to be carefully placed, leaving the way open for the other person to step back if he is not ready to commit himself, and if badly timed (often by being put too early before the tension has dropped) can backfire. In this sense leading questions are *permission seeking* ('Could/Would/Should we do it this way?').

You can use questions to get at the other person's perception of the facts. Psychologists call these *directed* questions. They require something more than 'yes'/'no' answers but may not elicit a great deal more information than the specific answer to the specific question. For example:

What sum of damages are you seeking?
When did our services drop below the standards you expected?
How many man-hours were tied up in the search for the compressor?

Their counterpart are *non-directed questions, which leave the other person discretion on how much he wants to inform you by his answers:*

How do you calculate the consultant-day rates you charge?

What benefits do you see in applying an Equal Opportunities code to my part of your operations?

Why do you insist on our tenders remaining at a fixed price for 12 months?

Would you outline for us how you assessed the losses on the Jordan contract?

Another version of a non-directed question is barometric, in that it gives you information about the other person's feelings, state of mind, or degree of flexibility:

How do you feel about training black labour for the South African project?

Do you mind if my colleagues sit in on our discussions?

How does the idea of a 12-month lease option strike you?

Is there any scope at all for relaxing the documentation procedures within the construction compounds?

Have you any views on our making a new site agreement with the union?

The barometric question is often a good lead-in to a decision because judging by his response you can make a proposition that could form the basis of a joint decision. That decision may only be to look at the implications of what you have uncovered by testing his feelings and attitudes.

The skilful use of questions is aimed at opening up the discussions from the narrow tracks they have been on or shifting them from the massive issues of principle they have broken down over.

Questions suggest potential packages of proposals on 'how' the dispute can be resolved (partially or wholly) or outlines of what the proposals could look like.

Instead of concentrating on too-narrow a package, your best interests are served by opening up the field to as many packages as you can think of. The very fact of searching for packages increases the confidence they have in your intentions, without committing you to any specific solution. (After all, *everything* is negotiable!)

The dispute can gradually come to be recognized as a mutual problem. Once it is in the domain of being a mutual problem it can easily slide into being recognized as suitable for a mutual solution.

The next step is the trickiest: fixing it so that some form of criteria is chosen against which the proposed solutions will be tested. This is to prevent the negotiations falling back onto brute strength, pressure or force for deciding who gets what out of the deal.

The search for acceptable criteria for deciding issues separates each side's threat capacity from the criteria to be used for deciding issues that separate them. Criteria for this purpose could include:

Comparability with similar solutions. (What is a 'similar' problem and is it analogous?)

General concepts of 'fairness'. (What is fair?)

Maintenance of traditional differential treatments – the weakest get the most support. (What is 'weak' and how much is 'most'?)

Accepting the given standards laid down by third parties, e.g. legislation, club rules, referees' reports, independent surveys, technical specifications, and so on. (How is applicability decided?)

Previous decisions. (But which 'precedents' should be followed and which created?)

Equality of sacrifice or gain. (How is 'equal' defined?)

Separate the issues and deal with them individually or link the issues and take the lot together on a 'swings and roundabouts' basis. (What happens if each has advantages and disadvantages?)

Majority votes to decide. (Referendum – who sets the question? Absolute majority or qualified majority? What constitutes a fair vote? Who can vote in the election?)

Of course, the selection of criteria is itself a negotiating problem (as the questions in brackets suggest) but the act of searching for criteria helps you towards a settlement if you take each obstacle in turn and apply the Lazarus Shuffle to it if deadlock threatens.

If they have problems in accepting a particular criterion then go step-by-step through the shuffle. Either an amended criterion or a new one will suggest itself. The one thing you must avoid is attempting to solve a deadlocked position without some criteria for testing the proposed solutions against. Otherwise it will come down to a con or intimidation.

If the issue remains deadlocked or the proposed solution is still unsatisfactory, you might have to return to the first step of the shuffle and reconsider whether you prefer the negotiated outcome to the alternative means of getting a decision that are available.

There is no dodging this requirement: if the alternatives are *worse* (in the sense of having unattractive consequences or having little chance of making much difference to the outcome on offer) you are bound logically to take the negotiated outcome or continue with the negotiations (though, of course there is no accounting for our 'irrationality').

To do otherwise is to fall back onto pure subjectivism: 'If the bastards won't give in to me, then screw 'em!'.

If the alternatives are better for you, i.e. they have manageable consequences or a good chance of securing your goals, you are logically bound (with the usual *caveat* for irrationality) to choose them – as long as you take into account the damage this might do to your relationship with the other person.

Clearly, for example, one alternative to agreeing to the landlord's new lease or fighting him is to move out altogether. Giving up is not entirely dishonourable if you have tried and, having failed, you prefer to use your life for something more constructive than beating yourself against a brick wall.

Accepting the fact that we can't win 'em all is no disgrace as long as we try our best to do so! This sometimes is the best outcome of the Lazarus Shuffle.

You become so separated from the emotional ties to your original entrenched positions that you see no point in trying to fight or to rescue them, and you decide to fold up your tent and depart. For we don't always get what we want or what we deserve.

That, after all, was much the fate of poor Lazarus himself!

Answers to self-assessment test 20

1 *(a)* What good does that do?

   (b) The first step to finding a negotiable solution.

   (c) Argumentative questions only get you a fight.

   (d) If they know that it won't help and if they disagree it won't find your container.

2 *(a)* You obviously want to go to jail!

   (b) You rarely win public arguments with politicians.

   (c) Correct. You clearly need some behind-the-scenes 'clout' and the best way to get it is not to make it difficult for political friends to support you. Public rows entrench people in positions they find difficult to move from without losing face.

257

3   *(a)* Should be resorted to only after *(d)*, *(c)* and *(b)*.

(b) Only if it is likely to produce the result that negotiating hasn't managed so far, otherwise you are using up energy better spent in your business.

(c) Could be the only alternative to *(a)*.

(d) *Everything* is negotiable! But recognize that you can't win 'em all.

Self-assessment test 21

1 You are stopped by a policeman in Ogoland and he demands that you pay him 50 quonks (about £20) not to book you for speeding. You were almost stationary at the time and could not have been speeding at all. Do you tell him:

   (a) Not before you see your consul?
   (b) Does he take bribes?
   (c) Certainly, if he has change for a 100-quonk note?

2 Sanctions have been imposed on Ogoland by the United Nations but, by dint of your highly specialized knowlege, you know of a way to supply Ogoland with consumer goods with small risk of detection and with a certainty of high profits. Do you:

   (a) Approach the Ogoland Government with details of your scheme and a cash contract to implement it?
   (b) Decline to do so and instead approach your own government with a view to having the gap plugged that you have spotted?
   (c) Approach somebody else whom you know is sympathetic to Ogoland and offer to sell the scheme to him?

3 An Indian importer owes you £100,000 and you demand payment before any more shipments take place. He tells you he is going through a short-term cash flow crisis and needs more time to pay and that he cannot pay if he does not get more of your products. Do you:

   (a) Tell him he cannot get more deliveries unless he pays what he owes?
   (b) Tell him that if he does not pay you will sue him?
   (c) Decide to visit him in India and see for yourself what his financial situation is really like?
   (d) Tell him if he pays you £20,000 on account you will make another delivery?

Chapter Twenty-one

Negotiating close to the wire
*or how to trade
in the Third World*

First, we should dispose of the bad news. The Third World is a long way from being a happy and prosperous place in which to do business. Apart from having some of the worst poverty on the planet (though they are not by any means *all*, nor even the majority, starving), some of the worst records in health and hygiene, many of the worst records in education and welfare, and a long history of neglect and failure, the countries that comprise the Third World also have an unenviable record for both local violence and general warfare.

Since 1945, the majority of wars (119 out of 124) have taken place in the Third World, while most systems of government are of military origin, and many of the governments that have come to power there have done so not by means of an election but from military coups or by violent civil wars and revolution.

Hence, low levels of personal income, political instability, and local violence are features of the Third World that have to be borne in mind by the international business negotiator when contemplating business in these countries. Legal foundations for conducting business have been laid in most of these countries, and for many of them there is more than a semblance of law and order. But the fact remains that there are wide variations in standards and conduct in many of these countries and it is not alway possible to seek, let alone get, redress for breaches of contract – in fact, in some places even to seek redress is to invite judicial and extra-judicial reprisals against one's business and, sometimes, one's person.

Standards of public service in respect of personal ethics and morality are not always of the kind that is expected by a person living in a relatively uncorrupt Western democracy. It is always dangerous to generalize about moral issues – 'let he who is without guilt first cast a stone' etc. – and you are not advised to do so except in an abstract fashion (and always while safely in your own backyard). But corruption, the great unspoken feature of business in the Third World, is a reality of business which few are prepared for when they are confronted with its scale and, what appears to be worse, its total acceptance as a way of life.

In corrupt societies (that is, those judged to be corrupt by normal Western standards; though be careful of being too pompous about this in case tomorrow's papers expose some local scandals in your own country) the norm is for almost everybody who has some discretionary power, no matter how trivial, to use that discretion to personal advantage in return for some small (or not so small) consideration.

Passports get stamped faster if a small token payment (called 'dash' in West Africa) is left within the pages when it is handed over – otherwise, you might be left to the end of the queue even if you were first to get to the counter. Similarly, in customs, immigration and the baggage reclaim area.

Success in securing airline reservations tends to be correlated with a small bribe to the booking clerk; seat reservations likewise. Anything that needs rubber stamping is a goldmine to the clerk who has the rubber stamp. If he has to consult another clerk's list or check with the supervisor, you had better bear this in mind when handing over the bribe because what is divided by two or three is often not enough to generate an interest in your interests in those with no incentive to take an interest in your interests!

Hotel reservations can appear at the drop of a 100 cedi note, and disappear if somebody got there before you with a 200 cedi note. The lift shaft vista awaits those foolish enough to trust to their confirmed reservation with the ocean view, if they forget to 'dash' the desk clerk. A table by the toilets in the restaurant is your best chance if you forget to look after the head waiter, and you might as well be *in* the toilet if you forget to demonstrate to the waiters serving the tables your goodwill and intention to see them all right – the best way to ensure the latter is to tip them when they take the order and imply that there is more to follow.

As for official forms, you have little hope of even getting near one in many countries without paying the clerk the local 'tax' on those forms which are a devolved responsibility of the clerk who collects the forms. Pay up and you get the form; don't and you will wait, perhaps for ever.

Once petty corruption becomes a way of life and spreads right

261

across the entire fabric of society, it is something you have to accept as a visitor if you wish to do any business at all. You should take local guidance on the state of play regarding corruption and follow the advice of the 'old hands'.

It is not only an expensive business but also a risky one. If you assume everybody is corrupt and they are not you might get into serious trouble for attempting to bribe an honest clerk, or worse for you, an honest policeman. Several businessmen at any one time are in local jails for trying to corrupt officialdom. Perhaps the (corrupt) authorities are trying to make an example of them for PR purposes, or perhaps the businessmen did not offer a big enough bribe in the negotiations and they are in jail for the 'insult'.

A stranger in a Third World country has no means of knowing whether the police (or army) have stopped him or her for a real offence or because they want to collect some extra pocket money.

Two basic rules should be applied in these circumstances. First, and without exception, you should never stand on your dignity and imply either by word, grimace or gesture that the official who has stopped you does not have authority to do so, or that he is in any way unsuited to be in the position he is in, or that he is in some sense incompetent, a candidate for the gestapo, or 'typical' of his race, religion or nation.

Secondly, you must not make a direct approach to the subject of bribery (unless, as can happen, they tell you straight out that they want some pay-off for letting you go, in which case, pay up and go).

Your best bet, when not sure of the scene, is to apologize for whatever wrong they claim that you have committed (even if you feel indignant because of your saint-like innocence) and say words to the effect: 'I am a stranger in your country, officer, Sir, and I am very sorry for my mistake, Sir. In my country we pay on the spot fines for similar offences and if you tell me, Sir, what the fine is I will pay it to you immediately, Sir.'

Either (unlikely) he will tell you that you do not pay fines on the spot in Ogoland but will have to appear in court next Monday and pay any fine then, or (more likely) he will tell you what you have to pay him. As long as you say the above with no money in sight (don't reach into your pocket for your wallet until told to do so), you are unlikely to be charged with attempting to bribe an officer of the law. If he asks you for money and you pay him you are unlikely to have further trouble.

Cash or kind

Exchange regulations and controls can be extremely tight in certain countries because the government desires to use the country's foreign currency earnings with the greatest care and attention to political priorities. The penalties for breaches of these regulations can be severe – imprisonment for offenders, confiscation of property (and not just the bag full of dollars you were caught with) and heavy fines are among them.

Many have been tempted to engage in illegal dodges to get round the problem.

For example, in some countries you can arrange to have payment made to you not in the form of cash but in real goods which you then sell-on to recover your money. If you are unable to get paid in dollars in Ghana but can acquire good quality cocoa against payment in local cedis you can ship out the cocoa to Europe and sell it for hard currency. The fact that you have to pay CIF may mean you taking a loss on the original amount owed to you – but in a choice between a loss and a total loss you don't really have a choice!

To obviate the cost of shipping real goods out you can try some high-value item which you can take with you, though here you run the risk of being stopped at customs and searched. Diamonds, gold, artifacts and such-like are too obvious for even the dimmest customs official to miss (and by no means assume that customs officials in other countries are any less smart than they are in your own).

I know of a negotiator who has avoided currency regulations for years by the simple expedient of using local currency to buy rare stamps which he sticks in his wallet and sells in London. Two things favour his choice of payment: he knows a rare stamp when he sees one and, though he has been searched at customs several times, nobody has yet noticed his postage stamps!

So keep your smart comments to yourself, pay up and get going.

If you cannot bring yourself to do this, well and good. But in that case be ready for a long hassle, an uncomfortable time in detention and perhaps, in some countries, a few indignities and bruises to your person. While the latter is going on you may wish to review your decision to be an international negotiator in the Third World.

In India, until recently, public corruption was so widespread that it was a safe bet that you could offer a bribe – even for a rail ticket – and expect to get appropriate treatment. Many members of India's many governments are widely suspected of being involved in big pay-offs from this or that interest to smooth the way over the many obstacles to the conduct of business that have been created by India's central government.

Believing, as it does, that intervention is necessary if India is to be developed industrially and commercially, the government in New Delhi has introduced thousands of regulations and licences for all forms of trade, including exports and imports, and these have become 'dripping roasts' for the officials who have discretion on how the regulations are applied and to whom the licences are doled out.

Whenever a government is persuaded by somebody to have a quota for this or that (in the 'national interest') they create a meal ticket for the clerk who has control of the quotas. In Nigeria and Ghana businesses have grown up in the trade of licences and quotas –not of the goods that are meant to be licensed or quotad!

An official quota to import shoes is traded across the business community for fabulous sums long before a single pair of shoes reaches the country. I know one businessman in Ghana who bought the production licence for shirts and is sitting on it until somebody else comes along to buy it at a price considerably more profitable to him than actually laying out the capital to make shirts.

When somebody does come along who wants to manufacture shirts he will still have to get another permission to erect the buildings and that permission too can provide a good living for the person who gets hold of it first, without them ever having to go through the trauma of actually building and operating a manufacturing plant.

Negotiating in these conditions to set up an import distribution network for your shoes, or a plant to manufacture them locally, is not going to be a simple process of putting up a proposition to somebody and letting them evaluate the commercial prospects. You will have no idea how serious the opposite number is about actually doing anything about your proposition. He may only be interested in tying you into a deal to secure the appropriate paper licence for somebody (anybody) to implement your proposition so that he can re-sell the licence to a third party.

If the project is complex and on a large scale, the number of officials that have to be 'squared' can reach formidable numbers. The costs of 'seeing them all right' will not be trivial, and for that reason they are not likely to be accountable (that is, you have no assurance of the efficiency of your bribes nor whether the people whom you thought, or were persuaded to believe, needed to be squared received anything at all). You could be the victim of a con as well as a candidate to become a convict (and in much of Africa there are more conmen out of jail than in it).

The market in official permissions is only one side of the deal; in many areas where central control is not as strong and certain as it should be (and sometimes even under the very noses of official personnel) you might be subject to an unofficial market in permissions.

You will have to pay off the local 'bosses' (or those who convince you that they are local bosses) or suffer the risk of severe retribution to your person and property (if your trucks are burnt out you know they were not kidding you). Lawlessness of this kind is a natural by-product of the system of official corruption. For the unofficial 'tax' collectors who do not have an official goldmine of discretion at their disposal, their remedy is to invent one, and where necessary to back it up with threats, intimidation and outright violence.

If this seems incredible, you should consider the well-known operations of the Mafiosa in parts of southern Italy and the pay-offs they require, in addition to whatever permissions you have obtained from the authorities. You might also consider the very large-scale operations of the 'Godfathers' of Northern Ireland who 'tax' all kinds of businesses, allegedly to replenish their paramilitary funds but more often to support their personal life styles – and this with the armed authorities patrolling the same streets looking for them!

Large-scale projects are likely to be negotiated at the highest levels. Nobody ever did much in the way of large-scale projects in Kenya who did not pass before the Presidential desk when Jomo Kenyatta (and Mrs Kenyatta) ran the show. Similarly in President Sadat's Egypt, though the front man there was his brother, while in the Philippines everything was run for many years through President and Mrs Marcos.

In Nicaragua the Somoza family ran the entire country as if it was a private bank account and they went to such excesses that most of the population preferred to take their chances with the communists

Baksheesh, backhanders and dash

You will not spend much time in certain parts of the world before you come up against petty bribery – if you hang around long enough and have the right contacts, you will also become aware of *big* corruption, but that's another story (and I don't want my book banned for discussing it!).

In West Africa they call petty corruption 'dash'.

If you want *anything* done by an official you ought to know about *dash*, because if in your innocence you don't, you will wait ages for even the most routine of transactions.

Aeroplane reservations in Ghana (and Nigeria, etc.) mean nothing unless the guy at the front desk has been paid his dash –a few cedis or whatever – out of which he pays the guy in the back office for the use of the rubber stamp, or signature, or even a sight of the passenger list.

Likewise with hotel rooms, appointments to see the boss, the civil servant, the tax accountant, or to use the telex.

This is common practice wherever you have to use the services of people who by virtue of their positions can extract a few dollars here for a few favours there.

In Egypt, the ministries are riddled with locally created monopolies. Maps are not published openly but are kept in locked drawers to be extracted for a 'little something', statistical tables are treated likewise, i.e. sold page-by-page like ancient Scrolls, and official forms and licences can be little gold mines to the clerk who is in charge of them.

In India, the fastest – indeed, sometimes the only – way to move paper through the bureaucratic labyrinth (courts, tax offices, even railway stations) is by paying a *baksheesh* (tip or 'bribe'):

> Baksheesh! Baksheesh!
> Sixteen Annas, One Rupee
> One Rupee, One Baksheesh!

How you approach this petty corruption is a personal matter, but don't moralize about it, unless you *never* give tips to taxi drivers, waiters and the kids who find your golfball!

rather than continue to live under the family's rule. This shows how desperate they must have been, for communists in power are every bit as despotic as those they throw out – only worse, no communist government yet has left office once it has established itself.

If you are dealing with the top you are sure of at least one thing: if you get the go-ahead the project is likely to become a reality eventually (though if they tap your brain and discover that they can do the job themselves and cream off the profits, you might find yourself the creator of a good idea and *persona non grata* on an early flight home!)

You will need presidential level approval to get the otherwise lethargic system to move in your favour. But presidents and their families cannot supervise everything and you will have to rely on people a little lower in the structure to get things moving. This might cost you (I avoid any reference at all to what 'presidential approval' could cost you in some countries and, in the interests of not having a future visa blocked, certainly cast no aspersions on the countries mentioned above!).

Open or thinly disguised corruption – paying off go-betweens for securing multi-million dollar business – has proven to be vulnerable to inquiry and, if established, to prosecution in the home country of the business concerned (even if ignored in the country where the pay-off for the order occurred). Hence, big-business negotiators have become more subtle about disguising the bribes – known euphemistically as 'commissions' – and they have become more careful to cover their tracks.

To use a go-between in itself indicates that you expect a commission will have to be paid, for no go-between (yet) has got business for an overseas company for nothing.

Some large corporations contribute to party funds in the country they do business in and, in return, they are allowed special concessions to do their business.

You will have to decide how you are going to cope with this problem. At the lowest level of getting into and around a country you will have to tip, bribe, dash, baksheesh, or commission those whose co-operation is necessary for you to function there. Once you cross that line (and be sure that you will have to do so) you will be faced with another line (and yet another!) as the sums at stake become progressively larger.

You can leave it to a go-between and let him deal with the officials that 'need taking care of', or you can take care of them yourself. But be clear: there is no legal way to bribe somebody and you are personally vulnerable once you attempt to do so.

Paying them in their own country out of the money for the deal is one way to settle up (which leaves you exposed when you hand over the cash), while paying them through bank accounts abroad (the famous numbered Swiss account system) is as risky.

To set up a money deal with a Swiss bank on behalf of somebody else will involve your own staff and you are then vulnerable to their mood and sense of grievance in future if something goes wrong with your relationship with them (many 'office romances' that go sour end up with the boss in court on charges varying from income tax evasion to bribery – 'hell hath no fury' etc. – so protect yourself from the same by *never* chasing your own staff).

Your go-between may swear undying loyalty and confidentiality to you and your company in accepting the bribe but, given the human rights records of many of these countries, you cannot be sure that he will remain so adamant in defence of your interests once handed over to the tender mercies of interrogators who do not recognize the Geneva Convention when they question prisoners, and have orders to find out who gave them the money, how much was given and where the money is now.

Your next, innocent, visit to that country could be the prelude to some very uncomfortable experiences (if you think Third World hotels have a long way to go before they are comfortable, you should compare them with their prisons!).

Competition selects winners and in doing so also selects the losers. Not everybody approaches losing with the same philosophical acceptance as you or I do, and we must therefore be aware of the pressures on those who don't like losing to try to do something to improve their chances.

The world of business is populated with people, and people in business are like people in most other lines of life: they are susceptible to gossip, rumour, innuendo and outright deceit. This gives rivals a potential life-line if they are feeling pessimistic about their chances of getting the deal. They can blacken you in the eyes of your potential clients.

The use of dirty tricks in the search for business is legendary across the whole world. It is not confined to people in dirty macs selling dubious postcards and video nasties. Complaints about the use of dirty tricks have emanated from some of the most prestigious of board rooms, though naturally what constitutes a dirty trick depends very much on the perception of the 'victim'.

You will hear negotiators complain that their rivals cut their prices to get the business, which seems to me to be unfortunate more than unfair. Some time ago, when a British shipyard lost an order to a Finnish yard, it complained that, on its calculations, the Finns could not even pay for the materials for the ship for the price they were quoting and therefore the government must be subsidizing the deal. The Finns replied that they were not subsidizing anything and challenged the British to prove it. The row went on for a while, but the feeling that there was something underhand going on persisted, though no evidence was forthcoming to establish this.

Pre-emptive 'underhand' moves are likely to be justified on the grounds that if they are not undertaken the result will be that the business goes to a rival who, anyway, is suspected of being willing to sink to underhand moves!

Dirty tricks are comprised of two major techniques: blackening, or bad-mouthing, you and your company to potential or current clients (which stops you getting or keeping the business); and unauthorized access to information about your negotiating position or business operation (which enables a rival to pitch their deal in a more attractive and devastatingly competitive way).

In foreign trade you are doubly exposed to dirty tricks, if only because of the distances between you and your customers. In your absence, your rivals can be in contact with your client's personnel and, by dint of charm, plausibility and outright lying, inculcate a picture of you and your operation that is at variance with the facts. It is common in business to find individuals in any company more disposed to one supplier than to another – each supplier has its supporters and detractors in a client organization and, like anybody else where something is at stake, you have to pay attention to your constituency.

It does not take much to knock you out of the running and, if you neglect your supporters (fail to visit the country enough times to be on hand to support them supporting you, or visibly let the client down in some way with deliveries, quality or spares), your rivals will use these incidents in the constant propaganda war against you.

A single failure could let them in the door on a 'trial' basis and you could be out of the door for good, or at least have to share the business with somebody else. Hence, visit your clients regularly and maintain contact with them in between through letters, faxes and telephone. Get your people to back up your hard won negotiated deal with an all-levels approach to communicating with all levels in the client's organization. Thus, when your rivals turn up and try to set hares running against you, the initial defences of good, because there are regular, personal relations between your people and the client's should see them off. At the very least you will get an early warning of any moves in this area by rivals because you can be sure that their people will tell yours about what was said.

How about the dirty trick of industrial and commercial espionage? Here again you have a problem when you are negotiating abroad. You are a long way from home and you are forced to use insecure communications to refer matters back or to get some guidance on a new issue.

Look at the issue of security. The clerk in the postal department may have been bought by the opposition to open and copy your correspondence, complete with price quotes and specifications. Nor can you be sure that your client's filing cabinets are immune to similar intrusions. There is not a lot that you can do about this (though you can refrain from using your client's post room to send messages home – use the post office instead).

Your own communications to your home base and the security arrangements there are within your control, up to a point. Those companies that engage in proper security procedures for sensitive commercial information are better placed to ensure some immunity from dirty tricks than those that are completely lax.

If what you have is worth stealing then somebody somewhere might endeavour to steal it. So you should take simple precautions to keep your valuables (in this case information) to yourself.

Negotiators who have to report everything back while abroad are more vulnerable to having their information intercepted (listening in on an extension, bugging the hotel telephone, copying your fax messages, photocopying your price lists and conditions and other papers left in 'safe' places etc.). It is better to give long distance negotiators as much authority to settle as possible and allow them to minimize home calls for guidance.

For convenience, negotiators often carry with them vast amounts of information, only a proportion of which is needed for a particular negotiation. For example, a company price list and procedures manual will contain materials relevant both to domestic and international business, and yet only one or two pages of this may be relevant to the particular deal being negotiated. If this is accessed by an unauthorized person, then the information damage to you is extended way beyond the specific negotiations that you are in the country for. A simple stripping out of all unnecessary material from your file before you leave will minimize the damage (it will also give you less to carry).

In sum, you should support your overseas negotiation on a 'need to know' basis and select on a 'need to go' basis the materials that are to accompany the negotiator. The negotiator should be made responsible for the security of the company's commercial information and should be required to demonstrate the measures taken to protect that information while he or she is abroad.

What happens if you come across commercially-sensitive information regarding a rival? That would depend on how you came across it. If you have stolen it or engaged in some illegal acquisition of it, you are obviously in breach of the law, and risk criminal charges. If, however, you come across it fortuitously (your rivals should be more careful with their secrets), I can see no reason why you should not use that information, if only by sending it to your home base.

A negotiator I know was engaged in detailed discussions with an overseas client. He returned to his hotel and unpacked his briefcase to work on his figures and found a set of papers included in some material given to him by the client which were his rival's quotation. He dithered for some time about this and decided to hand them back the next morning (having not dithered over reading them!). This he did, to the obvious embarrassment of his client. He did not get the business and has long wondered whether the client disbelieved his story that he acquired the papers accidentally and decided not to do business with a 'spy'.

Many negotiators acquire a facility for reading upside-down the papers in front of their opposite number! Many negotiators do pencil in their negotiating positions, especially figures, and these can be seen across a table. It is, of course, a silly thing to do – to pencil in your price limits like that – and the remedy is in your hands. Also, if you leave the room with your sensitive papers on the desk, you must expect your opposite number to lean forward and read them – and he must assume that this is what you intended him to do.

Answers to self-assessment test 21

1 *(a)* He could think you were impugning his character and this could get you into more trouble (of the 'more than it's worth' kind).

(b) You are impugning his character and you are now in deep trouble (his four colleagues lounging about by his jeep are itching to show you damn foreigners who's in charge of Ogoland now!).

(c) Very good, you may now drive off unmolested – though you may not get your 50 quonks change.

2 *(a)* Why not? I suppose it depends on how you feel about the reasons for the sanctions (and the UN can be more than a little hypocritical in what it condemns and condones). You had better be sure that you have a serious scheme and do not waste the time of Ogoland officials as they might make an example of you.

(b) Only the most pressing of humanitarian reasons would incline me to follow this line. The fact that you are prepared to do so without knowing why the sanctions have been imposed indicates a less than free trade attitude to business. Perhaps you are a career civil servant?

(c) Nice one. It manages to meet one's own ideas about ethics and also make a profit out of somebody else's. It could get you awarded the Gold Star of Ogoland with Oak Leaf Clusters as well as a couple of million quid.

3 *(a)* Hard headed approach. It might not get you your money. Something is always better than nothing in the debt business.

(b) Poor response and it puts your company's £100,000 at the mercy of the Indian legal system.

(c) The best move initially. See for yourself and make a judgment (that's what being a manager is all about). If his story is true you could go on to try *(d)*; if not you go to *(a)*, with the threat of *(b)*.

(d) A step in the right direction, best after *(c)*.

Chapter Twenty-two

The long distance negotiator
or a salute to those who go out and get the business

This final chapter is by way of a short salutation to the men and women who go out at all times of the year and negotiate to get the business that their country depends upon. Without exports we could not pay for our imports, and without imports we would be both poorer and at the mercy of over-protected domestic producers who know (and they all do!) how to take advantage of the lack of international competition.

Undertaking business abroad is no easy task and it takes a special breed of executive who is willing to fly off (often at too short notice) to a distant land and negotiate on behalf of their company, many employees of which care little about what is being done in their name and know even less about what is involved in doing it.

Faraway places, like green fields, can look very attractive at a distance. Go through the hassle of getting there and of functioning in what is, after all, for you a strange environment, and you begin to appreciate the kind of job which keeps you close to your hearth.

This is not to say that international business negotiators are all tired, worn-out and boring. I met a fresh-faced lass only last month who was simply oozing with enthusiasm for her new job as an international representative for a designer clothes company. She was on one of those round robin trips that take in a handful of European capitals in five days, and she was positively keyed-up to go out and get the job done. I admired her enthusiasm though I could not share it, as I was returning from a particularly gruelling sixteen-hour a day week with a client in Sweden.

There is no doubt that the international negotiator is one of the great unsung heroes of modern times. As world trade increases, the role of the international negotiator is growing commensurate with the job in hand. Goods do not sell themselves – would that they could! – and it takes hard work in many different environments to get the business to keep the goods flowing from one country to the next.

In international business many are called and few are chosen but still hundreds and thousands of new faces join the ranks each year and try their best to extend their company's business or hold on to what it has already. Those that fall by the wayside are the necessary casualties in a continuous striving for business deals the world over; those that persevere deserve their material rewards, for they certainly do not acquire them easily.

International negotiating requires travel and travel soaks up energies as sure as any sport, only the strain is prolonged over longer periods.

At any airport you will see scores of negotiators embarking or disembarking, or more likely waiting between flights, each carrying with them the hopes and the future of their company. What these men and women do when they get to where they are going can determine whether there is a company to come back to, or one worth making long-terms plans for.

You can tell the negotiators from the tourists. Negotiators travel more often to more places and consequently they are more at home in the complex tangle of an airport. They move about with an air of certain purpose about them rather than fidget their way from the indicator board to the gates.

The smarter negotiators seldom have too much luggage with them (tourists always have too much of everything, except patience) and they are organized for their flight. If they are in company they form a merry band, swapping stories of their last deal and their hopes for the next. In this sense, they are like sales staff the world over who regale each other with tales and jokes, mutual 'atrocity' stories of this or that dealer they all know; when, that is, they are not slashing into the reputations of their colleagues in other functions who don't understand anything about how tough it is out in the field.

There is a camaraderie among international business negotiators, partly expressing their competence and their pride in their work, and partly their inner tensions about the next deal that they must tackle. True, some of them (all of them at one time or another!) talk-up the deals they have negotiated – a little exaggeration here or there is as surely par for the course among negotiators as it is among those who would catch fish by rod and line. Mostly these little peccadilloes are harmless invasions of personal integrity and are mostly caused by the need to appear worthy of one's trade in a world where it is not always sensible to go into the details of a private commercial deal.

When you next sit in an airport lounge – for, be sure, if you travel at all by air you will sit in some lounge for some time, perhaps for longer than you planned – look around you at your fellow travellers. Having separated out the tourists, check over the others. Most of these will be travelling on business. If you count them you will be surprised just how many men and women fly out for this reason only.

You will spot the first-timer, nervously checking and re-checking his or her ticket, ever-willing for someone to talk to them so they can confirm their status and appear more confident than they feel. The old-timer will probably be pretending to be totally relaxed, even dozing to prove it, though his ears will be well attuned to departure announcements through his deepest of cat naps. Their faces will show the years, in some cases better than others, but the lines will be worn with the pride of experience. So will the condition of their bags – working bags, a trifle battered but everywhere serviceable in every condition they might encounter – no smart Sunday supplement luggage sets for them!

Between the new and the retiring come the vast mass of business negotiators, in all shapes and sizes, in all temperaments and moods, waiting for the 'off' like a marine-packed landing craft on D-Day. Those who want to talk and socialize will – it is from this band that you get all the advice on where to stay and what to do about foreign exchange rip-offs – and those who want to travel in solitude and contemplation will try to do so, either by physically slinking crabwise away from the hearty souls looking for a foursome for a bridge game from London to Bahrain (or just somebody with whom to drink their duty-free), or they will immerse themselves in a large paperback.

I know one guy in search of being left alone who prominently displays about him a couple of issues of *Watchtower*, a Jehovah's Witnesses newspaper, to ward off potential talkers!

The best of the breed of international business negotiators have several things in common. Observe them at work, imitate them, improve upon what you learn, and you will joint their ranks. Here are my ten rules for negotiating for business anywhere:

● **First**, you must get used to the idea of being a foreigner. There is

275

no substitute for the acquisition of a little national humility. You don't have to go overboard the other way and renounce your birthright ('go native' it used to be called in the Empire). But you must accept your place as a foreigner in the order of things, and this means above all accepting that the world neither owes your country a living nor does it necessarily owe it a good turn. What you get from them will depend upon how much they think they need what you are offering in exchange, and if they can get a better deal elsewhere they should and will take it.

- **Second**, you must get yourself organized for international business travel. Those who want to be the most successful negotiators fly first or business class, stay in good quality hotels, take with them only that which they need, do not regard a long flight as an excuse for a boozy party and are sensible about the very real problems of jet-lag (they only go to bed in other time zones when it is time to do so there, not when they feel like it on arrival).

- **Third**, you must learn something about the manners and customs of the people with whom you want to do business. You should not assume that anything that is quite acceptable in your culture is necessarily acceptable in all other cultures. One way to improve your acceptability as an international negotiator is to learn something of the language of the people with whom you deal.

    This advice also applies to those countries where the people speak a language akin to your own. For example, Australians and most North Americans speak recognizable English, but you would be foolish to leave it at that when you go to these countries to negotiate. The English-speaking peoples are separated by their common language, and you would be well advised to gen up on the local slang, dialect, and manners if you want to do business with your 'cousins'.

    If you have any doubts on this score think about the differences in approach within the tiny British Isles between the English and the Scots, and then consider how different the Australians etc. have become from both English and Scots over the years of separation.

    When dealing with non-English-speaking peoples the advice is the same, only more so. Japanese manners and courtesies are entirely different from those of the Mid-West of the United States. Fortunately, once you observe them, you can adjust without too much discomfort to your sense of what is right or wrong – though Japanese bathtime might be a tiny surprise the first time!

- **Fourth**, you must adjust the pace of your negotiating to that of the people with whom you are keen to do business (they might have to do the same if they visit you in your country). It is no good trying to do anything much in a hurry, and it is absolutely hopeless to expect to be able to ginger them up just because Father Time is knocking on *your* schedules.

  In most parts of the world you will have to slow down (in the US of A you will probably have to speed up), and it does not matter whether the delays are caused by bureaucratic procedures (the Soviet Union etc.) or by the way they make decisions (Japan and the Middle East). Have patience, take longer, and don't give yourself unrealistic schedules.

- **Fifth**, you must develop those skills of negotiating that are the same the world over. Beginning with preparation (or knowing your own business better than your rivals), you must know how to listen, react to what you hear, make conditional propositions ('If, then perhaps'), re-package creatively and bargain using conditional, and only conditional, offers ('If, then').

- **Sixth**, you must always remember that in a negotiation with anybody anywhere you always have the option of saying 'no' to a deal that is in any way suspect, whether your suspicions concern the contract they want you to sign, the terms they want you to agree to, or the business ethics they want you to abandon.

  You do not need to sign anything that does not meet your best and long-term interests, but if you do sign something you ought not to have then you will have to live with it (or without it).

  This is all the more true when you have been working hard for a long time to get some kind of deal. You must adopt the attitude that 'bygones are bygones' and previous investment in time and energy can never be recouped, and certainly you must never try to do so by agreeing to something that is not strictly what you can live with.

  Hence, if Soviet negotiators want you to take goods in place of cash, or Germans want you to accept penalty clauses for delivery commitments, or Chinese negotiators want you to cut your prices on a 'sell cheap, get famous' promise, or Australians want your goods on a consignment only basis, or Americans

277

want exclusive US of A rights, or Arabs want 15 per cent commission, or Ogolanders want side-payments in a numbered Swiss account, or whatever (and there will be many 'what-evers'!), you should always remember that, though you have the authority to say 'yes', you also have the responsibility for what you say 'yes' to. So perhaps you should say 'no' a little more often?

- **Seventh**, you must cultivate the habit (until it requires no effort whatsoever) of never getting involved in discussions or comments upon any country's politics, religion, way of life, ethics of doing business, racial mix, legal processes, constitutional arrangements, methods of selecting their leaders, public or private morality, prevalence of tips, bribery and corruption, modes of dress or undress, laws regarding your personal preferences in sex, booze, drugs, porno videos, press freedom and citizens' rights.

  If you wish to combine a business career with reforms of other countries you should reconsider your personal prospects. The internal affairs of other countries are none of your damn business and in many parts of the world they do not take kindly, or treat lightly, interfering visitors who forget what their visas say they are there for.

  Your wonderful views on democracy, feminism, the free market, income distribution, social welfare, local wars, racial strife, the treatment of offenders and such-like should be left at home, and if in your case that is not possible then you should stay at home too!

- **Eighth**, you must treat everybody with whom you deal with the greatest of personal respect, no matter how you feel about the way the negotiation is being handled. This applies to personnel on your own side as well as on the other side (even if you feel some of your people seem to be working for them too!). Respect for the individual in business life is always a rare treat if you are on the receiving end of it, and, for that reason alone, it is well worth adopting as a policy for your own behaviour towards others.

  No matter how new and strange to you any culture is in the world, and no matter how intricate are the social obligations of the people you deal with, you can be sure of being accepted anywhere, in spite of any courtesy gaffes you make out of your ignorance or forgetfulness, if you display constant evidence of your respect for your opposite number as a person. There are no parts or peoples of the world where you will find exceptions to this principle; everybody reacts more warmly to those whom they can see respect them than they do to those whom they suspect do not.

- **Ninth**, you must always endeavour to the best of your ability – and sometimes beyond that – to meet the terms of the contracts you negotiate and agree to. Each deal for you has to be a personal as well as a company commitment. Your role does not finish when the signatures are recorded. In many respects it continues through the lifetime of the deal.

You must take a personal interest in what happens thereafter and be ready to use your good and best offices to get things put right that manifestly are wrong. Good and enduring personal relations between negotiators will lead to long-term relationships between their companies and it is from this that the mutual prosperity of trading partners grows.

Your best action is always to follow through on a deal – call the other person on the phone, or drop in to see him on your next visit, to check that everything that you agreed to is actually happening and that he is well-satisfied with the outcome. In other words, you do not sign the contract, grab the cash and run. Follow through and follow up if there are any problems. Your pride alone should incline you to do so, but your long-term best interests should make it mandatory.

- **Tenth**, in deciding how to conduct your business affairs abroad, particularly when operating in parts of the world where social licence is somewhat slacker than it is elsewhere, you must be guided by what you feel comfortable doing rather than by what you feel is right or wrong.

This is by no means a prescription for abandoning the distinction between right and wrong – quite the reverse! – nor is it a prescription for turning you into a hardened cynic. The facts of life are that many parts of the world with which your country trades do have different standards of personal conduct and these standards influence whether you get business, or even get around the country itself, and you will have to learn to live with this and adapt to it, or you will not do business there.

Deciding on what is right in the circumstances is no easy matter, and it is, therefore, a highly personal decision which you cannot pass on to somebody else. What you will be advised to do by people sitting on their safe and comfortable seats back home may be fine for an assembly of ostriches approaching a sandy beach but absolutely useless for you as you go down the ramp from your aircraft and approach the ranks of officialdom at customs and immigration (and the serried ranks of their colleagues along the corridors of the ministries you need to get past to complete your negotiations). It is you that is faced with the moral dilemmas in Ogoland and you who must decide what to do about what you face there.

It is presumptuous of me to advise you on this matter, except perhaps to suggest that you talk to the older hands about it on a country-by-country basis. Listen to what they have to say, reflect on the fact that billions of dollars worth of business is being conducted every year in that environment, and decide on a case-by-case basis what you feel most comfortable about doing (remember the sixth rule about your right to say 'no').

For every set of ten rules there is always an eleventh. The eleventh commandment is usually to the effect that you must avoid getting caught while breaking any (or all) of the other ten. My eleventh is somewhat different. It is to remember, when all else is said and done, that *everything is negotiable*. Practise that commandment and you will reap opportunities in the bleakest of circumstances, the most forbidding of environments and the unremitting of pressures. Moreover, the same principle will reward you endlessly when circumstances are favourable, when environments are welcoming and when pressures are relaxed or in your favour. What more satisfying way is there to make a living than negotiating for it?

Index